Praise for *It Stops with Me*...

Charleen's courageous story and writing give strength to all of us. We are survivors from generations of joy, sorrow, violence, and love. And we have the responsibility and privilege, like Touchette herself, to say, 'It stops with me.' From now on we will be about love and a good life.

—WINONA LA DUKE
Native American Activist
Anishinaabe, White Earth
Indigenous Women's Network

A spellbinding journey that through self-discovery demonstrates the magic found in our every day lives. Every page rings with authenticity, involving us in the world of child abuse, metaphysical learning, and, finally, the triumph of self-empowerment. This one is one book that demonstrates the full-chanelled embroidery of modern American life.

—GORDON BASICHIS
Author, *The Constant Traveller*

Touchette's words weave personal experience and cultural background into an historical tapestry of light and shadow. Her vision conjures images both ethereal and concrete, creating a literary tension that is earmarked by the remarkable precision of its prose.

—SANDRA HUGHES
Producing Artistic Director
Gateway Performance Productions,
Atlanta, Georgia

Not only is her work moving, an important piece of literature about women and an addition to the growing body of work about childhood trauma, it is beautifully crafted. She has a way with words, a gentle descriptive style that only slightly covers the powerful images that lie there...The reader never has to wallow in her problems, but rather learns, experiences, and comes to many points of humor and joy... People will be fascinated and moved.

—SHARON STINE
Professor Emeritus
College of Environmental Design
California State Polytechnic University

I was so spellbound and deeply moved by this wonderful memoir that I found myself reading in the dark as the sun was setting. I could hardly get up to turn a light on; and when I did, I couldn't put it down until I had finished. Riveting, compassionate, heartbreaking, descriptive, historical, fascinating are just a few words that come to mind...This book is an inspiration.

—KAREN EDWARDS
Former National Geographic Manager

Querida Charleen,
Mazeltov! Mazal bueno!
You are an inspiration in truth, courage, beauty...
Your paintings look beautiful!

—CONSUELO LUZ
Sephardic Ladino Singer/Songwriter

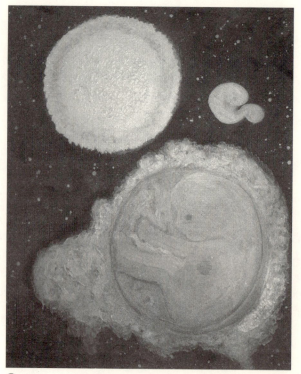

Genesis

It Stops With Me

Charleen Touchette

Also by Charleen Touchette

Preface to *Women Artists: Multicultural Visions*, by Betty LaDuke (Africa World Press) 1991

"Multicultural Strategies for Cultural Revolution in the 21st Century," *Feminist Art Criticism: Form Identity Action* edited by Arlene Raven, Cassandra Langer, and Joanna Frueh (Ikon Press HarperCollins) 1997

ndn art: contemporary Native American art, New Mexico Artists Series (Fresco Fine Art Publications) 2003

Forthcoming

IAIA Rocks the '60s: The Painting Revolution at the Institute of American Indian Arts

Real and Fake Indians: Adventures in Indian Art Country

IT STOPS WITH ME

Memoir of a Canuck Girl

CHARLEEN TOUCHETTE

TouchArt Books

SANTA FE

Published by: Touch Art Books
　　　　　　　 PO Box 4009
　　　　　　　 Santa Fe, NM 87502
　　　　　　　 www.TouchArt.net   Touchart@aol.com
Editor: Beth Hadas
Copy editor: Jacques Paisner
Design and production: Janice St. Marie and Charleen Touchette
Art Photographs: Sage Paisner, James Hart, Addison Doty, S. Barry Paisner, Charleen Touchette
Portrait Photographs: Jennifer Esperanza, Carolyn Wright
Paintings: Charleen Touchette
Do Not Enter photo: Sage Paisner
Copyright © 2004 by Charleen Touchette

The author and publisher have made every effort to ensure the accuracy and completeness of information in this book and assume no responsibility for factual errors or omissions. Some dates and names of people and places have been changed. Descriptions pertaining to people, places, and organizations are solely the viewpoint of the author.

Publisher's Cataloging-in-Publication Data
Touchette, Charleen.
　　It stops with me : memoir of a Canuck girl /
　　Charleen Touchette. – – Santa Fe, NM : Touch Art
　　Books, 2004.

　　　　p. ; cm.
　　　　Includes reproductions of art by Charleen
　　Touchette.

　　　　ISBN: 0-9746545-0-7

　　　　1. Indian women artists—United States—
　　Biography. 2. Women artists—United States—
　　Biography. 3. Children of alcoholics—United
　　States—Biography. 4. Victims of family violence—
　　United States—Biography. 5. Indians of North
　　America—Canada—Biography. 6. Family violence—
　　Psychological aspects. 7. Feminism—United
　　States—20th century. 8. Feminism—Indian
　　influences. 9. Women—United States—Social
　　conditions—20th century. 10. Self-actualization
　　(Psychology) 11. Art—United States—20th
　　century.
　　　　I. Title. II. Memoir of a Canuck girl.

N6538.A4 T68 2004　　　　　　2004100228

759.13 [B]—dc22　　　　　　　0404

Printed in the United States of America on acid-free recycled paper
10 9 8 7 6 5 4 3 2 1

To my grandmother Mimi,
for helping me get through my first nineteen years,
and to Barry, for everything else.

For my children—Jacques, Sage, Raoul, and Liesette-Mimi—
and the seven generations that follow.

In Gratitude

My gratitude to all who connected with me on this path—you were my teachers. Special thanks go to my parents, who gave me the story; my sisters, who lived through it with me, my grandmother Mimi and pépère Archie who inspired and sustained me, ma tantes, mon oncles, and cousins, and all my ancestors who prevailed so I could have a better future. I am indebted as well to my in-laws and their extended family who welcomed me into the joys of Jewish family life.

I am grateful for the women who became my sisters through this journey, especially Betty and Winona LaDuke, Shadi Letson, CeCe Whitewolf, Janeen Antoine, Juanita Espinosa, Joan LaBarbara, Consuelo Luz, Theresa Blackowl, Joanelle Romero, Liz Gorman Paisner, Akary Busto, Maya, Kay Miller, and Carmen de Novais, for the gentlemen who became my brothers, particularly George Morrison, Alfred Youngman, Bernard Pomerance, Mort Subotnick, George Burdeau, Guy Cross, Victor di Suvero, Zarco Guerrero and Billy Soza Warsoldier. I am forever indebted to many healers, principally Naomi Fiske, Dr. Phillip Whitely, Avis Archambault, Kristie Seibold, Thia Luby, Paula Jensen, Dr. Vito Hemphill, Iswari, George Poirier III, and Dr. Justina Trott.

Special appreciation goes to the American Indian Community House Gallery/Museum, the Smithsonian Institute's National Museum of the American Indian, Barbara Goldman and Sandra Wechsler of the Santa Fe Rape Crisis Center, Klaudia Marr and the Van de Griff Gallery, the University of Colorado at Boulder's What Follows Visiting Artist Program, Hortensia and Elvira Colorado of Coatlicue Theatre, and Jackie M of the Georgia O'Keeffe Museum, all of whom sponsored preview exhibitions, readings and/or performances of this work.

Many people were instrumental in getting the book to press. I am indebted to countless advance readers for their invaluable suggestions, especially Gordon and Marsha Basichis, Bernard Pomerance, Sandra Hughes, Raquel Ortiz, and Mort Subotnick. I am eternally grateful to my brilliant editor, Beth Hadas of the University of New Mexico Press. Thanks to Ellen Kleiner of Blessingway for author's services. Kudos and gratitude to Janice St. Marie for her elegant graphic design and to Jacques Paisner for his astute copy edit. Always my deepest gratitude goes to Barry, who has been there throughout, and our children, who gave me the reason to do the work.

Contents

UN

DEUX

TROIS

Mes Ancêtres: Connu et Inconnu

Art in *It Stops with Me*

Front Cover and Frontispiece
Boom Boom Boom, oil/canvas, 20 x 16, 1999

Back Cover
Nursing Mothers' Circle, mm/paper, 8.5 x 5.5, 1986

Interior Art
Genesis, mm/canvas, 34 x 30, 1994
Mes Ancêtres—Connu et Inconnu, mm/sculpture, 12 x 12 x 12, 1989
Do Not Enter photo by Sage Paisner
Four Serpents Dream, wc/canvas, 12 x 9, 2001
Chez Mémère Lavallée's, acrylic/canvas, 60 x 48, 1984
Mes Ancêtres—Canuck, mm/sculpture, 12 x 12, 1989 (detail)
Fleeing with my Treasures, acrylic/canvas, 20 x 16, 1998
Jaguar Woman, acrylic/canvas, 20 x 16, 1998
Flashback Memory, oil on canvas, 20 x 16, 1999 (original 1977)
Oil Spill, wc/paper, 14 x 11, 1976
Good Daddy, charcoal/paper, 30 x 20, 1995
Offering on the Mountain, mm/paper, 44 x 30, 1989
Floating in My Mother's Womb, mm/canvas, 40 x 30, 1994
Floating Child, mm/canvas, 34 x 30, 1994
Healing Hands, wc/paper, 12 x 9, 2001
She Wanted to Die, oil/canvas, 20 x 16, 1998
La Bête, wc/paper, 12 x 9, 2001
Swimming with Orcas, wc/paper, 6 x 4, 2002
Elk Woman's Shield, mm/canvas, 9 x 6, 1990
My Cup Runneth Over, acrylic/canvas, 20 x 16, 1999

Art Gallery 1974-1997
Sky Mother, mm/paper, 44 x 30, 1988
Le Rêve d'une Jeune Fille, pastel/paper, 20 x 17, 1985
Mimi Parle de son Travail, pastel/paper, 22 x 30, 1986 (original *Mimi Combing*, 1983)
Mimi Parle des Grenouilles, pastel/paper, 22 x 30, 1985
Mémère's Boat, wc/paper, 11 x 8, 1974
Mimi Fait la Lavage, pastel/paper, 22 x 30, 1985
Listening to the Fiddling, pastel/paper, 22 x 30, 1985
Serving Cake to the Grandmothers, pastel/paper, 17 x 20, 1985
Only Women Bleed, mm/sculpture, 12 x 18 x 4, 1977
Womanspirit Body Print, charcoal/paper, 65 x 65, 1975
Birth, charcoal/paper, 18 x 24, 1976
Mother Earth, pastel/paper, 12 x 18, 1977
Medicine Egg Dream, pastel/paper, 20 x 18, 1985 (original 1980)
Grandmother Leads Us to the Mountain, serigraph, 21 x 22, 1983
On the River Again, charcoal/paper, 35 x 29, 1982
Sweat Lodge Northwest, acrylic/canvas, 24 x 30, 1984
Pink Pontiac and Painted Tipis, pastel/paper, 22 x 30, 1987
A Wolf is Coming, pastel/paper, 30 x 20, 1985
Chinle Horses, acrylic/canvas, 30 x 40, 1984
Dreaming a Crystal Path, acrylic/canvas, 36 x 48, 1984
Holding Up Half the Sky, acrylic/canvas, 30 x 40, 1986
Shima Telling Stories, acrylic/canvas, 30 x 40, 1987

Shadow Mama in Santa Fe, pastel/paper, 30 x 40, 1987 (original 1983)
We are the Same, But Different, acrylic/canvas, 40 x 30, 1988 (for Oliver Lake-original 1983)
Elk Woman at Twilight, mm/paper, 17 x 20, 1988 (original 1983)
Elk Woman with Twin Serpents, mm/canvas, 60 x 48, 1988
Elk Woman Gestating, mm/paper, 40 x 30, 1994
Her Miraculous Birth, 30 x 22, pastel/paper, 1990
Deer Mother Vision, pastel/paper, 30 x 22, 1987
Communication about the Spiritual Path, mm/canvas, 30 x 42, 1989
Offering on the Snowpacked Mountain, pastel/blk paper, 44 x 30, 1989
Offering à la Mer, pastel/blk paper, 44 x 30, 1989
My Vision is My Shield, mm/canvas, 40 x 113, 1990
You Can Get AIDS, mm/canvas, 70 x 40, 1994
Confined Gestation, mm/canvas, 36 x 30, 1994
Dreaming of Her Birth, mm/canvas, 48 x 102, 1993
Tikkun Olam, mm/canvas, 120 x 60, 1995
It Took Them All to Save Her, mm/canvas, 120 x 30, 1997
Toxic Pain, acrylic/canvas, 12 x 10, 1997
Illumination, acrylic/canvas, 12 x 10, 1997

Art Gallery 1998-2001
Not a Picture Perfect Family, oil mm/canvas, 20 x 16, 1999
Daddy Spanking, oil/canvas, 20 x 16, 1999
Daddy's Fist, oil/canvas, 20 x 16, 1998
Daddy's Wine Jug, oil/canvas, 20 x 16, 1998
Drinking Daddy, oil/canvas, 20 x 16, 1998
I'd Run and Run, oil/canvas, 20 x 16, 1999
He Always Caught Me, oil/canvas, 20 x 16, 1999
Daddy's Closet, oil/canvas, 20 x 16, 2000
The Strap, oil/canvas, 20 x 16, 2001
Caught in the Schoolyard, oil/canvas, 20 x 16, 1998
Nun Sees the Bruises, oil/canvas, 20 x 16, 1998
Peeping Daddy, oil/canvas, 20 x 16, 1999
Don't Look at Us Daddy, oil/canvas, 20 x 16, 1998
Scary Daddy, oil/canvas, 20 x 16, 1998
Boom Boom Boom, oil/canvas, 20 x 16, 1999
Daddy Hugs Too Tight, oil/canvas, 20 x 16, 1999
Ugh, oil/canvas, 20 x 16, 1999
Drowning Baby, oil/canvas, 20 x 16, 1997
Is She Alive?, oil/canvas, 20 x 16, 1997
Can I Save Her?, oil/canvas, 20 x 16, 1997
She's Alive, oil/canvas, 20 x 16, 1997
Laughing Levitating Baby, oil/canvas, 20 x 16, 1999
Zen Baby, oil/canvas, 20 x 16, 1999
Indigo Snake Tattoos, wc/paper, 12 x 9, 2000
Protecting the Artist with Light, wc/paper, 12 x 9, 2000
Tree of Life Ceremony, acrylic/canvas, 20 x 16, 1998
Light Shower, oil/canvas, 20 x 16, 2000
Depression, wc/paper, 12 x 9, 2001
Rebirth, wc/paper, 12 x 9, 2001
Mountain Chakras, pastel/paper, 12 x 9, 2001
Ocean Chakras, pastel/paper, 12 x 9, 2001
Water Illumination, wc/paper, 12 x 9, 2001

Do Not Enter

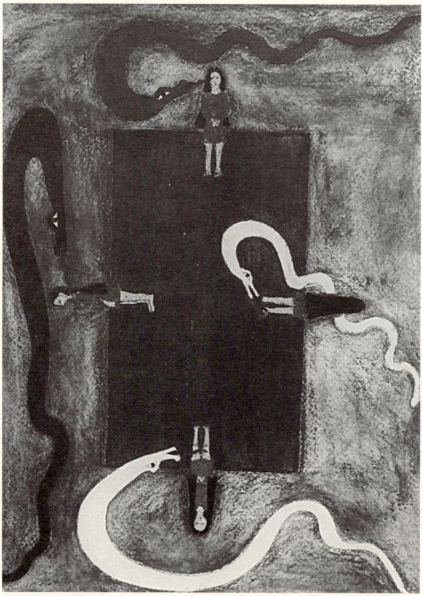

Four Serpents Dream

Un

Fifties Snapshot

W HEN I LOOK AT THE FADING BLACK AND WHITE PHOTOGRAPH
dated February 17, 1954, I see a young woman with porcelain
skin and raven black hair smiling benevolently upon a tiny
baby. The infant's eyes are deep dark pools locked on her mother's face.
She is swaddled in a hospital receiving blanket, dependent, defenseless, and
totally trusting.

I know Maman loved me. I remember feeling safe cuddled in her
arms. As I grew, she told me over and over again the story of the day I was
born. She was only nineteen years old and had married my dad nearly
two years before. Her labor began in the dead of night, but she waited
until dawn to wake my father to drive her to the hospital. She labored for
eighteen hours, most of it alone in a cold sterile delivery room. They
anesthetized her with ether for the delivery as they did in those days, so
she missed hearing my first wails when I was born at 7:58 that night.
Even so, Maman was entranced by my birth. She told me she forgot all the
pain of labor when she saw my face. She was transformed. I had made her
a mother. I grew up knowing the day of my birth was one of the happiest
days of Maman's life.

Colleen was the mother of a daughter in a clan where the women were the center and force of the family. I was her firstborn daughter in a family and culture that valued daughters above sons. Sons moved away. A son's child belonged to his wife's family and was not as directly tied to the maternal line. Daughters stayed close to home and could be counted on to cherish and carry on the family traditions. Maman's oldest sister had four boys, so Colleen thrilled my grandmother Mimi and the entire family when she delivered the first granddaughter.

Like most dads of the 1950s, my soon-to-be father arrived at the hospital after work, and was relegated to the maternity waiting room. Other fathers-to-be paced, but Archie outpaced them all. He was a nervous man, gyrating, lanky, all arms and legs in perpetual motion. Archie did not walk; he marched at a clip, his arms swinging, his long knobby fingers crossing and re-crossing and his mouth jabbering on and on in English punctuated with thick Québécois French.

Eight years Maman's senior, he was tall, dark, and handsome with classic chiseled features and deep-set eyes. People often compared him to Clark Gable and Cary Grant. His movie-star looks and recently opened dental practice made him quite a catch in Woonsocket, Rhode Island. But when he opened his mouth, there was something not quite right about Archie. As Maman discovered soon after their wedding, his good looks masked a troubled soul.

I wonder how he felt on that cold February night as he waited. He adored my beautiful mother. She was his prize, the love of his life. My growing presence in her belly had placed a wedge between them, an excuse for his devoutly Catholic wife to refuse his sexual advances. He must have worried that I would be even more in the way once I was born.

A sepia-toned photo captures petite Colleen at thirteen, made up, wearing a low cut leopard print dress, looking glamorous and sexy beyond her years. By the time she chose Archie at seventeen, Colleen had already refused two other prospective grooms, one whose proposal came with a 3-carat diamond. Years later, my dad would badger Maman about Dog Biscuit and Fido, as he had christened the unlucky but still offensive suitors. Though he had won Colleen, Archie still seethed with jealousy against them. He often accused Maman of secretly harboring regrets that she had not married one of them instead. Her regrets were real, but more because Archie was so different from the knight in shining armor she had hoped to marry.

Dog Biscuit and Fido—when I was little, I thought those were their real names—I tried to imagine what they looked like and wondered what Maman could have seen in them. As I grew older and got to know my father better, I wished so hard she had chosen either one of them. I dreamed about what my life could have been like if Maman had picked a different father for me. I promised myself I would find a kind good daddy for my own kids. At eight, I wrote a letter to my future grown up self. *Never forget how it feels to be a little kid with a crazy mean daddy.*

There is another snapshot, one I did not see until I was grown and pregnant with my second son, twenty-eight years after the photoflash blinded my baby eyes. I stuffed the photo in an album and forgot about it for over a decade. When I was forty, I found it again.

My father looks into the camera. He is holding me facing out, with his arm crossing over my belly. Even with his strained nervous smile Archie is an attractive man.

But looking at his image filled me with dread and revulsion. It was confusing because I loved my father, but something inside me hated and feared him.

The baby in the picture wears delicate pale clothes. Pretty in pink coveralls, she grimaces and leans away from her daddy's face pushing away from him.

For the first time, I saw the deep sadness in those tear-filled eyes.

Place of Many Falls

I N 1954, WOONSOCKET WAS STILL ONE OF THE STRONGEST and most intact strongholds of Franco-American culture in the United States. Generations of mixed blood Métis immigrants left hunger and persecution in French Canada and trudged down to New England to work in the mills in the 1800s. Tired of religious and cultural discrimination in Québec Province, they sought a country where they could speak their language freely and raise their children without subjugation.

As they left La Belle Province, they repeated, *Je me souviens* so often, over so many generations that it became the motto on provincial license plates with the *fleur de lis*. *Je me souviens* means I will never forget. Almost a million *émigrés* fled Canada vowing never to forget the injustices the Québécois endured. The rate of immigration increased after the French Canadian Rebellion was thwarted in 1838, and destitute *émigrés* fled imprisonment, hanging, forced exile, and brutal reprisals by the British. The refugees traveled south with their hungry children, ten to twenty in a family, bundled in threadbare homespun clothes that were scant protection against Canadian Arctic winds.

They came to Woonsocket in the heart of the Blackstone River Valley, the birthplace of the American Industrial Revolution. These heroic people fueled that revolution for pennies a day with backbreaking toil in the unsafe mills. They were oppressed by the industrialists who lived in mansions on the North End while their workers subsisted in dire poverty in the tenements below.

Despite the hardships they endured, my ancestors developed a mystical bond called *survivance*, literally survival. Rooted in the three pillars of our culture *foi, langue, et famille, survivance* kept our community intact and relatively untouched by mainstream America until the advent of radio, and later, television. *Foi* was Catholicism, the faith our ancestors brought from France, or learned from the Jesuit missionaries and practiced in Québec. Any other faith was unthinkable. *Langue* was French, either Québécois with its peculiar accents frozen in the style of the early 1600s, or Parisien, learned from the French nuns at École Jesus Marie. Everyone was proficient in French and had mixed feelings when their children returned from school in the thirties and forties speaking English. Though the families stressed speaking French, slowly the primary language of their adopted country became dominant, even in Woonsocket. *Famille* was the large extended families with grandparents living surrounded by numerous children, grandchildren, and great grandchildren within a radius of a few blocks or miles.

When I left home and told people I was from Rhode Island, they said, "Oh that is a beautiful state." I laughed, "Obviously, you have not been to Woonsocket." Pronounced *Woone soc két* by the natives, Woonsocket is a small industrial city in the northeastern most corner of Rhode Island. It is totally different from the quaint re-gentrified city portrayed on the television show *Providence* and a world away from the mansions of Newport and white sand beaches of Narragansett that form most people's impressions of Rhode Island.

Woonsocket, Rhode Island is in America, but when I was a *p'tite fille*, it was still French Canadian in heart and soul. When Maman and her sisters were children, almost everyone in Woonsocket was French Canadian. Some were bilingual, but most spoke no English at all. Both my parents spoke only French until they went to grade school where the classes were conducted in French for half the day and English for the remainder.

The neighborhood children taunted *petite* Colleen with the chant, *Mwi puis twi fait deux pompiers. Moi puis toi fait deux Chinois.* Mwi and twi was the Canuck pronunciation of me and you favored by the majority in Woonsocket. Moi and toi was the Parisian pronunciation adopted by the middle and upper class mill owners. The other mill workers' children on Rodman Street teased Colleen for talking with the Parisian accent her mother taught her. Canuck was the derogatory term used to insult French Canadians. Colleen did not want to be tied to people who were called such a disgusting name. Though they tormented her, she had no ambivalence about her loyalties. She was born poor but she did not intend to stay that way. Her children would not be called Canucks. Speaking with a Parisian accent was the first step.

When I was a child half of Woonsocket's population spoke little English. I had to answer my dad's phone in French because many of his patients did not understand a word of English. Over the years, French speaking at École Jesus Marie gradually diminished to one French class, and the conversations at Woonsocket's dinner tables became a mixture of French and English. But by the sixties, the relentless infiltration of the outside world there crumbled the defenses of *foi, langue, et famille* that had set us apart. We did not realize then that the changes had begun generations before. By the time I entered high school, the world had exploded into Woonsocket, and the culture I grew up with was evaporating before my eyes. But it was not until I got to college that I saw how different the America I experienced in Woonsocket was from the America my classmates from other places experienced in the sixties. I decided to reclaim the name Canuck with pride.

When I met my husband-to-be Barry, I tried to tell him Woonsocket was different. "Woonsocket is in America, but not of it. It's culturally French Canadian." He just could not get it. Though he was born in Canada and retained Canadian citizenship, he always felt American by culture because his family moved to Minneapolis when he was a little boy. Though I was American born, I never felt American at all because I grew up in Woonsocket. Barry insisted, "If you were brought up in America, you grew up in American culture." I could not convince him otherwise until I brought him to Woonsocket. Even in 1973, enough vestiges of our Québécois culture remained for him to see how different it really was.

The Woonsocket I showed him that day was just a pale shadow of the rich, foreign culture of my childhood. In many ways, I missed being immersed in that complex milieu, which was already becoming lost to me as I entered adulthood and the outside world. I wished I could make dioramas to capture the good memories of what it was like when I was a girl. One would be a scene of me and my schoolmates in our uniforms walking *deux à deux* up the hill to Église Precieux Sang for the French and Latin Mass. Snowflakes would fall on the French and Indian girls' lace mantillas and on their black hair, and you would hear our little girl voices singing *Il est né le petit enfant*. Maybe I would paint the entire school lined up in pairs from the tallest high school girls from Ste. Clare to the littlest first grade boys and girls from École Jesus Marie walking from Greene Street to the Stadium Theater. Clad in identical navy blue uniforms, they marched prim and erect with careful steps, delighted to be on the way to a movie theater in the middle of a school day. The line snaked from École Jesus Marie across the slippery metal Court Street Bridge, continued past the dilapidated train station at Depot Square, and wound down Main Street to the once fancy, now run down movie theater at Monument Square. Or I would make a diorama of Christmas at Mon Oncle Gilles and Ma Tante Claudine's upstairs apartment with everybody laughing, singing Québécois songs, and dancing to fiddles and accordion. Or, I would paint Papi and Mon Oncle Leo going frog hunting before dawn in hip high wading boots with young Mon Oncle Gilles holding the flashlight to blind the croaking bullfrogs—*les grenouilles*. In the painting Mimi would be frying onions in butter, awaiting the sunrise, and the returning men bearing the delicious treat. I would show them to my wide-eyed children who will never be lucky enough to see our culture in its fullness, a culture that is now irretrievable.

I wished I could have captured these cherished memories and held them close to me forever. I wanted so much to share our lost culture, but even then I knew that no matter how eloquent I was, something would always be missing. Just by hearing the stories, Barry could not taste the golden brown *crêpes* cooking in Mimi's skillet or smell the *Tourtière* baking in the oven for Noël. He could never hear the melodies of French and English words intermingling in a glorious cacophony as we gathered in Mimi's small apartment, all her children and eighteen grandchildren laughing and talking in a bilingual bicultural *fricassée*. Those days were gone forever. We were losing our language as over the years English words replaced French ones, until we spoke mostly English sprinkled with remnants of French, and the richness of our Québécois culture survived in its fullness only in our memories. I want to share those days with my own children. But there were other memories too, the ones that I did not want to pass down to them.

Woonsocket—it is thought that the name came from two Indian words, *Woone*, meaning Thunder, and *Suckete*, meaning Mist referring to the majestic Woonsocket Falls. Some historians think the name derives from another Indian word meaning "Place of Steep Descent," but when I was little, I was told that the Indians called it "place of many falls."

It must have been beautiful when Eastern Woodland Indians first saw the steep banks of the wide Blackstone River that rushed through rolling hills thickly forested with maples, massive oak, and weeping beech trees teeming with deer, black bear, bobcats, and wild turkey. When I was a child, I often imagined how amazing this place was when Nipmuck, Wampanoag, and Narragansett Indians hunted in the lush forests bordering the river following it as it surged over glacial boulders making innumerable waterfalls, while weaving in and out of the green valley. I wondered what they thought when they came to Woonsocket Falls where the river cascaded over steep rock cliffs and formed cataracts that poured into a basin as big as a lake. The sunshine refracted through the spraying water would have created luminous rainbows suspended in a brilliant white mist, and the water would have smelled fresh then, and tasted pure and sweet.

That was before the destruction of the river began. When the industrialists harnessed the rushing waters to propel the mills in the early 1800s, the Blackstone's deterioration accelerated. By the time I played in those forests in the mid-1960s, the Blackstone was polluted and rats as big as cats were the only wildlife I ever saw on the river's shores.

Though poisoned, the Blackstone River was the economic and physical lifeline of our community. Mendon Road ran parallel to its western shore. It was the main artery between our house in the insignificant suburb of Cumberland Hill and our family, school, work, and community in Woonsocket.

Riding the five miles north to Woonsocket thrilled me. Mimi was there, along with the rest of our family. Pressing my nose to the car window, I watched as Daddy sped down the curving road, and it became congested with an ugly hodgepodge of shops, manufacturing factories, clapboard houses, and tenements, as well as the increasingly omnipresent fast food and chain stores the nearer we got to Woonsocket. White colonial homes sat crammed between used tire yards, mobile homes, strip malls, and run-down tract houses.

I smelled Woonsocket miles before I could see the towering smoke stacks spewing gigantic billows of toxic fumes into the sky. When we reached the crest of the hill the land dropped off sharply, and I saw the Hamlet Village textile mills spread out below, flanking each bank of the roiling Blackstone River. The mills and the river dominated the landscape. The river's rushing falls provided energy for manufacturing. The district was comprised of mammoth textile factories; Lafayette Worsted, Florence Dye, and French Worsted, where Mimi worked thirteen-hour days as a young girl. The mills covered several city blocks apiece. Each had thousands of frosted windows that stared blankly down on the landscape and culture they were destroying.

Cumberland Street was on the other side of the Hamlet Street Bridge. My parents said the people who lived there were dirty and unrefined. When they wanted to teach me to act middle class they scolded, "Don't act like you are from Cumberland Street." The narrow road was crowded with distinctive wooden three-deckers whose porches were decorated with cornices and spindled railings on each floor. The multi-family structures were built of cheap clapboard, with thirteen and even fifteen people stuffed into each apartment. Fires were common, often trapping the inhabitants on the upper floors. Stories about huge rats that crawled up from the river to bite the children as they slept crammed four and five to a bed scared me when I was a child. The poorest families lived at Social Coin (pronounced *Quin*) at the other end of Cumberland Street where welfare moms struggled, and streetwalkers offered their services amid densely-packed tenements.

Église Ste. Anne sat in the middle of Cumberland Street surrounded by this misery. It was an elaborate Gothic style church, with a sumptuous interior embellished with gold leaf and intricate carvings of the Saints and the Holy Family. The people were mesmerized by the pomp and circumstance, and dropped their hard earned pennies into the collection baskets so the Church could be adorned and the priests dressed in finery, well fed and fat as turkeys.

I saw more churches as we continued the drive around Woonsocket following the river as it wove in and out of neighborhoods, slums, and cluster after cluster of textile mill villages. I learned that the workers breathed in cotton and wool fibers that eventually gave many of them brown lung disease during grueling days in the factories, then went home to inhale chemical fumes from the smoke stacks through their open windows, and drink water fouled by a hundred and fifty years of contamination.

The Blackstone River's waterfalls produced spouts of sudsy rushing water that could be breathtaking, but only from a distance. Close up, the fetid smells were overwhelming. The foaming water at the base of the falls was a putrid pea green from the chemicals. All kinds of offal and detritus floated and roiled about in the murky chemical stew. We wrinkled our noses and covered our faces with embroidered handkerchiefs to protect ourselves from the poisonous smells as we crossed the bridges.

Chez Mémère Lavallée's

Pearl Street

I WAS CONCEIVED IN MASSACHUSETTS AT FORT DEVON where my father
was stationed after his stint in the Korean War. My parents set up their
first home in the married-housing there. When Mimi visited, people
often assumed that she was the prematurely gray Lieutenant's wife, and
Colleen who was nearly a decade younger than Archie, was their teenage
daughter. Archie had enlisted to avoid being drafted and served as a lieutenant in the Medical Corps. In my teen years, I was quick to explain to
everyone that although my dad was in the Army, he did not kill anyone. I
joked, "My dad went to Korea to fight tooth decay." Somehow, at the
height of the Vietnam War while riding buses to anti-war protests, I could
stomach my dad's military past as long as I knew he never shot anyone. But
when I was a little girl, I treasured the pictures of my handsome daddy in
his lieutenant's cap. I played with his uniforms and imagined this mysterious
stranger courting Maman. I understood what she saw in him. He was dashing,
a real dreamboat.

Colleen never did anything she did not want to do. While Archie was
courting her, she went to bed at her regular nine o'clock bedtime even
though he was visiting, playing cards with his future in-laws on the sun

porch. When Archie returned from Korea, she sat him down and gave him an ultimatum. She had heard through a rumor that her in-laws had renovated their third floor apartment for their returning son and his new bride. Colleen was a tiny five foot two inch one hundred pound seventeen-year-old, but she told her six foot tall, one hundred eighty pound lieutenant that if he did not move them into their own place, she would leave him. She was not afraid to stand up to Archie, even risking the stigma of divorce in Woonsocket.

Maman's goal was to become middle class and live in the suburbs. My father, the dentist was necessary to achieve that end. But the suburban dream house came later. For now, she took me home to the apartment she fought so hard for on Pearl Street. Maman often talked about that apartment on the top floor of a two-story house. The clapboards were painted dark forest green on the bottom floor and pale mint on the second. The boxy house was topped with a slanted charcoal tarpaper roof. Matching screen porches, one atop the other, faced the street. The windows were plain rectangles. There was nothing interesting about this square house on a corner lot. It was like all the others on the end of quiet Pearl Street, but Maman adored her new home. The modest upstairs apartment in the tenement was much like the one she left behind when she married, but it was hers.

I have no clear memories of this house, although we lived there until I was three. But my mother told me stories of our time there. Even years after we moved away, she took us to visit the neighbors who befriended her in those early days of her marriage when she was often left alone with her babies while Archie was playing poker or drinking at L'Union St. Jean Baptiste. From the time I could listen, Maman told me stories about the early years of her marriage. One was about the life-threatening birth of my baby sister Kim. Maman hemorrhaged and nearly bled to death trying to push out Kimmy's eight pounds seven ounces. The doctor wrenched the baby from her womb with cold steel forceps, and ripped her apart. The pain and swelling from the tear and stitches was so bad she had to sit on a rubber donut for weeks. All her life, my parents told my middle sister who was as thin as a sapling that she almost killed our mother with her excessive birth weight.

"Your dad was always gone at work trying to build his practice or out with the boys gambling and drinking. He wouldn't even stay home when I was sick after Kimmy was born," Maman often said. Mimi wouldn't help because she was busy tending Maman's oldest sister during one of her twelve pregnancies. Maman refused to share her feelings with either of her sisters and was too proud to confide in friends. So she did it all alone. She woke in the middle of the night, alone in an empty bed, drenched in sweat. "The bedclothes were soaking wet," she said as she pantomimed wringing out the sheets.

In my earliest memory I lay on the changing table. I saw Maman's smiling face coming toward me to blow on my belly. My entire body convulsed with pure joy. A little later, as a toddler, I remember playing with my parents on their bed and being disappointed when Maman put me back in my crib in my own room. Wanting to be with them again, I dove out of the crib, cutting open my chin and getting stitches.

Now I wonder about this memory. Is it really my own, or was it suggested to me to explain away the jagged scar on my chin? Maman told me how my father refused to take me to the hospital, so she put a Band-aid on the wound. When she returned from Sunday Mass, she was horrified that my chin was still bleeding and the little white smocked shirt she had put on me was covered with blood. Approaching hysterics, she finally convinced my father to take me to the hospital for stitches.

Every time Maman told this story, my father got angry when she described the shirt and soft rose-colored corduroy skirt I wore in detail. He said, "And what color was the ribbon in her hair, Colleen?" and, "Are you sure the shirt was smocked, Colleen?" and, "Did it really have a Peter Pan collar, Colleen?"

There is a black and white photo of me sitting in my stroller under a striped awning wearing a bonnet with an outrageously wide ruffled brim, my eyes locked on those of my sweet young Ma Tante Collette. She is a slim adolescent in pedal pushers and a sleeveless cotton shirt, her dewy young face framed by soft black curls. Our matching broad smiles show how elated we are to be with each other.

Maman's twelve-year-old sister came over occasionally to watch me. Her younger sister's help gave my overworked Maman some respite, but Ma Tante Collette was a schoolgirl busy with classes and homework, not to mention the many beaux who courted her as she blossomed in her teens. Maman spent a great deal of time alone.

A generation later, as we chased after my firstborn son in an airport, Maman revealed she put a leash harness on me when I was a toddler. "I *had* to." She insisted. "You walked when you were nine months old. You were always into everything. I had to carry the laundry down from the second floor. So I had to tie you to the clothesline pole in the back yard. I had to. It got worse when I was pregnant with Kimmy, and even harder after she was born. You were only twenty months apart. It was nearly impossible to make sure you stayed out of trouble while I took care of a newborn." As she talked, I saw my baby face streaked with tears in the wind of a New England September day and imagined how I must have felt when Maman tied me to the metal pole, hung each piece of laundry, hoisted her empty basket, then turned her back to get another load.

In Maman's world the housekeeping was always paramount. There was not time to run after a curious toddler. The floors had to be swept, then cleaned and waxed on her hands and knees. The windows, walls, and every surface in the apartment had to be washed and polished to a soft sheen, the wash and ironing done, even my dad's underwear pressed. There would have been piles of laundry with a new baby and a toddler under two, both in cloth diapers. I knew. I could barely keep up with Jacques' laundry and I sent his diapers out to be washed. But we played in a messy house with the sink full of dirty dishes singing songs, reading stories cuddled up on the couch, or lounging outside smelling roses in our herb garden.

After I was a mother myself, my grandmother Mimi told me her memories of Pearl Street. "It all started in the second floor apartment on Pearl Street," Mimi said. "You were just learning to walk the first time I saw your daddy hit you. Your father was furious because you would not go to bed on time. He chased you all around the apartment raging and yelling. When he caught you, he totally lost control. He kept hitting you over and over again. I hated going to your house because there was always so much fighting."

"I always thought you liked the other cousins better."

"Non *ma belle*, Mimi loves you. It was because of your dad."

Maman's "Dream House"

FROM OUTSIDE, THE HOUSE ON CLARK ROAD was like any other in a lower middle class suburban neighborhood in the 1960s. Color coordinated shutters framed custom-made curtains in all the windows of the small three-bedroom ranch style house. My mother paid attention to every detail of her dream house. She made sure that her house looked like the homes she saw in the glossy pages of *House Beautiful*. And from the exterior, it did seem like the perfect suburban home on the perfect tranquil suburban street. The milkman, Mr. Fluette, in his crisp gray uniform and cap, delivered the milk regularly in thick glass bottles with the cream floating at the top. The bread man Mr. Dupré, also in uniform with his name embroidered on the chest pocket, delivered fresh baked bread, muffins, and pastries once a week. We had a fluffy orange tabby cat named Puff and a white toy poodle named Pierrot.

Maman wanted her three daughters to look perfect too, like miniature replicas of our elegant, impeccably attired mother. She took great care that we should never have a wrinkle in our clothes, or a hair out of place.

A classic Easter snapshot shows us picture perfect in pressed organza dresses and voile Easter bonnets. Top to toe, Maman attended to every detail, from lace trimmed white anklets and shiny patent leather shoes to tiny white gloves and mini patent leather purses, just like our maman's. She is chic in a cream colored knit suit splashed with bright magenta crewel stitched flowers, an elegant ivory silk hat, and soft creamy kid gloves. Our father is dapper in a dark suit, starched white shirt with French cuffs, and striped silk tie. Each of us has jet-black hair and dark brown eyes. We look like a perfect 1960s family.

My friends liked playing at my house because I had the youngest of all the moms on the street. Maman taught us how to make cakes with creamy frostings, flaky pies, and dozens of different cookies. Every night she whipped up a delicious dinner accompanied by an amazing dessert. *Si on veut on peut*, Maman would say. "If you want to, you can." She sewed, knitted, and crocheted, and showed me how. Every year she made us Halloween costumes. When I was about eight, Maman cut angel's wings out of shiny gold paper, carefully glued them to bent and shaped clothes hangers, and affixed them to white angel dresses she had sewed. Then she attached gold paper halos to our wings so they floated above our heads. At night Maman brushed our hair, gently pulling one hundred strokes through our three shades of silky dark locks. In the mornings when we got ready for church or school in the bathroom, she combed our tresses into pretty styles. She taught me how to comb my sisters' hair so I could help. We giggled as we primped and preened together, just Maman and the girls.

Twice a year, fall and spring, Maman took us shopping for clothes. We ran from store to store, trying on outfit after outfit, until we returned home after dark, exhausted but exhilarated with full shopping bags, excited to show Daddy our new clothes. Oblivious to the scowl he was turning on Maman, I tried on the first dress and happily modeled for Daddy's approval. But he never complimented our choices. Instead, he got angrier and angrier as we showed him each new outfit until he was screaming by bedtime and we went to sleep crying.

Daddy was an avid athlete and sports enthusiast. He played nearly every sport as a child, was the quarterback on Assumption's football team, and excelled in tennis as a youth. One of his most bitter disappointments was never having a son to share his passion. Since Maman was totally uninterested in anything more athletic than vacuuming, Archie tried to raise his daughters as sports fans.

Maman bundled us up in ruffled dresses, velvet collared wool coats with matching hats and muffs to keep our hands warm to travel with Daddy to arenas throughout New England. We three little girls sat in the bleachers next to our daddy, surrounded by burly cigar-smoking, roaring fans. We hollered with them as Bobby Orr slammed the Boston Bruins' opponents into the boards and shot the puck to score. We were usually the only little girls in the noisy crowds of drinking, smoking men. Like all good Canucks, I liked hockey best. Along with the rest of the Bruins' fans, I jumped up and screamed with delight when the players threw their gloves down for a fight on the boards. In basketball season, we cheered Bob Cousy at his final game for the Boston Celtics, and were awed as Bill Russell's lanky body flew across the court to score. Though Daddy liked baseball least of all, he drove us to Fenway Park to eat hot dogs and pretzels, and we rooted for the Red Sox. When New England got its own professional football team, Archie bought season tickets to the Patriot games. Wrapped in red plaid wool blankets, we sipped steaming hot chocolate poured from a thermos Maman packed.

Daddy and I stood in the little hallway between the bedrooms and the bathroom. Daddy gripped my arm with his left hand, and hit me with his right. I was screaming at the top of my lungs.

"*Tais-toi. Ferme ta grande gueule*, Shaaleen Gail."

Daddy repeated over and over again.

"Shut up. Close your big mouth."

I could hear Maman's classical music humming from the stereo in the living room. I understood. I meant nothing to him.

"You don't care what you say to me. You don't care if you hurt me. All you care about is the neighbors finding out what you do to me."

My heart froze when Daddy's face distorted, and he bellowed, "Shut up. Shut Up. *Tais-toi.* Shut your big ugly mouth or I'll shut it."

I was about eight or nine. He pulled back his fist and began pounding me with his white knuckles. I had gone too far.

The night I first remember blurting out those words, Daddy was especially uptight about my screaming because our next-door neighbors had called the police a few days before about the ruckus at our house. I repeated the challenge many more times with slight variations over the years. Always, I got the same response. "*Tais-toi*. Be quiet. Don't tell. Don't you dare tell."

Appearances were everything to Maman. But she could only create the illusion of perfection. We lived in a perfectly coordinated décor we were afraid to mess, formal furniture we were scared to sit on, and pastel guest towels we were not allowed to use.

I grew to hate Maman's house. Over time, each room held sad memories. At the polished drop leaf kitchen table I watched Daddy get more and more drunk as dinner progressed until he was out of control screaming and yelling at me. In the dining room I raced around and around the long wooden table trying to outrun my raging father on so many nights that all the memories melt into one continuous nightmare.

Then there were the bedrooms. My parents' big double bed piled high with decorative pillows was under a large impressionistic oil painting of a lovely Parisian lady who looked like Maman holding a parasol. I crawled into their room to find comfort on the pink rag rug at the foot of the bed when I woke from my nightmares.

The bedroom where I slept with my sisters was down the hall from my parents' room. Baby Lori slept in my old white enamel crib with its red spinning balls. Kim's matching railed junior bed was on the adjoining wall under a high wide window that glowed from the ambient light outside. My bed was across the room nearest the door until I turned seven.

Maman converted the den so I could have my own room. It was a pretty room with a big picture window, pretty eyelet curtains, and a hand-painted Hitchcock bedroom set. But the family used it as a hallway. They ran through the two sliding doors at each end to get from the kitchen and front door to the other bedrooms and bathroom. The louvers in the doors let light and sound in and out. I could not close them securely, let alone lock them to keep my father out. Daddy came into my room through those doors without knocking. I woke in the middle of the night and saw him standing by my bed. Often, I caught him hovering over my desk reading my mail or journals by the light from the street lamp that shone in through the big window.

The corners of the house were filled with disturbing memories. Especially the niche behind the toilet in the lavette where I tried to squeeze when Daddy chased me, then held me down to yank a tooth out of my mouth, and where Maman ran after me to administer enemas for constipation.

My parents scrutinized every inch of my body. They noticed each change and imperfection, and commented on them incessantly. But it did not stop with my body. Everything I said and did underwent the same intense observation that yielded fodder for round-the-clock teasing and nagging. I could keep nothing to myself. I was always on edge, nervous that my clothes, body, words, or self would fail to pass muster. If my hair was not perfect or lint had attached itself to my sweater, they picked at me until the offending stray hair was tamed and the sweater was immaculate.

The first day of pre-school, I was only four years old, but I remember being elated, and a little scared. It was my first step outside the house and the beginning of my struggle to escape.

There is a color snapshot of me that day standing as tall as I could stretch in front of the fireplace in our living room. My hair is bobbed and big curious eyes look out from under thick black hair. I wear a red and black plaid dress with mother of pearl buttons down the front. My fist grasps a leather book bag. Lace-trimmed anklets top my black and white orthopedic oxfords. My smile is huge.

Mlle. Lusignan's school in the parlor of her cramped first floor apartment was dark and smelled musty like an old lady, but I could not wait to get there everyday. Mademoiselle taught us in both French and English. Soon I knew my numbers from one to a hundred, letters in both languages, and how to read. My daddy picked up my best friend Marie Frances and me every day and while we waited, we helped Mademoiselle clean the blackboards and wooden desks and sweep the worn floor in the cloakroom. If we were lucky and Daddy was late, we sat with Mademoiselle while she ate her spinster's lunch of fricasée and sliced bread in the kitchen and listened to her talk about books.

As soon as I learned to read, books were my escape from home. After I read the few volumes in my father's one bookcase, I spent weekends pouring through the big family Bible from cover to cover. When I got bigger, I went to the local public school library every Saturday, took home the maximum number of books, read them cover to cover, and then returned for a new batch the next week.

Stories about children enthralled me, like *David Copperfield* whose escape into a better life gave me hope. I was so engrossed in Victor Hugo's *Les Miserables* when I was in fourth grade that I defied Maman's rule against reading at the dinner table, and hid the book on my lap, sneaking peaks when my parents were not looking. I might have gotten away with it, but big tears started running down my face and I could not stop sobbing when I read about Jean Valjean dying in Cosette's arms. Though I was punished, it was worth it to live fully for seven hundred pages in a safe fantasy world. My godmother's crazy husband was the one who gave me the wonderful book. Even the most ruthless men have redeeming qualities.

Reading did not endear me to my parents. On weekends they berated me for doing "nothing but lying around reading." They said reading with contempt, as if I had been soiling my pants. Books were a waste of time. I should have been helping Maman with the never ending cleaning. Why couldn't I be a good little girl like my sister Kim who quietly dusted and mopped, swept, and polished at Maman's bidding? I did not care. I could never be a good girl in my parents' eyes without selling my soul. So, I read, and read, and read.

When I was in grade school, my parents refinished the basement. The downstairs rooms were the only places in the house where I could relax a little and not be afraid to touch or break Maman's things. On rainy days we played hide and seek in the boiler and oil tank rooms and the storage closets, and shuffleboard on a game stenciled onto the linoleum floor in the "children's room." Swinging doors like those in saloons on TV westerns separated our playroom from the laundry room. We pushed them open with bravado pretending we were cowboys or dancing girls entering a saloon. Sometimes when we watched the black and white television on the comfy couch in the rumpus room, my boy cousins turned off all the lights and closed the shutters to scare us, and we pretended we were at the theater watching horror movies. On rare Saturday afternoons Daddy and I sat together on the couch watching war movies. He especially liked anything featuring Kirk Douglas. Sometimes we shared cheese and crackers while he mixed his drink at the bar. On hot summer afternoons when my father was at work, Marie Frances and I retreated to the cool basement and brewed witches' potions behind the bar. Then we swiveled on the barstools and sipped ginger ales pretending they were highballs like Daddy mixed.

I filled my days with school and creative activities, and tried to be a good productive girl doing lots of laundry, washing, folding, and ironing for Maman. But I was happiest when I was making things. Once I learned to sew, I sat in the cellar for hours pressing my thigh to the magical lever that ran the machine. It whirred as I carefully pulled pinned fabric pieces under the needle to form straight seams and intricate embroidery stitches. I transformed colorful remnants of cloth I bought at factory mill outlets into anything I could imagine, tablecloths in rainbow colors, aprons made of cotton batiste, gingham, and elegant voile, doll clothes, embroidered fancy-edged handkerchiefs, dresses, skirts, and blouses. Under Maman's skilled tutelage, I made costumes for Halloween and Christmas gifts for my teachers and family.

My favorite safe haven was the boiler room. It was the only place where I could make things and not be yelled at for making a mess. An elephant sized black oil tank held the fuel for the furnace, and the room was permeated with the smell of oil. There were naked, decapitated, and limbless dolls in boxes strewn around the clutter, discarded toys that became spare parts for new creations. I spent hours there, making all kinds of things.

Even as a young child, I knew that school was my way out. I have my mother to thank for that. Unlike my dad, who could see no use in educating a girl, Maman greatly valued education. She encouraged and pushed me to do my best at school. When I returned home with my tests, she always asked how I did. If I got a ninety-eight, she said "Why didn't you get a hundred percent?"

Wanting to please Maman, I became obsessed with doing well in school. Some nights I dreamed I had not done my homework and found myself in the middle of class facing the disappointed nun, or in the cloak room in the school's basement standing naked holding my empty book bag. I woke from those nightmares and jumped to my desk to begin doing the homework still half-asleep with my pencil in my hand. Then I spotted the work already sitting in my book bag on the floor.

After Mlle. Lusignan's school, the nuns skipped me from first to second grade on admission. I was six years old. I adored my teacher, Mother Mary of the Visitation. When my third grade teacher noticed I was smart and encouraged me in my studies, I worked even harder. I was a classic over-achiever, trained by Maman to always do my best. But after I reached each goal, I felt hollow. I recorded my thoughts in lined journals. The paper became my confidante to share my sadness and my hope for a better future. Why was I born? What was I here to do? Why did Daddy hurt me? Why didn't Maman leave him?

Fights over money were constant. Maman did not work outside the home, and Daddy kept a hawk eye's vigilance over every penny she spent on the household, so she had no control over any money of her own. Maman overdid everything year round, but at Christmas, she outdid herself. She worked the three of us to death for weeks, cleaning, making presents, sewing, cooking, and baking to prepare for the holidays. Some years, we started in October. Everything was exquisite, from the wreath on the mantel, the decorated tree topped with a fragile angel, the clay crèche, the tender roast, and mouth watering pies, to our lace trimmed velvet dresses, and perfectly combed and beribboned hair. As the holiday approached, Daddy waved bills and receipts in Maman's face demanding explanations for every expenditure. He criticized and questioned every penny she spent, especially if her relatives were coming for dinner. The tension built up each day as Christmas Day neared.

We were bursting with excitement in the first moments after dawn when we began opening our presents, but Daddy got more and more furious as we opened each gift. He glared at Maman, and badgered her about the price of everything. By the time I stuffed the torn wrapping paper into the trash, my stomach was twisted in knots. As soon as Mimi and Papi, and the other relatives arrived for the noon time dinner, Daddy greeted them loudly and offered to mix drinks for everyone. He drank more than usual and poured wine around the table. Soon he was insulting and berating Mimi or the other guests. Maman's only brother was his favorite target. Archie put Mon Oncle Gilles down because he was a car salesman and weighed over three hundred and fifty pounds. Whenever he visited, Daddy hurled his most vicious fat man jokes at him until a full-blown argument erupted that made Maman cry. We helped clear the table and wash the dishes.

One year, we started saving money months before the holidays to buy Daddy a hunting rifle. Pilfering spare change he emptied from his pockets into a dresser drawer each night, we became experts in taking just the right number of coins, so Daddy didn't notice we were siphoning off pennies, dimes, nickels, and quarters. We kept the pirated coins in a big jar, and added the money we earned from babysitting, and saved from our fifty cents a week allowances. Just before Christmas we counted our accumulated loot, and finally had the hundred dollars to buy the rifle Daddy wanted for deer hunting. When we wrapped it up, I was so hopeful that Daddy would like his present and not be angry this Christmas. But it was always the same. No matter how hard Maman tried to save money, Daddy's drinking, horrible temper, and miserliness always ruined the holidays.

Every year on Christmas night, we piled into the pink Pontiac to drive to Ma Tante Giselle's for supper with Maman's family. I shivered in the back seat after the day filled with Daddy's yelling. I worried about making Maman angry by wrinkling my dress, but looked forward to seeing my relatives. When we arrived, Mimi, the ma tantes, and the cousins greeted us and enveloped me in their warm embrace for a few hours. They called me *ma belle*. After we ate, the women and girls cleaned up in the kitchen, and the men went upstairs to play poker.

I took Barry to Ma Tante Giselle's for Christmas night supper in 1973. He had never seen so many pies. "Your family is obsessed with pies. It's like a Pie Religion." Maman and the ma tantes thought they were bringing us up Catholic. But the smoky incense Latin incantations of the pre-Vatican II Church could not capture my devotion like the aroma of flaky pastry baking, and the animated chatter of the femmes as they rolled and cut dough.

My first memories of pie-making were of reaching up on my toes to receive a piece of raw dough which Maman dropped ceremoniously into my mouth the way I had seen the *curé* put the host on the outstretched tongues of the girls receiving First Communion. I looked forward to the day when Maman would dress me in a pure white ruffled dress and miniature bridal veil, and I would finally get to taste the translucent wafer. I wondered if the *Body and Blood of Our Lord* would taste as delicious as Maman's pie dough.

Every Christmas, all sixteen of Mimi's grandchildren in assorted sizes with hungry eyes framed by shiny hair, gathered around the table gently pushing and tugging at each other. We enjoyed bickering over whose maman made the most delicious pies. Being the oldest girl, I was the bossiest. Once I could make pies myself, I knew what it took, but my *stupid* boy cousins could not see the obvious. One cousin refused to acknowledge my mother as Pie Queen. He was a little older than me and thought he knew everything, but Maman's superior baking skills should have been clear to everyone. Did they not know Maman was perfect?

When Barry met Colleen, he said, "You know, your mother is not perfect." How could he not see that Maman was a saint? I had always believed my daddy was the devil and Maman was perfect.

I was in the pink baby doll pajamas Papi gave me when I was five and had measles. This time, I had German Measles, and had stayed home from school. My father stood at the open refrigerator door by the bar, ranting. He picked up a gallon jug of red wine and hurled it at me. I ran as fast as I could to the other end of the long room, but I could not get away. The jug slid fast down the polished linoleum tile floor. I crouched and tried to cover my head as it crashed against me. Glass shattered everywhere. The bitter wine splashed over my face, hair, and body, over the floor, and walls. My thin pajamas, soaked in wine, clung to my skin. I whimpered quietly, drenched and shaking.

I do not know how I got upstairs, or who cleaned the dark burgundy spills off the floor and walls. I do not remember who washed the wine off my skin, and bleached the stains from my pajamas, or who picked the glass shards off my skin, the walls, and the floor. I have a vague memory of wiping the red wine from the floor, shivering, and crying, but I can not be sure if I did it all myself, or if Maman did. What I do remember is my father coming to me in my bed later that evening and apologizing. He was crying. It was the first and last time he ever told me he was sorry.

Forsythia Blossoms

OUR HOUSE NEARLY COVERED THE SMALL LOT IT SAT ON, and the outside spaces were manicured meticulously. Nature was my refuge. I spent every moment I could out in the fresh air. I climbed over the rock wall that separated the houses in our plat from a field of wild knee-high grasses. At the far end of the field, there was a copse of maples and elms. I liked to bushwhack to my best friend's or to Ma Tante Giselle's down the hill. At the opposite end of the field, a swampy area froze over in winter to become the neighborhood skating pond. Like most French Canadian kids, I learned to skate before I could walk gracefully, and skated on the pond's edges, my blades gliding over the lacework of frosted golden grasses.

I met my best friend Marie Frances at Mass when we were three years old at St. Joan of Arc Church. She was the oldest of ten children, and I had all my cousins, so there were always lots of kids around. We climbed the spreading maple trees along Mendon Road and jumped into crunchy waist high piles of red and orange leaves. I ran through the neighborhood skinning my knees and running relay races with my boy cousins. Nearly every day, I dashed to a stable a few blocks away with my girlfriends to feed the horses apples, carrots, and sugar cubes so we could rub our hands down their silky necks and inhale their musky scents. We met a new girl who moved into the neighborhood from faraway Boston. Merita was a strapping Irish lass with bright blue eyes and freckles. She was the first non-French Canadian girl we ever met, and we were fascinated by her tales of Salem witches. The three of us were so inseparable the neighbors dubbed us the *Three Musketeers*. On long hikes, we explored the wild overgrown forests at the bottom of the subdivision that separated our suburb from the Blackstone River. Maman gave me a small flowerbed in the back yard. I tilled the soil and felt its dark loam between my fingers. The small seeds I pressed into the soil grew into velvety pansies I gathered into bunches to give to Mimi and Mémère on Sunday visits.

When my dad was away at his poker game or working at his satellite office above the bank in North Grosvendale, the house was peaceful. After putting my little sisters to bed, Maman let me stay up to keep her company. She stopped washing, mopping, vacuuming, dusting, cooking, cleaning, baking, and ironing, and we sat close on the couch downstairs drinking hot chocolate with marshmallow fluff floating on top. We watched ABC's *Saturday Night at the Movies* on the television in the rumpus room and stayed up late. I made Maman laugh by insisting Shirley Temple's dress was red when it really looked gray like everything else on the black and white television. Some winter nights, we wound balls of yarn from skeins stretched across each others' spread palms, then knitted together, soothed by the soft clicks of our needles and the crackling of the fire.

One Saturday when Marie Frances slept over, the movie of the week was about a baby that was beaten to death. My best friend and I sat close together on the soft couch, both skinny in our flannel pajamas, me petite and dark with big eyes, and she taller and lankier with flaxen bangs framing a long narrow face. We both sobbed over the tiny baby who was battered and bruised.

My heart went out to the baby in the movie. I cried and cried, not realizing I was also crying for myself. Part of me believed I deserved to be punished when I was bad, but even then, another part knew I did not deserve to be hurt so much and so often. I do not know when I started fighting back. I do not have a memory of when Daddy started hitting me. I was too young. But I do remember clearly the moment when I looked up at my dad's face, and realized he was a fool. I was seven.

But I could not tell. Even unspoken, the message was clear. Do not tell that your father hits you. Do not tell that your father drinks. Do not tell that your father enters your room at night. Do not tell that your father tries to see you naked in the bathroom. Don't tell what your father does. "If you tell, he will go to jail. How would we survive then?"

Today, I understand Maman's fear. She could not let herself see what he was doing to me. No one said daddies shouldn't hit little girls, and drink and scream night after night. There was no language then to describe what was happening in our house. Maman could not admit that what he was doing was abuse. Children who did not bend to adults' wills were punished. He wasn't wrong. I was a bad girl. My daddy had to hit me.

Maman could never leave. How would she support three daughters with a tenth grade education and almost no work experience? She dreaded returning to poverty more than she hated Daddy's temper. Her older sister's husband was more brutal than Archie and certifiably crazy to boot even before he got a blood clot on his brain. Mon Oncle Renée hired thugs to burn down Ma Tante Giselle's first apartment with all her wedding gifts in it while they were away on their honeymoon. Everything her relatives had saved to give her went up in flames so he could collect the insurance money. After she pushed out a new baby nearly every year, Mon Oncle Renée's viciousness intensified, and he regularly beat the four older boys. All eight children were afraid of their father's temper. I often watched as he chased my cousins up the stairs panting, and roaring, screaming wildly, his four hundred pounds heaving and jiggling grotesquely, his knuckles stretched white, tautly wrapped with a wide leather strap.

Mama fooled everyone with the facade of the perfect family she managed to project to the outside world. Archie and Colleen and their three beautiful daughters dressed for church. Who would have thought that before Mass our family had violent fights with screaming, yelling, and hitting? No one saw the bruises underneath my starched skirt and voluminous petticoats. We were all experts at subterfuge.

When I was eight or nine years old I took some seeds, the ones with wings that we split and put on our noses, from under the wide spreading maple in my friend Jackie's front yard across the street. I planted five seeds in my flowerbed and watered them. Slowly a tree grew.

There is a photo of me, skinny with wide eyes and black pigtails, wearing a madras sleeveless camp shirt and pedal pushers, standing tall and proud towering over my maple tree.

That tree was one of the few things that were mine. I planted and tended it. As it grew, I measured my height against it. My torso thickened as its trunk did, and I spread out into the world as its branches spread out over the small backyard, over the ancient New England stone wall, and over the neighbor's fence shading his garden. After I left home, my parents periodically threatened to chop it down. It did not fit into Maman's landscaping plans and their neighbor never ceased complaining about his hard green tomatoes. I threatened to never return to the house if they cut my tree down.

A forsythia hedge grew near my flowerbed. In the spring, it exploded with bright yellow blossoms right next to our swing set. We spent hours swinging, chanting sing-song chants as we swung. We three girls pumped fiercely, our little brown legs straining to touch the bright yellow blossoms. I always felt so free when I was swinging, stretching my feet up to the perfect blue sky trying to reach the blossoms with my toes with my sisters. Kim was the sweetest kindest person I've ever known and Lori-Ann was my precious doll.

In 1991 Kimmy sent me photographs of us, "Archie's beautiful girls," bronzed and pig tailed with sad eyes swinging in the backyard. Kim sent the photos, but she does not approve of my work. She hates it that I make paintings that juxtapose my daddy's fist with the happy girls we pretended to be. Kimmy does not want me to tell. I understand why she wants to remember only those clear blue skies and reaching with our toes to the fragile forsythia branches. She only wants to hear our laughter pealing out into the neighborhood. She can not bear to remember the screaming. I wanted to forget too. I am from Woonsocket; I am one of Archie's beautiful daughters. But there was an underside to the picture of three little girls swinging in the backyard.

Maman trained me to remember my dreams. Each morning she asked, "What did you dream last night?" She was not a dreamer, but recognized that my youngest sister Lori and I both had amazing dreams. Maman taught me to value the dreamworld. Even when I had nightmares, she never said, "It's only a dream." Early on, I learned to recognize the symbols that recurred, and saw that some dreams held messages or clues to help me understand what was happening in my waking life.

There were a few months when Daddy had a pale blue 1958 Chevrolet convertible parked in the garage alongside his pink Pontiac with the outrageous fins. When I was four, I began dreaming about this magical car. I dreamed I rounded up my sisters from their beds, and we climbed into the blue car and drove away. Sometimes we drove up and down the hills watching the trees disappear behind us into the night. Other times, the blue car rose up into the sky, and Kimmy, Lori, and I, cozy in fleece robes, flannel pajamas, and fluffy *pantouffles*, flew across the continent speeding by the clouds and up into the blinking stars. One day, the real Chevy convertible was gone. But that did not stop me from dreaming about it.

Nous Allons à la Plage

Mimi

W HEN I WAS YOUNG MAMAN'S OLDEST SISTER LIVED down the street from us and always had a new baby for me to help feed, change, and cuddle. Besides being her godchild, I had a special place in Ma Tante Giselle's heart as the firstborn granddaughter. Maman's little sister Collette, who was more like a cool big sister than an aunt, lived in Woonsocket. After she married, I walked to her apartment after school to keep her company while she recovered from her miscarriages. If both ma tantes were busy, I visited my best friend's house and helped care for her nine brothers and sisters—anything to get out of the house.

The best was visiting Mimi at her second floor apartment on Rodman Street. I helped her cook *provençal* meals for Papi's noontime dinner, listening to her melodic French chatter all the while. Mimi's print dresses were always covered with a handmade apron.

There is a photo of her standing in her narrow kitchen. She is in her fifties. Her silky hair, still pure black, frames her face with its ever-present smile like raven's wings.

Mimi cooked feasts fit for a king in her cramped kitchen, leaning out the window to hang laundry as she told me stories and the aroma of baking pies filled the air. The piercing noon whistle meant her husband was on his way home for dinner. I held onto Mimi's apron as she leaned out the window to get a glimpse of her beloved Romey. I could see the factory with its many gray windows and billowing smoke stacks over her shoulder. Though they had been married for over forty years, Mimi was as excited as a newlywed when her husband came home at noon each day.

Every visit with Mimi was filled with magic. Her *joi de vivre* was infectious. Mimi kept rabbits and pigeons to feed her family, and grew vegetables and flowers in a small garden she let me help weed and water. Her capable hands could do anything and she taught me I could do the same by watching, following, and imitating her. She taught me in the Indian way and rarely gave explicit verbal instruction. I was expected to watch carefully and do as she did. Mimi could do all the traditional handwork like tatting, knitting, crocheting, and sewing, and she could skin rabbits, pluck pigeons, gut frogs, clean fish, and cook them into gourmet meals. She made me thick slabs of *toast daughty* in a cast iron skillet and covered them with real maple syrup. I played in her attic, listened to the Victrola on the front porch, and explored her back bedroom where boxes overflowing with this and that were piled floor to ceiling. A large print of *Custer's Last Stand* hung in the back stairway, a tribute to the only major Indian victory in the conquest of North America. As a child, I looked at it for hours, reliving that brief triumph.

Mimi taught me with her stories, vivid imagination, and ribald sense of humor. She had a hard life, but she rarely complained. Mimi saw life as an adventure and encouraged me to face adversity with a positive attitude. Mimi was the first person who loved me unconditionally. She showed me how to be strong, and remain gracious and refined. She was beautiful, but she would tell me, "Beauty is as beauty does." The beauty of her soul surpassed her extraordinary physical beauty. She taught me that a good heart was what really mattered.

When she was born at the dawn of the twentieth century, Mimi's fraternal twin brother died at birth. The doctor pronounced that *petite* Florence would not live more than a few days. He put her emaciated body in a box on the floor by Mémère Philômene's bed, covered it with a makeshift oxygen tent, and told my great grandmaman not to hold her premature baby because she was doomed and would not survive. But Philômene, would not accept this death sentence. Mémère took Florence's frail body to her breast, nursed her, and willed her to live. Still, the doctor predicted that Mimi would not live past adolescence.

Born Florence Lavallée in 1904, Mimi grew up on her parents' farm on a hill at Bernon Heights near where the Catholic boy's school, Mount St. Charles, stood when I was a girl. Though her family was very poor, Mimi had class and moved with grace in any circle. Her long silky black hair reached past her knees. I loved climbing onto her lap to listen when she told us stories. She called me, *ma belle*.

As I sat in Mimi's lap and rested my head on her bosom, she described how each night at dusk she walked to the pasture and rung a big copper bell to call the cows back to the barn. One particularly fierce cow always tried to butt her with its enormous head. I pictured the backs of the heifers glowing in the evening light and my brave Mimi shaking the bell as she perched atop the pasture fence keeping a watchful eye out for that *vâche*.

Mimi told me our tribe was Pied Noir from western Canada. Our Indian grandmother was very tiny, under five feet tall. She was very religious and lived to be one hundred four years old. We think she met Pépère Lambert at David Lambert's Trading Post situated among the *Kainah*, the Blood Nation of the Blackfeet Confederacy. Pépère Lambert was captivated by the Pied Noir beauty in the shadows of the craggy Canadian Rockies on a bluff overlooking the Kootenay River in Alberta, near Stand Off.

Their daughter, the mixed blood beauty Philomêne Lambert, married a handsome trader and salesman, Antoine Hébert, who traveled all over Canada and New England with his rickety wagon buying the remnants of farmers' harvests to sell on his next stops down the rutted Post Road. Pépère Hébert's stock changed constantly depending on the season and the produce of the area he passed through. I never tired of hearing Mimi describe the mouth-watering contents of his wagon, pints of summer berries, and Mohawk ash splint baskets overflowing with the Three Sisters, corn, squash, and beans crammed between crates of crisp apples and pears. When Pépère Hébert passed near the coast, lobsters, littleneck clams, and shrimp packed on ice and piles of seaweed became ingredients for clambakes. In winter, the wagon sagged under stacks of Indian tanned deerskins, beaver pelts, and other hides. Spring greens, eggs, and wild asparagus shoots replaced them along with crockery jugs of pure maple syrup when the sap began running in the spring thaw turning the Post Road to mud. Listening to Mimi's stories, I saw them huddled on the buckboard against the spring rain headed to each farm with a loaded wagon, and felt relief when they made each sale.

Many times rain, snow, or pestilence destroyed the harvest and left no surplus leaving Pépère's buckboard and belly empty. He tired of coaxing his half-starved horse to drag the wagon through biting snow during interminable New England winters, so he settled in Woonsocket with Philomène. Their daughter, the second Philomène, was born on their farm there in 1875. Philomène was strong and long suffering. Her husband Alphonse Lavallée was a notorious philanderer, but Philomène prevailed and was known for her honesty, hard work, and dependability. Mimi told me, "Once my mother said she would have a bushel of *haricots verts* ready for a customer who came to the farm and she picked the beans by moonlight rather than not keep her word." When she was still a young mother and my grandmother Florence was only ten years old, Mémère Philomène's mother became blind and died. Afterward, Philomène's full-blood Indian grandmother was her confidante and support as she raised her brood and ran the farm. One of Mimi's first memories was watching her Indian grandmother walk to Mass every morning at dawn.

Like her maman and mémères, Mimi was resourceful and religious, even as a little girl. She wanted to go to École Jesus Marie to fulfill her religious obligation, but her father would not pay the tuition. So Florence convinced the nuns to let her and her siblings attend free of charge. Then she tricked Alphonse by walking the little ones to the Catholic school after he had dropped them off at public school each morning.

Pépère Alphonse Lavallée was a barber. He was muscular, very tall, and strikingly handsome with thick wavy coal black hair and a flamboyant curled mustache. Alphonse was smart and charismatic with many friends in Woonsocket. He loved to cook, but he humiliated Mémère Philomène by flaunting his mistresses all over Woonsocket.

In those days, barbers were often surgeons too, and Alphonse relished any opportunity to play the doctor. Once a man came to his barbershop with a nearly severed arm, and Mimi's father sewed him up *good as new*. Another time, Mimi was jumping from the hayloft and landed on a pitchfork hidden in the hay on the barn floor. The tine pierced right through her foot. Her brother Leo gathered her up and rushed her into the kitchen, where Pépère Lavallée was cooking chicken and dumplings. Though he had no anesthesia to dull her pain, Pépère seized the opportunity to display his surgical skills, and sewed Florence's wound while she watched.

Mimi, who was usually talkative, had little else to say about her father. Alphonse forced her to quit school in fourth grade to help support his large family. Little Florence started as a bobbin girl at French Worsted. The mill owners hired small children to change the bobbins because they could fit into the narrow spaces between the looms. Florence spent grueling days scurrying back and forth between the fast moving machines refilling bobbins on the huge looms as they emptied. It was hazardous work. As she ran between the machines, she worried her braids would get caught. Florence knew that would mean a sure and painful death. She and the other children worked thirteen-hour shifts alongside their older relatives. In the middle of each workday, she retraced the three steep miles home to her maman's kitchen to eat dinner, and then trudged back to the factory for the rest of the shift.

At the end of each week Florence resented handing over her entire paycheck to her father. She knew he used the money to keep his current mistress in finery while her little brothers and sisters walked to school in the snow with cardboard plugging the holes in their shoes. She bit her tongue every payday when Alphonse opened his hand to take her salary, then ceremoniously presented her with a single quarter. Whenever one of the women in my family mentioned Pépère Alphonse, they acted as if saying his name soiled their mouths. Nevertheless, Mimi worked steadily at French Worsted for years and gave her father her pay, until she married Romuald.

On their first date, the suave, meticulously groomed Romey took Mimi to the elegant Stadium Theater with her sister and her beau on a double date. Mimi asked her older sister to walk behind and tell her if her new date was shorter than she was because if he were, that would be their last date. Fortunately, her sister liked the gentle Romuald, and though she was an honest girl, this time she lied. Florence and Romuald were meant for each other. Their fathers had both lived in the same tenement house in Canada before they immigrated to the United States, and both married years later on the exact same day in different churches in Woonsocket.

When Florence became pregnant with their first child, Romey insisted she quit working. He did not want the mother of his children to endure the dangerous conditions at the mill for one more day. Mimi was grateful. She had one daughter, a son, and then my mother Colleen was born in 1934.

Colleen was just a baby when my grandmother Florence was diagnosed with tuberculosis and put in quarantine. Mémère Philomêne passed out cold and fell to the kitchen floor when the doctor told her Florence had to be driven to the sanatorium at Wallum Lake. She endured her faithless husband's pampering an endless string of mistresses for decades, but hearing about Florence's illness was too much for the normally formidable Philomêne. She could not bear to lose her special daughter to the coughing disease.

In the previous eighteen months Mémère Philomêne had placed the burial *crêpe* on the front door and waked and buried three children, Raymond and Loretta from TB, and Frank, the artist. Frank was twenty years old when his hand was mangled in a mill accident, and he got pneumonia and died after surgery to amputate it. Three times, my Ma Tante Giselle saw the huge ominous black satin *crêpe* hanging on the front door of her mémère's house signifying a family in mourning. Three times, Mémère Philomêne waked a child in the same farmhouse where she had birthed them. During that interminable year and a half, three times the family stayed up all night sitting in the front parlor with the bodies of their barely grown children. Each time they gathered around Mémère Philomêne. They rocked her in their arms and tried to comfort her, knowing there was nothing they could ever say or do, to soothe the pain.

When she heard about Florence getting TB, Philomêne's youngest, preteen Oscar was already quarantined at Wallum Lake Sanatorium where he battled the deadly lung disease for four years. Still, Philomêne held back her tears as they drove Florence to the sanatorium. My grandmother Mimi was confined there for an entire year. She took the cure sitting outside on a broad porch in a wheelchair bundled up in blankets against the biting wet winds. To my mother who was just beginning her life, the year seemed interminable, but to the doctors at Wallum Lake, Florence's speedy recovery was phenomenal. Mimi said it was unheard of for anyone to be released from the sanatorium after just one year, but she was determined to get well and return home to her children. She left the sanatorium despite the doctors' warnings predicting early death. For ten years, the family accompanied her to Wallum Lake every Saturday, where little Colleen watched a doctor insert a foot long needle into her mother's back to collapse her damaged lung. Mimi laughed when she told me that the doctors predicted that even if she got over the TB, she would not live long with the collapsed lung.

Mes Ancêtres—Canuck

Pépère's Lake

ARCHIE'S FAMILY WAS SOLID QUÉBÉCOIS WITH NO PRETENSIONS. Pépère did manual labor all his life. He was an honest hard worker, the kind of man who inspired trust and confidence. People went out of their way for Big Archie because they knew he would always be there when they needed him to unclog a drain, snake a toilet on a holiday, or lift a truck out of a ditch.

There is a black and white snapshot of Pépère and his apprentice standing in front of his plumbing van, both wearing starched uniforms. Pépère towers above the top of the van. His brimmed cap shades a broad brown forehead. The words, *Plumbing Shop on Wheels, Archie J. Touchette*, are written on the side of the truck.

Big Archie made a good living as a plumber. He and Mémère were parsimonious. They preferred to sit in the dark rather than pay more for electricity. They scrimped enough money to send my father away to prep school, college, and dental school at Georgetown University. But the family never assumed the middle class airs that Maman's family did. Pépère Touchette distrusted banks so much he buried his savings in a hole in the basement. When my father discovered it, he told his dad to put the money in a bank account. But Big Archie just squirreled his stash away in a pipe where it sat growing mold but no interest, until he died.

Mémère Touchette was far different from Pépère, and the exact opposite of Mimi, who was the epitome of refinement. Mémère Louisia was down to earth and gritty.

There is a faded black and white photo of her standing with Little Archie when he was twelve in front of their square shingled three-decker house. He wears a baseball uniform and swings a bat. Her hair is already pure white and she wears the same dirty wrinkled shorts and a camp shirt topped with a Red Sox cap she wore throughout her life. Naturally my fashion-plate mother despised her mother-in-law.

Mémère probably earned her only daughter-in-law's dislike. From the time Archie began courting Colleen, his mother took every opportunity to torment her. Maman told me the story of the day she went to tell her mother-in-law about her engagement to her precious only son. Archie was afraid to inform his mother he was marrying the seventeen year old daughter of a mill worker, so he made Colleen do the dirty work while he was safe in Korea.

Maman described her trepidation as she approached the imposing three-story brick house on South Main Street opposite Église Ste. Famille. The gothic church's towering brick steeples cast a cold shadow on Colleen as she climbed the steps at the end of the long walkway and knocked on the big oaken door. Mémère would not let her get any farther than the entry foyer that doubled as a waiting room for my grandfather's plumbing and heating office. There was a long dark wooden bench where people sat and waited to see Pépère or Mémère Touchette behind the big desk on the other side of the heavy office door, and a grand coat rack with big hooks and baroque carvings surrounding a mirror where visitors who came to play cards with Mémère stopped to check their lipstick and straighten their veiled hats. But that day in the winter of 1951, Colleen Ethier was not invited to sit on the bench, nor did her future mother-in-law offer to hang her coat on one of the shiny brass hooks. Instead, she had to stand and state her business right then and there in the narrow entryway. Colleen gathered all her courage in the face of the scowling white haired witch and began, "Madame Touchette, your son Archie asked me to tell you that we are engaged…" Before she could finish, Louisia collapsed into hysterics, moaning and groaning. Screaming for Pépère, she fell to the ground feigning a faint. She had to be carried away.

Maman never forgave her. Their mutual hatred grew bit by bit, year by year, as they took little snips at each other, each one getting insulted in turn, until they despised one another, and both were justified. Maman turned us children against our grandmother, demonizing her until we were frightened to be near her. Mémère's appearance did not do much to assuage our fears. Her wild white hair, deep set crazy eyes, and skeletal body made it easy for us to believe she was an evil witch.

My parents rarely went out alone together, but when they did, Mémère and Pépère Touchette babysat. I dreaded those interminable Saturday nights. Mémère arrived wearing smelly old clothes and nylons so filled with runs, Maman used to say it was a miracle they stayed on her bony legs. Maman was convinced that her mother-in-law came to our house dressed this way to embarrass her. As soon as our parents left for the evening, Mémère would plop us down in front of the television set between her and Pépère. I still smell the pungent odor of mothballs mixed with Avon perfume when I see the floating bubbles opening the *Lawrence Welk Show* and hear the Lennon Sisters sing.

Even though Mémère frightened me, I was fascinated by her house despite Maman's running monologue about how it was hideous and in bad taste. Mémère turned the solid brick mansion into a Canuck paradise. The tacky decors that disgusted Maman were a child's fantasy. There were stars, planets, and comets painted on the blue ceiling of the sun porch. The upstairs bathroom had all kinds of odd sized tubs and plumbing fixtures with tall pink flamingoes painted all over the walls. Mémère's big bedroom was dimly lit and covered with burgundy red brocade with a heavy carved double bed in the center, and a big vanity mirror flanked by heavily draped windows, and Pépère's Spartan room at the top of the stairs had a metal twin bed and simple furniture. We explored each room and then bounced down the thickly carpeted stairs giggling until Mémère caught us. Downstairs, a narrow secret hallway had several little doors that opened into narrow closet sized rooms where my sisters and I invented games that sent us on mysterious errands in and out of the fascinating cubicles.

Despite his mom's fun decorating style, my father told us his childhood was miserable. His mother never showed him the slightest affection. "I used to go over to the neighbor lady and she would hold me in her lap. She wasn't really related to me, but I called her mémère." Little Archie was afraid to disappoint his huge father. "When they sent me away to prep school, I was twelve years old—only twelve years old. I felt abandoned." Daddy got angry whenever anyone talked about sending children away to school. "Promise me you'll never do that to your children. Never send them away to school. It is the most horrible abandonment to send children away at a tender age."

When Archie returned to Woonsocket years later after graduating from college and dental school, he was an insecure adolescent in a grown man's body. His parents continued to manipulate and control him. I was a girl when I first saw him sneaking a drink in the pantry while the rest of the family ate Thanksgiving dinner at Mémère's house. Maman explained that Daddy's parents were convinced their son never had a drink until he was thirty. She thought her in-laws were hypocrites because she often caught Mémère sitting in the dark in the middle of the day with a nearly empty bottle of wine on the table.

My grandparents worried that Little Archie would become an alcoholic like one of Mémère's brothers who met a tragic death. They made him promise he would not drink until he turned thirty, and bragged to their friends about their upstanding and abstinent son. Archie did not want to disappoint them so he lied and hid, sneaking drinks for years behind their backs.

Daddy's large extended family lived in North Grosvendale. In the graveyard by Ste. Josephs' Church, the names of my great grandparents and many of their descendants are engraved on the tombstones—Touchettes, Aucoins, Simards, Sylvestres, Robillards, Dorvals, and LaRochelles. My grandfather's parents Gustave and Caesarie Touchette emigrated to northeastern Connecticut to find work in the mills. North Grosvendale was a dirt-poor town—even smaller and more impoverished than Woonsocket—and more remote surrounded by miles and miles of identical wooded rolling hills. My grandfather, Archie Joseph Touchette, was born in one of the grim stone tenements that housed millworkers along the swift river that cut through the French Canadian town powering the mills.

Pépère, his two sisters Rose and Blanche, and their cousins worked from the time they were little, alongside the adults in the dank noisy mills where they breathed wool fiber day in and day out. They woke coughing in the icy mornings as they left before dawn for work. Pépère seized the opportunity to apprentice with a plumber for seven dollars a week to escape the drudgery.

The Touchettes had strong muscular bodies and handsome faces with broad brows, piercing eyes, chiseled cheekbones, and prominent hawk noses. Pépère was a big man and his sister Blanche was a formidable woman, tall with capable shoulders and a solid stance. Rose was more feminine, but still a stately woman. They had thick black hair. Pépère's stood straight up.

Mémère Touchette's father, Pierre Aucoin, was born in Ste. Victoire in the Notre Dame Mountains of Eastern Canada south of Québéc City. He and his wife, Delima "Sylime" Sylvestre, traveled throughout Québéc Province where their first eight children were born. They continued journeying through the New England states, then trekked down south to Louisiana where they spent time with extended family in Lafayette, returned to Québec for a while, then moved south again to Natick, Rhode Island where Mémère Louisia was born. Eventually, they settled in North Grosvendale and raised their fourteen children in a big white house with black shutters, a wide wrap around porch, and steeply gabled roof. One son became a doctor, another, a priest, another was the brother lost to alcoholism; the rest worked in the mills. There was even a nun or two. My grandmother, Louisia was the nervous one.

When Big Archie, whose loving ways endeared him to everyone in North Grosvendale, chose Louisia the odd withdrawn Aucoin girl with deep set eyes, everyone was surprised and a little disappointed. Shortly after they married, Archie's oldest sister Rose wed Louisia's older brother Ovid, so the Aucoin and Touchette families were doubly tied.

There is an old black and white photo of the entire family from both sides posed in front of the white three-story farmhouse on the day Rose married Ovid. When the two families gathered together they numbered the size of a small town. Literally hundreds of my relatives dressed in their best finery smile out from that photo snapped on a sunny May day in 1917. The young women's raven hair sets off their delicate white Gibson Girl dresses. Covered head to toe, the mémères wear the traditional black matrons' dresses with high collars. Their hair is piled high in chignons atop heads they hold high gazing sternly over their broods. The men wear dark three-piece suits. Both the *fleur de lis* bedecked blue and white flag of Québéc, and the Stars and Stripes wave proudly from the porch.

Nearly every summer Sunday from the time I was born, my parents drove to visit Mémère and Pépère Touchette at their camp on a little pond near North Grosvendale. The pond was named Little Schoolhouse Pond, but we called it Pépère's Lake. Pépère won the lakeside site in a card game. Both sides of my dad's family were obsessed with playing cards. They played gin rummy, poker, and cribbage, but their favorite was canasta with its three decks of cards and mind-boggling rules. For hours on end, they sat on folding chairs at a flimsy card table on the screened porch, their gossiping in French accompanied by the sounds of the cards being shuffled and slapped onto the table, punctuated by soft giggles and occasional roars of laughter.

Colleen was an outsider in North Grosvendale. She was purposeful, always busy working to accomplish something. Maman hated card playing and never understood the point of passing time idly conversing. Moreover, she could not comprehend why her in-laws took card games so seriously. She never got over the insult when she brought me to the lake for the first time and Mémère refused to pause from her card game to greet her infant granddaughter.

Pépère adored his granddaughters and his face lit up when his *petites filles* arrived at the lake. As soon as I could walk, I followed Pépère everywhere, visiting his sister Blanche in her simple lakeside cabin, the Archambaults on the choice peninsula site surrounded by water that they won in the legendary card game, and Tessie's screen porch tar paper cabin deep in the woods with only a distant view of the lake. I watched Pépère as he worked; sawing wood for stairs, digging, pouring cement steps, painting, and making a giant sandbox. When he laid a flagstone patio by the lake he caught me staring at the liver colored wounds the size of leeches covering his legs. "Don't worry, *ma petite fille*, that's just Pépère's sugar. I bump my legs at work, and it takes a long time to heal." Both of Pépère's parents had diabetes. Mémère Caesarie went blind and had to wear dark glasses. His father Gustave died young. My Pépère Archie was diagnosed as an adult.

Maman hated the camp and spent most of her time inside cleaning and complaining about the dirt and spiders. As soon as she said I had helped enough with the cleaning, I escaped to visit Ma Tantes Blanche and Rosie whose skin was the same deep burnished brown as Pépère's. They had soft bosoms and wide laps perfect for curling up to hear a story. Many of Mémère's thirteen brothers and sisters were still alive and lived nearby so I got to know them well. Walking from cottage to cottage along the shore, I could visit with many relatives. Lolling on a porch swing, huddling by a wood burning cookstove, or fishing in the still hours of dusk and dawn on the wharf, I learned family history and culture.

On Sundays the relatives gathered around the barbecue Pépère had built brick by brick, and sat down at a picnic table as long as a tennis court, with plates piled high with hamburgers, hot dogs, cole slaw, and buttered corn. Once a year we had a big clambake with fish, clams, crabs, shrimp, corn, and lobsters steamed in seaweed. After the feasts, Maman put us to bed and the older people traveled by boat or car to another camp across the pond where people took out fiddles, accordions, and guitars and played traditional French Canadian music. The grown-ups danced the night away at the *fait dos dos*. I fell asleep to the sound of the waves gently lapping against the shore, the fiddle and accordion music punctuated by the beat of the dancers' feet hitting the ground as they whirled around the circle under the moonlight. I only went to these dances a few times, but I will never forget how magical it was to finally see the dancing I had only been able to hear before.

As soon as I was old enough, I helped Mémère cook and clean for the chance to spend a few weeks away from home during summer vacations. At Pépère's Lake I felt at home. I sat in nature undisturbed for hours. The smell of the pines, the croak of the bullfrogs, and the crunch of the pine needles underfoot soothed me. The pond changed constantly, and I never tired of gazing at the reflection of the full moon floating in the center of its expanse that could be as still and smooth as a mirror, or ragged with white-caps. I woke at dawn to see the liquid reflection of the morning sun floating on the calm pool and watched as the wind picked up until the light sparkled like millions of diamonds refracted off the water's rough surface by midday.

Ma Tante

URING MY SEVEN YEARS AT ÉCOLE JESUS MARIE, the nuns, Maman, and the ma tantes tried to condition me to fit into Woonsocket, but men had little influence on my everyday life. Daddy was at work most of the time. My uncles were not around much either. My mother's father was kind, but not very interested in his granddaughters. Papi was overwhelmed by the stress of his job as a foreman at a faltering mill. He had worked most of his life at Bonin Spinning, but it could not compete with the mills down South. After struggling through the fifties, Bonin closed in the early sixties when Papi was nearing retirement. He was forced to find jobs at other mills and ended up at one thirty miles away in Massachusetts where no one knew him. The pressure of the job took its toll. Papi had the first of a series of heart attacks when he was sixty-two. He often said he felt useless being disabled and unemployed. A year later in 1964, Papi had a massive heart attack and died sitting in his armchair on Memorial Day. He had just finished eating one of Mimi's midday dinners and was watching his favorite television show, *Jeopardy*. I was in the fifth grade.

Maman was overcome with grief. She was close to her father and was convinced no one would ever love her as much as Papi had. I envied her. I could not imagine loving my father that much.

An elegant widow at fifty-nine years old, Mimi looked more like forty, and was pursued by many suitors. Several offered proposals of marriage, but she always declined. Romey was the love of her life. No one could take his place.

I was close to my boy cousins but like most boys of that era as they got older, they were uninterested in their little girl cousin until I started developing. Early on, I was attracted to boys, but they were not real to me at first. Since I had no brothers, as I approached puberty, I had to learn what men were about. But I don't remember thinking what they did was more interesting or desirable.

My childhood universe was woman-centered and the heart and soul of our family was Mimi. My maternal grandmother was an empowered matriarch with a happy marriage and four children, eighteen grandchildren, and twenty-seven great-grandchildren who adored her. But there was a chasm between the values Mimi tried to pass down and the values her daughters embraced.

Maman and Ma Tante Giselle were mistreated by their husbands and alienated from many of their children. The women in my family were not at all like the retiring mothers of friends I later met at Wellesley. They were limited by their poor choices of mates, but were strong women in the tradition of their mother. Far from patriarchs, the husbands who aggravated them were buffoons in the eyes of their children and most of Woonsocket. Maman's revenge was to belittle and scold Archie. The only places he could sit to read his paper were the straight back chairs in the kitchen and the couch downstairs in the basement. The rest of the house was Colleen's domain. Maman and her sisters were feisty. They could shrivel you with the glare from their passionate eyes, and melt your heart with their warm smiles. Most often, they were strong and colorful, gesturing with graceful hands as they chatted in melodious French splattered with English phrases. They were the real power in the lives of their children.

When I was little, the rituals of the Church were mysterious. The esoteric Latin Mass took place under spacious vaulted ceilings in elaborate, gilded and carved gothic-style churches. Rays of colored light filtered through stained glass windows illuminated the pungent incense that billowed around the priest in his embroidered vestments trimmed with gold and lace tatted by the women of the parish. I sat still and held my breath as the priest lifted the host and wine, and pronounced the words that turned them into the *Body and Blood of Christ*.

Like my classmates, I walked up the steep hill to Église Precieux Sang for my First Confession filled with trepidation. I had memorized the catechism with its myriad questions and answers. "Who made me?" "God made me." "Why did God make me?" "God made me to love and serve him." I believed that at every moment my eternal soul was in jeopardy. As I neared the church eagerly anticipating my First Confession, I was so scared I would be hit by a car and killed before I reached the sanctuary. The nuns taught me that I would be damned to spend eternity in the fires of hell or the doldrums of limbo, if I died before confessing my childish sins.

I read a little book about the saints over and over. Ste. Lucia who was impaled on a spiked wheel, and Maria Goretti who chose death rather than lose her virginity to a rapist when she was thirteen, were my favorites. Their deaths granted them the ultimate spiritual reward, instant admission into heaven. That was my goal. I prayed for martyrdom.

When I said my Hail Marys, I begged to be delivered from evil. All day, I prayed to the Virgin Mary. In my innocence, I believed she would rescue me. Often I thought I saw her standing at the foot of my bed reaching out to comfort me.

I anticipated my First Holy Communion for months. I was convinced I would be filled with the Holy Spirit by eating the *Body and Blood of Our Lord*. I had seen how much the Eucharist meant to Maman and the ma tantes. I walked up the long aisle to the altar dressed in virginal white. I knelt, tilted my head back, stuck out my tongue, ate the host, and prepared to be transformed. But nothing happened. I did not feel any different at all. I thought, my faith must not be strong enough. Maybe I was so evil that the blessed Baby Jesus refused to come to me.

I was photographed that spring Sunday in front of the ornate Gothic façade of Precious Blood Church flanked by Maman and Daddy in their Sunday best. I wear a pretty voile dress, tulle veil, gloves, and a rabbit fur cape. I look like a tiny *Bride of Christ* with the most disappointed look on my face.

At Ste. Clare's convent where the nuns who taught Maman lived, I saw another side of the Church. The nuns were semi-cloistered, kept apart from their families and the rest of the community, but they had a lifestyle that honored the intellect, which other women in Woonsocket were denied. One day when I was very small, Maman took me to the convent to meet her favorite teacher. We walked down long dark corridors through an elaborate carved door, and entered a long narrow receiving room draped in red velvet and brocaded fabric. The atmosphere inspired deep reverence in me. The gentle woman was covered from head to toe in a black wool habit with only her face revealed under a white pleated wimple. She was ethereal.

The red brick convent covered an entire block from Precious Blood Church down the hill to Greene Street. Once I started school at École Jesus Marie adjacent to the convent, I saw how the women there worked and prayed together unfettered by the demands of husbands and children. Sometimes Marie Frances and I managed to get into the convent at lunchtime. The dimly lit passageways and cellars felt sacred and powerful. We stood in the back of the chapel listening to the clear voices of the novices and mothers as they chanted the *Angelus*. The black-veiled nuns and white-robed novitiates genuflected when the priest raised a giant host enshrined in a gold and silver reliquary. In the basement, we watched buxom nuns washing and ironing, with billowing steam wafting around their sweating, flushed faces. They laughed and enjoyed each other's company, so different from Maman's solitary folding and ironing. I helped the sisters who made thin wafers for the sacrament in the basement kitchen. They carefully poured the batter onto huge baking pans. Once the transparent sheets baked, they used cookie cutter forms with dozens of quarter-size holes to cut the hosts to be transmuted by the priest into the Holy Eucharist. Obscured by the clouds of steam doing their baking magic, they looked as sacred as the priests at the altar did surrounded by incense. These true *Brides of Christ* worked together to feed and clothe themselves without the aid of husbands. Though they ultimately answered to men, the Bishop and their spiritual spouse Jesus Christ, their day-to-day lives were woman-centered. Once or twice, my sisters and I stayed at the convent for a week while our parents went on vacation. It was inspiring to be among women who were free and self-sufficient, and for a little while, to be in a safe place where the violence of men could never enter. The frustration inherent in their lifestyle was not apparent to me as a child, but the joy they shared in intellectual freedom was clear.

If Mimi and the ma tantes noticed I was afraid of Daddy, they never let me know. Archie was nicer than my godmother's husband, and Ma Tante thought her little sister Colleen was lucky to be married to Archie who was athletic. Maman was too proud to disabuse her know-it-all older sister of that naïve notion. Unlike Maman, Ma Tante whined about her cruel, faithless, and morbidly obese husband. I heard her complain about Mon Oncle Renée's cruelty from the time I was very little, and watched him beat my cousins while Ma Tante wailed and cried, begging him to stop. Later Ma Tante explained how she could not leave him because she would be excommunicated from the Church. She cried to Maman and Mimi with each new pregnancy, wondering how she would manage another baby with this horrible man. I marveled she was able to have sex with her corpulent husband at all, without being crushed. But somehow she did, because she had twelve pregnancies resulting in nine live births before she was forty. Ma Tante lost her precious third son at seven months old to pneumonia because of a drunken doctor's negligence when she was pregnant with son number four. She got pregnant year after year and couldn't use birth control because it was against our religion. Finally, after the twelfth pregnancy, the doctor forced her to go on the pill saying she would die if she got pregnant again. He knew Ma Tante would never take the pill without his ultimatum because that would mean defying the Church. Nor would she have divorced her husband, because then she would have been denied the sacraments. Ma Tante said she couldn't live without her Holy Communion.

The Church captured my godmother's heart when she was a little girl. On the ceiling of Église Ste. Anne on Cumberland Street, an image of her fresh thirteen year old face represents one of the angels amid the heavenly hosts in the Rococo murals. Ma Tante told me, "The little *hunchback* fresco painter from Italy who painted the church's ceiling was a boarder at my Grandpère Ethier's house. He wanted to paint my face." The artist took a fancy to Maman's sister, whose innocent visage embodied his vision of the angelic. The painter took the sketch he made of her face and placed it upon the body of the celestial angel. Decades later, Ma Tante Giselle glowed when she spoke about it. The artist chose Ma Tante's infant cousin as the model for the baby Jesus. Ste. Anne's Church became for us "the Church where Ma Tante is an angel on the ceiling."

The Church convinced Ma Tante and Maman that the promise of eternal salvation after death was worth living through hell here on earth. Embracing the spiritual ecstasy of union with the *ideal* man, Jesus Christ, they settled for real-life lovers who were cruel. I cringe when I remember how often Maman told me she welcomed death because then she would be with her sweet Jesus. Throughout my life, I begged her to leave my father.

I watched and listened and saw our young parish priest attend to my beautiful, unhappy mother. Like many young prelates, he enjoyed the attention he got from the frustrated wives of the parish. It is unlikely maman ever consummated her passion for the tall, handsome priest, but they had what looked like an emotional affair that lasted most of my girlhood. Archie despised the *curé* and flipped out whenever maman spent time with him while volunteering at Church. The strain during his frequent dinner visits was distressing. As a little girl, I could not help but be confused by the palpable sexual tension between maman and the priest. But I guess to Maman he was the perfect man. She could love him without committing adultery.

At Maman's and Ma Tante's knees, I learned my first lessons in feminism. To choose happiness for themselves and their children would have put them outside both the Church and their culture. *Foi, langue, et famille* were so intertwined. They could not forsake the teachings of the Church without severing themselves from French Canadian culture. That was unthinkable. Better to suffer and proclaim it God's will.

All three of my oldest boy cousins got their girlfriends pregnant in high school. My favorite, most handsome cousin got his childhood sweetheart pregnant. Her pious parents sent her away to an unwed mothers' home. She was forced to give up our new cousin for adoption, disowned, and left destitute. He never got over losing his true love and only child. I was an adolescent full of questions. I admired my cousin's sweet girlfriend who babysat us all. She was gentle and refined, and was going to college. Why did Ma Tante turn her back on them? How could she let her grandchild be taken away? I learned she was just following our religion.

My oldest cousin Butch's girlfriend got pregnant too. Her belly preceded her down the aisle as she walked to the altar six months pregnant in a white wedding dress. A discreet afternoon wedding with a simple suit would not do for that bride-to-be. The wedding was quintessential tacky

Canuck. I loved it. I was a preteen, and had grown breasts. My cousins, noticing my new figure, introduced me to their friends and treated me like a human being instead of a nuisance. At the reception, we snuck sips of wine from abandoned glasses, chewed rubber chicken, twisted to Chubby Checker, and danced the watusi to *Louis Louis*. We were all glad not to be the groom and bride. I babysat for them after that baby, and then another son was born, and saw how hard they tried to keep their young family together. But the love they could not live without at seventeen became a millstone around their necks as each year passed. They split up, and Ma Tante lost contact with two more grandchildren.

Then the cousin who was just a little older than me got his sixteen year old girlfriend *enceinte*. It was just too much. Not him. He was the smartest, and had been going to Capitol High. He was supposed to be the first grand-son to go to college. His girlfriend dropped out of Woonsocket High and was not interested in anything more intellectual than the soap operas she watched with her mother and grandmother all day. Like her sister-in-law, she chose a huge church wedding, and waddled down the aisle to marry my cousin. I could see the entire weight of the world plop down on him, when she said *I do*. In a few years, they parted, too late to spare their son from their disastrous teen marriage, and too late for my cousin to go to college. With only a high school diploma, he struggled selling anything from ency-clopedias to vacuum cleaners. Frustration overwhelmed him, until he escaped and found love and success in California.

After watching the lives of my boy cousins destroyed by the laws of the Catholic Church; I went to Planned Parenthood. The fictional hell promised by the Church for using birth control was nothing compared to the real life one my cousins lived.

Ma Tante's husband owned a coat factory in Pawtucket, and he bought her an exquisite turn of the century mill owner's mansion in the prestigious North End of Woonsocket. Her family had a few years of lovely summer teas on the broad porches, childrens' birthday parties in the solarium, Christmas Night suppers in the grand halls, and Ma Tante had a few more strawberry blonde babies. Until one day men in black suits and thin ties came to the front door to collect the back taxes owed from the factory. Mon Oncle Renée had abandoned Ma Tante and the kids. They thought he was in Chicago. The men from the IRS said, "There is a lien on the house, Ma'am." It was an enormous amount of money in those days. Ma Tante had no hope of paying the debt. She was forced to pack up and walk away, leaving the magnificent house behind. She crammed her French provincial furniture, and the five children who were still at home into a small rented apartment, and ended up working for a meager pension at the state employment agency.

The two oldest of the five cousins who helped Ma Tante move out of the mansion, spent their youths haranguing their mother to leave their father. But now they tormented Ma Tante and accused her of not trying hard enough to save her marriage. They became born-again Christians, married young, had several children apiece, and took on the roles of patriarchal father and suffering obedient mother. A third cousin was feisty and fought her way through therapy to get over her relationship with her dad. She married a good man from a solid loving family. Each cousin dealt with it in their own way.

I listened to Ma Tante tell Maman that another little girl cousin was molested by the Monsignor who was pastor of their parish in Woonsocket. My tiny cousin with her soft copper curls, elfish freckled face, and delicate pre-pubescent body visited Monsignor weekly for special instruction. Ma Tante thought she had a spiritual calling, until she discovered the disgusting old prelate had been molesting her and some of her little friends every week for months. Ma Tante was furious. She informed the Bishop of the crime. At first, nothing was done. "Just a slap on the wrist." But Ma Tante persisted. They sent the Monsignor to a parish where they said he would not work with children.

As I grew, I learned that the Monsignor was not the only priest who rewarded his parishioners' devotion by violating their sons and daughters and swearing them to secrecy. The priests who did not molest, protected their pederast colleagues from exposure and prosecution. Their guilt and shame made them overlook the sins of the husbands and fathers in their parishes, and prevented them from ministering to the women and children parishioners who trusted them.

Ma Tante endured so much suffering to follow the Church's tenets only to learn that one of its monsignors was allowed to sexually abuse her daughter without much more than a reprimand. Her strong faith had met an insurmountable challenge. She stopped attending Mass for a time. Instead she went to the nearby Lutheran Church where she found welcome and comfort from the warm tolerant minister and his cheerful wife.

But she missed worshipping with family and friends in her parish. The Church granted an annulment of her marriage because Mon Oncle Renée deserted her, and Ma Tante returned to the Church, and her sacraments.

The faith I was baptized into seemed arbitrary and destructive. I was baffled when the Church annulled a marriage that resulted in so many children as if it had never been consummated. As a child I could not see the invisible ties that bound Maman and the ma tantes to the Catholic Church. I wanted a religion that would let the women in my family seek happiness and a safe place to raise their children.

Maman and Ma Tante had a different example growing up. Their parents had a happy relationship. Mimi was the only woman I knew as a child who had a good marriage. She let me know it was possible to have a deep fulfilling relationship with a man. Mimi made it clear a good sex life was an important part of marriage. She made us laugh as she pulled out a secret box from under her bed and showed us silky negligees and peignoirs she wore for Papi. The sexy innuendoes that peppered her conversations delighted us, especially Mon Oncle Gilles, who called his flamboyant mom, *Flying Flo*. Mimi loved the moniker, and enjoyed seeing her son's three hundred fifty pounds jiggle when he laughed at her bawdy jokes.

The Church changed after Vatican II, and I saw the sordid reality behind the pomp and circumstance. The signals were so mixed, it was dizzying. Value *foi, langue, et famille*, but speak English. Women are powerful and equal to men, but divorce is a sin even if your spouse hits your children. Be proud of who you are and where you come from, but assimilate. You can be anything you choose, but stay in Woonsocket, marry a French Canadian and raise your children Catholic. Go to college and be the first woman in the family to get a degree, but do not learn anything that contradicts our faith.

By thirteen, I learned about the atrocities committed in the name of the Church, and saw the devastation Catholicism's rigid laws wreaked on the women in my family. In the middle of teaching a CCD religion class, I decided I could not be Catholic anymore.

The Mill Ladies

ON THE SHORT STRETCH OF MENDON ROAD that was Cumberland's only center sat the neighborhood hardware store, St. Joan of Arc Church, and Rowey's Drug Store, where my girlfriends and I sipped cherry chocolate cokes and lime rickeys and twirled on vinyl stools at a soda fountain. Woonsocket, by comparison was bustling and fascinating. In grade school I watched the mill workers come and go daily. There were all kinds of brick and stone mills and factories along the stretch of the Blackstone River near École Jesus Marie and I went to them all. My school was always doing fundraisers and I was a star seller because I went to the mills to hawk my wares. I got to know the mill workers and saw what their lives were like. Selling them a candy bar for fifty cents or a magazine subscription to *House Beautiful* or *Ladies Home Journal* was an entry into their world. I rushed over to the factories at lunchtime and after school to sit and visit with the women. They dropped their quarters into the nuns' envelope and took a break to taste the sweetness of a thick milk-chocolate bar filled with almonds.

The pride they took in their work sustained them through the long tedious days of repetitive labor. I enjoyed their gutsy, down to earth attitudes and warm hearts. Sitting with them, I got a glimpse of what life was like for all my grandparents when they were young working in the mills. I suppose that they in turn enjoyed a visit from a smiling young person eager to hear about their lives.

There were all kinds of mills alongside the banks of the turbulent river. Spinning mills where wool and cotton fibers were turned into thread; dyeing mills with foul smelling vats of boiling chemicals to color the yarns; and weaving mills, both cotton and wool, where the colorful threads were woven into woolen plaids or cotton ginghams. And there were factories where row after row of women sat at sewing machines doing piecework at incredible speeds. I loved to watch them whip off seam after seam like lightning and toss the finished pieces into the bucket at their side until it was filled, and they began filling a new one.

The workers came in all shapes and sizes, tall and wiry, soft and plump, hard and muscular, just like the supervisors in khaki shirts and chinos who paced the aisles. Some were mixed blood with the same dark features, high cheekbones, straight hair and prominent noses as my family; others had light hair and eyes, like some of my cousins with Norman or Celtic ancestry.

The older women wore simple print housedresses, covered by canvas shop aprons. The younger ones wore dungarees and cotton shirts. They covered their upswept hair with hairnets or cotton bandannas to keep it from getting caught. Some were cheerful optimistic women who always saw the bright side of life. Others were sour women whom nothing could please. Some were young and slim, and others were motherly matrons whose ample bosoms were often dampened by the tears of their coworkers. Some aged workers had humps from stooping over the looms for so many years, and many lost their eyesight from the strain, and their hearing from the noise. These women were different from me in so many ways, but we were all French Canadian and proud of it.

The sweatshops fascinated me with the noise and bustle of people interacting with machinery to make something. The ladies in the mills produced a product. At the end of the day the weavers could see a span of cloth they made and the sewers could see hundreds of sleeves they stitched.

Maman had no real product to show for her labor. A sparkling clean house was an elusive goal. There was no end to her work. There were no breaks to eat donuts and drink coffee. There was no fresh gossip to re-energize her at midmorning. No noon whistle to signal that it was time to pause and eat lunch, and no quitting bell to let her know it was time to stop and rest. Even Sunday, the day the Church set aside to fulfill God's commandment to keep and honor the Sabbath, was a day of work for Maman. There was no time to step aside from the grind and reflect on existence or the beauty of the world. The satisfaction of a clean kitchen with shining countertops or freshly made beds with perfect hospital corners was fleeting.

Of course, Maman had the advantage of not having to answer to a boss all day while Daddy was at work. Some of the mill bosses could be brutal, and sexual harassment of the women workers was a regular feature of life in the mills. But Maman was a harder boss on herself than the toughest foremen. Though she had the freedom to make her own hours, she worked night and day, rarely giving herself the permission to take a day off. "Maman, can you come play with us?" was answered by, "The walls have to be washed. The laundry has to be done. The sheets have to ironed. Dinner has to be made."

In the mills, the women welcomed me into their jovial circle. They perched me on a tall wooden stool and I sold them candy bars for fifty cents. In return, I got to hear about their lives in twangy accents of Québécois French and felt a wonderful sense of belonging.

Maman considered herself lucky because she didn't work in the mills, but she was isolated in the suburbs. The girlfriends she knew from high school had the solace of one another's company at work. They could talk about their no-good husbands with their co-workers and bring pictures of their brown-eyed babies for the ladies to coo over. When they had a celebration or a tragedy in their lives, there was a circle of friends to share both joys and sorrows.

Colleen was alone in her gilded cage. She saw her older sister tell their mother, all the ladies at Yvette Bibeault's Hair Salon, and almost everyone else in Woonsocket every detail of her unhappy marriage. She was sick and tired of hearing about her *pauvre soeur* from virtual strangers, and decided she would never make the same mistake. She was not anyone's poor sister and did not want to be a topic of gossip in her insular town.

Maman would not share her troubles with her sisters, and that left me as her captive audience and only confidante. She told me her complaints about her marriage. I thought I was standing up for Maman when I repeated them to Daddy, but it infuriated him to hear her words coming out of my mouth, and he lashed out at me.

One Drink

D ADDY ALWAYS INSISTED THAT HE ONLY DRANK ONE DRINK, but it was
a scotch on the rocks in a huge copper beer stein. Every night as
soon as he came home from work, he rushed to the basement and
poured his Johnny Walker Red. As he drank down to the bottom of the
stein, he would become more and more belligerent. When Maman complained he was drinking too much he snarled, "I'm only having one drink,
Colleen."

My place at the table was wedged against the window between the
stove and the opposite wall of the cramped breakfast alcove in the kitchen.
To get out, I had to squeeze behind Kimmy and Lori or crawl underneath
everybody's feet to get away from my dad. Sometimes, Daddy rose up furious
and caught me before I managed to escape so I crawled back under the
chairs to keep out of his reach. Other times I got to the dining room before
he did, and he ran after me and chased me around the long table until he
caught me and grabbed my arm. His eyes bulged when he wound back and
pounded me with his big gnarly hand.

I hated myself for screaming back at Daddy. My parents always made me feel it was my fault that my father hurt me. If I would just be a good little girl like my quiet sister Kimmy, he would not have to hit me. If I would "just drop it" like he warned me to, I would not be hit. "Just drop it. Just drop it. Just drop it." He shouted over and over again. I grew to despise those words. But somehow, I could not just drop it. My ideas were the only thing I had control over and I was not going to drop them. I could not give Daddy the satisfaction of knowing he dominated me. He could yell at me, he could hit me, he could beat me, but he could not make me agree with his medieval ideas.

I turned into a bratty kid. Not all the time, but often enough that it became hard for me to like myself at times. I do not think I was any worse than any other toddler when Daddy started hitting me. But at some point after years of being hit, or maybe when I started fighting back, I became a brat and could be nasty at times.

There were days when Daddy decided I needed to be taught a lesson. He brought me into his bedroom and held me by the wrist as I struggled to escape his grip. He made me stand still as he slid open his closet door with a theatrical gesture. It was full of suits, white shirts, ties, and belts with matching shoes lined up on the closet floor. Every item had been arranged according to color and size by my meticulous mother.

My father made a show of selecting the widest leather belt with the biggest brass buckle to whip me. He picked a belt that would impress upon me the seriousness of my latest transgression. Today, I can not recall why he punished me so vigorously, but I remember the way I felt as he chose the belt. And I remember how the thick leather strap felt when it hit my bony bottom.

Daddy pulled my cotton panties down past my knees. Then he ordered me to bend over. I watched out of the corner of teary eyes as he wrapped the leather belt several times around his big fist. The strap was so close to my face I could smell the residue of the saddle soap Maman used to clean the belts. The scent melded with the musky one of leather and Daddy's acrid sweaty odor mixed with the Old Spice aftershave I bought him for Father's Day. The frightening stench of his anger, and of the fear exuding from every cell of my body was overpowering. I almost swooned from the stench, and squeezed my eyes shut tight, so the tears could not escape.

Holding my breath, I waited while Daddy stepped behind me still gripping my arm to prevent my escape, and gasped, as he raised the belt high above his head. The moments between the crack of the leather snapping above him, and feeling its burning weight hit my naked bottom, lasted forever. I filled those interminable minutes with frantic prayers begging God to make Maman come to stop him. She never did.

I entreated the Virgin. *Je vous salue Marie, Plein de grace.* (Hail Mary, Full of grace.) *Mère de Dieu,* (Mother of God) *deliverez nous de mal* (deliver us from evil),... *deliverez nous de mal,... deliverez nous de mal,... deliverez nous de mal.*

The strap hit my *fesse.* The crack of the whip was sharp and loud. Again and again, Daddy lifted his arm and brought the belt down on my bottom. Again and again I prayed he would stop. I bit my tongue to keep from screaming, but cries escaped my lips.

His rage spent, Daddy released me, and I collapsed in a crumbled pile on the shiny hardwood floor. Sobbing, I crawled to the bathroom and washed my smarting skin each time he hurt me. The tender flesh of my fanny swelled up in raised welts that stung for hours and sometimes days afterward. The bruises took longer to disappear, changing from black and blue to deep purple before fading to putrid yellow. After the first whipping I always knew what was coming when Daddy pulled me into his room.

La Bête

MY PARENTS ALWAYS TOLD ME I WAS A BAD GIRL. They taunted me with the rhyme about "the girl with the curl in the middle of her forehead" who, when she was bad was horrid, drawing out and rolling their rrr's on horrid. They took delight in telling stories about what a horrible child I was. One of their favorites was about when I was a baby and although Maman locked me in my bedroom for a few hours every afternoon, I would not go down for a nap. She described how disgusted she was when she opened the door and saw I had made paintings everywhere, all over the walls and furniture with my poop. I sat in the middle of the floor with a delighted smile on my face pointing to my art with hands covered in merde. They told me I did this more than once, and repeated the story throughout my childhood. I was so embarrassed, and thought, they must be right. I am *dégoûtant*.

Of course smearing shit is a normal response to sensory deprivation. It is well documented that babies whose mothers are obsessed with cleanliness often smear feces to get their mother's attention. Maman, with her compulsive cleaning, fit the profile. She locked me in a sterile room with nothing to do, so I used an organic material I made myself. My artistic nature was already apparent. I bet that when Maman came into the room, I was grinning because I was proud of my artwork, not because I was a possessed imp. But when I heard them retell the story, I could only see myself through my parents' eyes. I was a *dégoûtant monstre* who played with *merde* to annoy Maman.

Daddy told me over and over again, *"Tu est bête. Regardez comment tu est juste comme une bête.* You're a beast. Look how you are just like a beast." Or he said, "You're different. You sure are different, Shaaleen Gail," as if it were the most horrible thing in the world. Or worse, he would accuse me of having a mind of my own.

When I was growing up, I hated the constant fighting and anger at home, but I didn't know that not all families were like mine. Like most children of alcoholics, I was embarrassed to bring my friends over when Daddy was home because he was so weird and I never knew when his temper would erupt. I vacillated between imagining that all other children lived in safe happy homes and believing that everybody's home was filled with violence and fear like mine and Ma Tante's. It was easier to think that all families had unspeakable secrets than to admit that our family was unusually sick.

Sometimes when I woke up, Daddy told me, "You're a bad girl for not wearing panties to bed." He said he came into my room in the middle of the night and saw my bottom up in the air all exposed. "I saw your *kitchewee*. Shaaleen Gail." he chanted. *Kitchewee* was the sick word Daddy used to describe our private place. It made me feel creepy that he was in my room looking at me at night. But Daddy always acted like I was a bad girl for not wearing panties to sleep, so I thought I did something wrong.

Daddy always tried to see us naked when we were in the bathroom. He prowled in the hallway and peeked in whenever the door opened, and one of us left or entered. We pulled the door closed and begged him, "Daddy, don't look at us naked." He leered at us and made comments about our bodies. It got worse after I reached adolescence.

My dad's constant sexual banter and inappropriate touching confused and frightened me. The strict teachings of Maman and the Catholic nuns had made me afraid of any kind of sexual feeling. It was made very clear from the time I was a small child that my pipi was evil. I was told that if I touched it or allowed anyone else to, I was committing a mortal sin, and would burn in the excruciating fires of hell forever. Still, I masturbated frequently from a very young age. Even though I knew it was wrong and I was risking eternal damnation, I could not keep my hands off my pipi.

Lying on my tummy, I tucked the covers tight around me. But no matter how hard I tried to stop myself, my fingers inched their way towards my pipi and I rubbed myself until I shuddered, not knowing I was bringing myself to orgasm. Because I had no privacy in my room and knew I was doing something bad, I made sure I was completely quiet and moved as little as possible. Before I climaxed, I could not control the drive to stimulate myself, but as soon as I did, I was overcome with the sickest feeling of shame. Then, I knew Daddy was right. I was *dégoûtant*.

I tried to stop. Sometimes I was able to go a day or two without touching myself. But the next day I made up for it. I did not understand why I could not control myself. Why couldn't I stop doing this dirty thing that I knew was so wrong? Why was I so evil? I did not know why my sexual feelings were activated so young. I thought I was a sinful monster with unnatural impulses. Overcome with shame, I was sure everyone else could see I was wicked. It took years to get up the courage to enter the confessional and admit I had impure thoughts. Telling the priest I masturbated was unthinkable.

Cauchemars

W HEN I WAS EIGHT I BEGAN HAVING A RECURRING NIGHTMARE of a big sound. It was a rhythmic boom that grew louder and louder. There were no visual images. I was in a dark featureless space with a palpable atmosphere. As the sound got louder, it seemed to get closer and closer. I knew it was coming to devour me. I woke up, frantically trying to escape the sound that kept booming in my ears even after I awoke and clapped my hands over my ears. It never stopped. I curled into a fetal position and sobbed, afraid to close my eyes and fall asleep. When I did doze off, the sound roared back, and the nightmare resumed.

On some nights when the sound grew unbearable, I went into my parents' room and crouched at the foot of their bed. Curling into a tight ball, I rocked back and forth whimpering and praying for the booming to go away. I grasped the pink fibers of the rug at the foot of the bed while tears rolled down my face. I heard Daddy snoring and Maman stirring, but my soft moans rarely woke them. Pulling at the threads of the rug, shaking in fear, my ears full of the big scary sound; I rocked back and forth until exhaustion overtook me, and after awhile, collapsed into sleep. Night after night, week after week, month after month, the nightmare continued. Whenever I closed my eyes, I was afraid it would return and I would hear the big sound booming again.

Keeping Secrets

I DREADED GYM CLASS BECAUSE MY NAVY GYM SHORTS did not always cover the bruises. I remember fidgeting and pulling my shorts down so the marks would not show. Maman made it clear that our world would be shattered if anyone found out about Daddy hurting me. I would be blamed if the nuns saw my bruises and he was sent to jail. But I need not have worried. Most of the time, no one noticed. Once, a nun spotted the contusions and asked about them, but she accepted my transparent lie about being clumsy.

In fourth grade, I stood in line at the school door after recess. There were bruises down my legs below my uniform. The nun in charge pointed, and asked, "Where did you get those bruises?" I made up a story about falling out of a tree. I felt faint. The world started to spin, and I blacked out and fell to the asphalt. That distracted Sister and she did not ask again. I wondered what would have happened, if she had persisted and helped me.

As I got older, the fights got louder and more violent. On several occasions, the shouting got so loud, the neighbors called the police. They lived right next door, barely ten feet away. The end of our house that abutted theirs, held the bathroom and my parents' and sisters' bedrooms. One night Daddy and I were fighting in the bathroom when the phone rang. Maman answered it and told the police it was a mistake. She said we were just having a loud discussion. Most of the time the police would talk to Maman on the phone, then drop it. But I have a vague memory of them coming to the door at least once, taking Maman's explanation and leaving.

When I was about ten, I began having headaches, and Maman brought me to Dr. Dashef. The pediatrician asked Maman if I was having difficulty at school. She told him a clique of girls was excluding me. Dr. Dashef and Maman agreed that was the reason for the headaches and the big sound nightmare. He was an intelligent doctor, and should have known that something was awry. When the headaches got unbearable, he ordered an EEG. I remember going to Woonsocket Hospital where technicians applied ice-cold jelly and electric sensors to my forehead. But when I asked Maman a few years ago if she remembered how old I was when I got the headaches, she had no recollection of them even though she took me to the doctor many times and to the hospital for the EEG and other tests. All she remembered was that Lori-Ann had migraines when she was ten. Maman did remember my nightmares lasting over a year and me coming into their bed.

I knew I had nowhere to go, but I was so frustrated, I often tried to run away from home. I would race out the door and climb over the wall into the field behind our house, and run fast to get to the thicket of maples and elms at its end. Then I jumped into the little patch of forest and went as far as I could until I found a pile of downed trees and soggy leaves to hide in. The musty odor of decaying leaves and damp earth filled my nostrils, mixing with the stink of my anguish. I curled up into a little ball and sobbed for hours. I was inconsolable, but it did not matter because there was no one to console me anyway. I always hoped Maman would come out to try to find me, but she never did. I cried until it began to get dark, then I got scared. When it was pitch black, I crawled out of my hiding place and returned home humiliated and defeated. I slinked through the garage into the kitchen where Maman stood at the sink washing the dishes, looking out the window onto Clark Road as if nothing were out of the ordinary.

The Sixties
and Woonsocket

I NTELLECTUAL ACHIEVEMENT BY GIRLS WAS NOT VALUED in Woonsocket. Throughout grammar school, my neck and neck competition with Robert Pepin for the distinction of top student was frowned upon by my teachers and peers. In Woonsocket it was unseemly for a girl to compete in academics with the boy whose father owned the successful Pepin Brothers' Lumberyard. The rationale was that while Robert would need a sharp mind to run his father's business, "You should be content to be groomed to find a rich husband. The only skills you will need are for cooking and entertaining."

When I turned twelve, Maman decided I should have some special evenings alone with my dad. I remember vividly how excited I was as I got ready for our big dinner at the Woonsocket Inn. When Daddy's steak arrived, he was not happy. "This is not cooked properly. I ordered it medium-rare. Take it back." The boy, a pimply graduate of Woonsocket High slunk away in his stained red jacket and clip-on bow tie. Daddy returned the cheap steak three times, getting nastier each time, while I prayed to fall through the floor and disappear from the face of the earth. My prayers unanswered, I sat chewing my steak across from my scowling dad who got more belligerent as he drank his second and third scotch, and waited for his food. I just wanted the check to come, so I could go home, crawl into bed, and sob myself to sleep.

To my perennial embarrassment, wherever we went, Daddy would strike up conversations with complete strangers and harrass them with his nervous babbling. He never seemed to notice that they did not want to talk with him. Once at Mystic Seaport in Connecticut, Archie was walking Maman's little toy poodle, Pierrot, when he stopped to talk with some passers by. It wasn't that he really did anything out of the ordinary that day. The difference was that for the first time, I noticed what a dork my father really was. Slinking off, I stood as far away from Daddy as I possibly could. My gawky dad, dressed in loud plaid Bermuda shorts and a bright shirt held onto a delicate pink leather rhinestone-studded leash with a groomed fluffy white poodle yapping sharply at the other end. When I saw the annoyed looks on the faces of Archie's unwitting victims, I was so embarrassed. I could tell they thought my dad was weird.

At thirteen, I began working at my dad's dental office. I would walk there after school across the Hamlet Street Bridge during the week, and drive with him to work on Saturdays. Working with Daddy gave me the opportunity to see him in a different context. He was good at his work, although he hated his profession and always regretted that his parents refused to let him become a real doctor. He was a demanding employer, but he treated his employees fairly. The office was his domain, and Daddy was a different man there, than at home. I liked earning my own money even if I had to stand up for eight hours suctioning people's mouths and washing blood off cuspidors. But when I wanted to spend the money I saved from my job, it was Maman who told me, "That money isn't really yours."

On the five-mile ride to the office on Saturday mornings in his champagne colored Cadillac, we stopped at the red and chrome Hamlet Avenue Diner, right next door to the French Worsted Mill. I felt proud and mature dressed in my bright white nurse's uniform, white stockings, and crisp starched cap sitting opposite my dad who looked so professional in his suit and tie as he greeted the breakfasting workers. We ordered a typical French Canadian breakfast, *two eggs, side by each, face the sun, jus d'orange, deux strips ba koun, café.* Friday nights, we stopped on the way home at Mrs. Petit's to pick up a bubbling pot of Boston baked beans and fresh steamed brown bread wrapped in tin foil. As we rode up and down the rolling hills past Pepin's Lumberyard, I often got carsick. Daddy would tell me to breathe in through my nose and count slowly from one to ten until my nausea passed. This rare kindness moved me to tears.

When I was in junior high, Archie got the skiing bug and, despite the considerable cost, bought us all equipment. Maman quit when she injured her knee on one of the first runs down the hill at nearby Diamond Hill, so we girls became Daddy's ski bunnies. One winter Friday Maman packed us up for a ski weekend in Vermont, and we stopped at a New England inn on the way for supper. As we waited for our order, I saw Daddy was reaching behind his chair rubbing the fanny of the waitress who was bent over the wait station table tallying a check. Archie continued to pat her bottom as I watched. Maman, her friend and my sisters noticed me holding back my giggles, then saw for themselves what Daddy was doing to the waitress. Soon we were all laughing so hard our noses leaked and tears ran down our faces. At last, Daddy figured out we were laughing at him and blathered, "I'm so sorry. I did not know that was your fanny." The waitress, who had not minded being rubbed by a handsome stranger, was insulted when Archie explained, "It felt so hard and big, I thought it was a piece of furniture. Fannies are usually soft." The more Daddy talked, the deeper he got himself into trouble. "Are you wearing a heavy girdle? You must have on one of those girdles with thick, thick rubber to make it feel so hard. It feels big and hard like a piece of wood. It does not feel like a fanny at all." I giggled through dinner and during the rest of the ride to Vermont.

When it came time for high school, Archie wanted me to go to Ste. Clare's because it was cheaper. But the idea of continuing my education at the provincial school was abhorrent. I already had enough experience with the school to know how repressive the nun's attitudes were and its academic reputation was shabby at best. I convinced them to send me to Bay View. It was the beginning of an enormous change in my life. Until then I had no idea how different the Québécois world I grew up in was from the mainstream. Bay View was in East Providence just forty-five minutes away but it might as well have been a universe away. The nuns were Irish Sisters of Mercy, known for being intellectual, liberal, and socially conscious. The students, mostly Italian and Irish, came from all over the state. For the first time, I interacted with people outside Woonsocket. I would never again be immersed in my native milieu, and would never feel the sense of belonging to my own people that I felt with the women in the mills.

But I was not able to see the repercussions of leaving Woonsocket until decades later. When I was a thirteen-year-old dressed in my heather blue Bay View uniform, I was eager to be in a new environment that valued intellect, where I did not have to be embarrassed about being smart. I did well in school and participated in extra-curricular activities, but I never thought I was good enough. I was pretty with a slim figure but I thought I was ugly and misshapen. Although a high school friend told me ten years later that I was considered popular at school, I always felt like an outsider. My parents had produced a daughter who was painfully insecure.

During my adolescence the Woonsocket that had changed fast from Mimi's to Maman's generation, was transformed. The turmoil of the times horrified my parents, but exhilarated and inspired me. News of the Vietnam War, Free love, anti-war protests, the American Indian Movement (A.I.M.), Black Panthers, Women's Rights, SDS, freethinking, and political uprisings came into our house via the nightly news. On the television in our basement, I saw injustice and the status quo challenged and defeated.

As a Métisse, I knew that from the moment Columbus "discovered" the Americas, brutality, rape, theft, and violence were American before apple pie. Despite the violence of the sixties, which corroded my idealism, the liberation movements of the time had a profound impact on my political consciousness. A.I.M.'s occupations of Wounded Knee, Alcatraz, and the BIA offices in DC in the 1970s elated me. It was as if the heroic warriors of Mimi's painting were resurrected before my eyes. At last, America was confronted with the ugly history of the conquest of its indigenous people. I was convinced the average American could no longer claim all Indians were dead.

Naturally, I was against the Vietnam War and my participation in anti-war demonstrations pissed off Archie who went without question to Korea. "A citizen should not oppose the government during wartime," he said, worried I would become an establishment-hating hippie. I was a sophomore in high school in 1968 and too young to be a real hippie, but I tested my own ideas and chose my own friends, clothes, and music. These small victories were exhilarating and made Daddy's wrath and Maman's disappointment worth facing.

Everyone in the family said *chienne*, *merde*, and *trou cul*. Papi's favorite expression was *moche merde du cul*, which translates loosely as *rotten shit of ass*. But if I said the same words in English, Archie would say, "Oh? Is that the kind of language you learn at your fancy school, Bay View? Shaaleen Gail. You think you're so smart, but you talk like a *sallop*."

When I was twelve or thirteen, boys of all shapes and sizes began hovering around the house. Like most girls my age, I was boy crazy. My girlfriends and I went to every football, basketball, and hockey game to ogle the boys, and hoped they would notice us. On weekends we roller skated or ice skated. Every event was an excuse to meet boys, which angered my dad. He abhorred the pubescent males with their unbridled sex drives. He told me never to sit on a boy's lap, but if I had to, I must put a telephone book between us. "Shaaleen Gail," he would say in his annoying nasal voice, "You have to be cawful with those boys, Shaaleen, because sometimes things rise that don't have flour in them, Shaaleen Gail." I had no idea what he was talking about. Like the nuns' admonitions not to wear white because it reminded boys of bed sheets, or patent leather shoes because boys could see the reflection of your panties, Daddy's warnings went over my head because I was far more innocent than the nuns or my father could have imagined.

Colleen had an acute mind and was always intellectually curious. She taught us to be critical thinkers and to question authority, but only other authorities. From her daughters, she expected blind obedience and loyalty. Though Maman was a devout Catholic, she was a fierce supporter of my right to freedom of expression. She did not hesitate to confront Mother Mary Virginia who called me an "evil temptress" because I wore bloomers and a shift dress, a style popular in 1970, on our eighth grade field trip. And she came to my defense in eleventh grade religion class when I said I did not believe premarital sex was wrong. I was still a virgin, but the Church's prohibition of sex before marriage seemed arbitrary and archaic, and I happened to say so in religion class.

The next day, the principal's bass voice boomed over the loudspeaker summoning me out of a physics exam to report to her in the school's basement. Her office was in a miniature house built to scale a decade before to train Bay View girls in home economics. I stood waiting outside, facing the incongruous clapboard façade with green shutters and window boxes overflowing with plastic flowers. If I weren't so frightened, I would have laughed.

It was the first time I had been called down to the principal's office in the three years I attended Bay View, and I was not used to being in trouble at school. One by one the other bad girls were called in to face the mother authority. When it was my turn, the principal bellowed my name. Clutching the wrought iron railing, I walked up the Astro turf covered stairs shivering with fear. She was formidable. Her muscular figure clad in a black habit dwarfed the massive desk she sat behind. The principal ordered me to sit in the chair in front of her. As frightened as I was, I could not help staring at the thick hairs sprouting out of her chin and a big mole on her nose. After an interminable amount of time, she told me I was evil to believe in premarital sex. I said, "I talk with God in my prayers all the time and I am convinced a just God would not damn people for eternity because they had sex before marriage." "You are not talking to God. You are listening to the devil instead. The devil is a clever disguiser."

Maman was summoned to explain why they should not expel her blasphemous daughter. My feisty mother overcame her deeply ingrained respect for the nuns and stood up for me. Her eloquent arguments proved beside the point. My sentence was commuted a few days later when the school got word that I was a National Merit Semifinalist and among the top four tenths percent of high school juniors in the country.

When I told my girlfriends about the encounter with the troll in the basement, I became the heroine of the moment. At a Halloween party with my classmates, I wore a devil's costume, and was a hit when I did a wild dance to *Light My Fire* by the Doors in the bright red spandex costume complete with forked tail and horns. For a moment, I felt popular, and liked the exhilaration of being an iconoclast and challenging authority. Thereafter I wore an outlawed red ribbon in my hair to mark myself as a rebel.

Wellesley

I N HIGH SCHOOL, I WAS IN SEVENTH HEAVEN dancing in a semi-professional company performing bit parts as an apprentice in the *corps de ballet*. I was a junior, and all my friends were applying to college, but my ballet masters at the State Ballet of Rhode Island thought I had potential, so I decided to become a professional ballerina instead.

Maman was appalled. She was adamant that I go to college. I did not understand why, since no woman in our entire extended family had ever graduated from college. Even among the men, my dad was the only one who had a degree. I would be the first woman in my extended family and the first of all my cousins to earn a college diploma. "Why do I have to be the first?" I complained. Maman revealed that she had never graduated from high school. She left Ste. Clare's in tenth grade to prepare for her wedding to my dad, and was mortified that she was a drop out. She was determined that her daughters would never make the same mistake. Maman was the smartest person I knew, but she had no confidence in her intellect because she never earned a diploma. She did not need one to convince me she was smart, and I thought I did not need a degree to prove myself either. I was sure I would be happier dancing.

The decision was taken out of my hands. Everything changed after I became a National Merit Semifinalist. The phone rang with calls and the mailbox overflowed with messages from admissions offices throughout the country asking me to apply. I was sought after for my intellect. It was dizzying. My teachers told me I should apply to Seven Sisters Colleges. I had never even heard of Seven Sisters Colleges. Under their guidance, I applied to seven colleges, including several of the Seven Sisters, and hoped I would not get into any. To my surprise, I was accepted at all of them. My initial disappointment soon gave way to excitement. Looking at the pile of acceptances with their embossed letterheads, I could not help but be proud of myself. Maybe I was worthwhile after all.

But I was still under Archie's control. When I was a teenager, my father's physical violence was less frequent, but the verbal and emotional mistreatment intensified. On my seventeenth birthday, I got so furious with him that I decided to run away again, this time for good. I left the house on that icy February day and began walking south down Mendon Road. I walked and walked, shivering and crying in the winter wind, the icy slush on the shoulder of the highway freezing my toes one by one. I had reached Lincoln, halfway to Providence, about a twenty-minute drive from home, when a police siren blaring behind me on the highway startled me and sent my heart straight up into my throat. My father had called the State Police. I kept walking, but my hopes for escape were dashed when the squad car with its lights spinning drove onto the shoulder and stopped in front of me, blocking my way. I was forced to get into the squad car sobbing as the rigid patrolman in his gray uniform drove me back to my father.

My parents took me to see six of the seven colleges within driving range. When we arrived at Wellesley, I recalled that we drove by there on a family outing to see the gigantic globe at Babson's Business College when I was a little girl. When I looked at the ivy covered campus and asked Maman what it was, she told me, "Oh, that's Wellesley College where the rich English girls go. You can't go there." You can imagine how thrilled Colleen was when her first daughter was accepted at the impressive school. I chose Wellesley over Bryn Mawr, Smith, Mount Holyoke, Vassar, and the others because I liked the campus best. I had been so starved for nature's unspoiled beauty that Wellesley's wooded acres with Lake Waban as its centerpiece seemed like paradise.

When we drove through the majestic stone and iron gates that separate Wellesley's five hundred acre campus from the surrounding town, I entered a different world. Unlike most of New England, which is parceled out into a cluttered patchwork of small lots, Wellesley's campus was sprawling with vast lawns of mowed grass spread between massive Gothic-style stone dorms and classroom buildings. Wellesley's "ivory tower" was a stone tower that sent melodies of clarion bells reverberating over the campus throughout the day, and cast a long thick shadow over emerald lawns where girls in cashmere sweater sets and pearls lounged on plaid blankets reading Ovid and T.S. Elliot.

When I arrived at the imposing stone dormitory, I had no idea how different Wellesley was from Woonsocket. Along with my trunk filled with clothes and books, I brought my Québécois accent and provincial ways, unaware I was about to meet young women whose mothers, grandmothers, and even great grandmothers had attended Wellesley. To them, girls like me were interlopers. I could not have imagined how impossible it would be for me to fit into this exclusive arena and remain true to myself, but I did drop my thick accent.

My single room in ivy-draped Claflin Hall overlooked the crystal-blue lake. Though I missed Maman and my sisters, the best thing about college was getting away from Archie. I could read all I wanted, and lock my door and have privacy for the first time in my life. Daddy could not barge in and read my mail or journals, or come into my bedroom while I was sleeping. Except for the occasional phone conversation or the visits when he squeezed me too tight, I was physically free from my father.

The library became my second home. Sitting in the stacks for hours on end reading, researching, and writing, I continued to develop and expand my love affair with books. But my primary love at Wellesley was the lake. All the lawns and paths on campus led to Lake Waban. It was a like a blowup of the little pond at Pépère's Lake and afforded me the same joy as it changed moment to moment and day to day throughout the seasons. Walking nearly daily around the wild lake nurtured me. Halfway around the lake sat the Honnewell mansion with rolling lawns sloping gently to the shore and a massive weeping beech tree on the far end that became one of my favorite refuges. I climbed its trunk to a wide perch and stretched out to gaze at the light filtered through the interlaced limbs and translucent leaves. Under its broad canopy, I felt embraced and at peace. When I could not take the time for a hike, I lounged on one of the benches overhanging the shore and read for hours. It was like being at an expensive summer camp.

The social world at Wellesley was not as comforting. Though I was shy, I was a friendly person. But most of the blue-blood coeds saw no advantage in being polite to a Canuck girl with a funny accent, and ignored me. In my first classes when the professors asked where we were from, gorgeous girls with thick blond hair and blue eyes wearing clothes from Abercrombie and Fitch and L.L. Bean looked down perfect ski slope noses and said, "Manhattan, Beverly Hills, and Paris," or "Shaker Heights, Palo Alto, and Rome." I didn't even know how exclusive those addresses were, but I had never met anyone who had more than one.

The afternoon teas at Claflin Hall were a challenge. Though I was no stranger to a silver tea service and had been taught proper manners, it was quite another matter to find something in common with the other Wellesley students. I was often snubbed because I did not fit in and my feelings went from fascination to boredom with the ritual until I met other girls, who like me found the convention and airs outdated. I gravitated towards women from minority cultures like my own and made friendships with Black, Hispanic, and Asian students. Wellesley had a long tradition of educating la crème de la crème from all over the world. My experience in a foreign culture within the United States gave me a commonality with the foreign students. My best friends were from Indonesia, Puerto Rico, and Iran.

Several girls invited me for weekends at weathered Cape Cod cottages, Long Island mansions, and summer lodges in the Adirondacks. But their acceptance was often superficial. One weekend a Wellesley friend invited me to join her and friends at a lodge on a large lake in the Adirondacks. The rustic compound was idyllic. The lodges were decorated with Hudson Bay and Pendleton blankets and artifacts made by Six Nations Indians, the people who were probably my paternal ancestors. Wide screened porches wrapped around each lodge offered perfect views of the lake. When we canoed at dawn, I felt that some ancient ancestral memory tied me to that land. It was as if I had come home. But my friends and I were scolded for insulting the hosts by curling our hair in rags. They said we looked like *pickanninies*, and blamed me. They thought I was criticizing their past, and insinuating they had been slaveholders.

The fall of my freshman year, Pépère Touchette had a severe stroke that paralyzed his left side. Pépère was used to carrying cast-iron bathtubs up four and five stories to the tops of tenement buildings. I had watched him dig huge holes in the front yard when the septic tank overflowed and pull a plumber's metal snake through the pipes when our hair clogged them. His big hands retained a stain from his honest labor no matter how hard he washed them with thick bars of Lava soap. Pépère was used to doing for everyone else. How could he endure being dependent?

It was painful to see my grandfather in intensive care, unable to move and barely able to speak. Seeing Pépère attached to tubes and wires, a part of me froze and I became paralyzed too, but with fear. I returned to Wellesley filled with guilt that I couldn't stay in Woonsocket at his side. The rest of the family kept vigil at Pépère's hospital bed. I buried myself in my studies and college life. With new material to master and midterms to prepare for, the semester passed quickly. I thought I would have plenty of time to see my ailing grandfather. Pépère was proud of me and knew I needed to be at school, but I regretted not getting back to Woonsocket to visit him more during his last months.

On March 21st, just a month after Pépère's stroke, I was in my dorm room with some friends giggling when the telephone rang. I picked it up laughing and heard Maman's angry voice on the phone, "Charleen Gail, your Pépère has just died. How can you be laughing?" I burst into tears as Maman told me Pépère had a massive cerebral hemorrhage and died instantly. He was seventy-six years old. It was the first day of spring.

When I returned home for the funeral, I was weighed down by grief, compounded by the guilt my family heaped on me for not being with them throughout the ordeal. There was a three day wake, and the tradition of an open casket let me see Pépère one last time. His huge body seemed too big even for the extra long coffin. It was strange to see his brown face without its usual smile, hard to see such a vibrant strong man, still and cold as stone. The funeral Mass was at Église Ste-Famille across the street from Pépère's house. Afterwards, the funeral procession drove to North Grosvendale and we buried Pépère in the cemetery where his relatives were interred next to St. Joseph's Church, where he married Mémère fifty-two years earlier. At Pépère's house, we fed the mourners who came to pay their respects. Pépère's death left a hole in our community and a chasm in our family. Archie could never fill Pépère's place.

When I returned to campus, the stimulating academic exchange offered a distraction from my grief. I had entered Wellesley as a political science major, but the most important class I took was Art 105, Introduction to Drawing. In art, I found my passion. It was a discipline that activated every aspect of my being. Art making became a way of meditation. At Wellesley, I took the first steps on my path to becoming an artist.

That summer I worked in Boston and shared a rundown room with another Wellesley girl in an MIT fraternity house at the seedy end of Beacon Street. Several nights a week I walked up Beacon to a decrepit brownstone where an equally decrepit French ballet master taught classes in the European tradition. The muggy heat, the filth of the streets, and the Bostonians aloof manner began to get to me, and I fell into a deep depression. In August, I moved back to my parents' house and commuted the forty minutes to Boston for the rest of the summer. I did not know returning home would just make me feel worse.

All my life, Maman told me I could tell her everything, and I had. During my teen years, as soon as I returned from a date, she would come and sit on my bed, and I told her every detail. I thought she was so cool that I could share anything with her. But I was naïve when I thought she would be happy after I told her my secret. Maman always told me sex was beautiful between two people who loved each other. But when I made the mistake of telling her I was no longer a virgin, she withdrew her love. It was the first of many periods when she would stop talking to me for months, and even years at a time.

She felt she was just doing her job, trying to bring me up to be a good girl, trying to be a good mother. Since she was the "good parent" and my refuge from Daddy's wrath, I had to please her to survive. When I was little, I tried to be clean to avoid making her angry. As I grew, I worked hard at school to gain her approval. But when I shared this news, she abandoned me. I felt totally cut off.

I saw my sisters dressed and coiffed like younger versions of Maman, and knew no matter how hard I tried to fit into her mold, no matter how many times I suppressed my own desires, it would never be enough. Maman would demand more and more compliance until there was nothing left of the real me except an empty clone that looked, sounded, and acted like her.

By the time I returned to Wellesley for sophomore year, I was in a full-blown depression. I slept excessively day and night, but awoke more fatigued than refreshed. I woke up bone tired, so exhausted I could not even hold my head up to study. Moments after I began reading after breakfast, I fell asleep over my books. Walking and lifting one foot then the other took superhuman effort. I felt as if I were in a deep dark well with smooth slippery sides and no hope of escape. I was so desperately unhappy, but too afraid to face the source of my despair.

Meanwhile, my passion for art grew. As time passed it became clear I was an artist, not an art historian. My professors encouraged me to leave Wellesley mid-year to apprentice with several artists at Brown University, Rhode Island School of Design, and Bard College. Maman was devastated by my decision to quit the prestigious college. The dream of her daughter entering the upper class would be dissolved by my decision to leave Wellesley. She was disappointed that I chose art as my profession, and often told me so. "You have so much more to offer the world. You should become a doctor or do something to help people. Don't throw away your intellect and education by becoming an artist. Besides, you need constant encouragement. You will never be happy in a profession that is so solitary."

But I was determined to be an artist. That spring I took classes at Brown and RISD before I headed to Bard in September to finish my degree. Studying Japanese art rekindled my life long interest in all things Asian. I began to experiment with mystical traditions and spent hundreds of hours in the art museum on Benefit Street with Buddhas enshrined in dim lit alcoves covered with intricate embroidered clothes and delicate Zen brush paintings.

I remember sitting in my red bikini on the raft at Pépère's Lake trying to follow my breath and still my mind. I would begin filled with hope. But no matter how long I sat in the lotus position, I could not meditate for more than a few minutes. For awhile, it would go well, but soon hope would wane, my mind would wander, and I would be filled with fear. Creepy feelings crawled up the backs of my legs, moved into my chest, and then turned to panic. Despite my efforts to find peace through meditation, the depression that began the summer before deepened until it almost swallowed me whole. I had surgery to chisel bone spurs off both my heels, and struggled up and down College Hill on crutches each day to get to my art classes. Things got harder. I was close to losing my mind and my very life.

One dark night, I found myself on the slippery, rain splattered roof of one of the seventeenth-century buildings on Benefit Street. I thought I went up there to get away from the noise of a party. Above the wet cobbled streets, surrounded by dark clouds illuminated by the moon, I was flooded with sadness and wanted to slide off the roof and end my pain and despair by crashing my head into the cobbles. I was so sad; I did not want to exist.

A classmate sensed something was wrong and climbed out to talk me down. I like to think I was just toying with the idea and would never have jumped, but I can not be sure. I told my rescuer, "Don't worry. I won't jump. The fall probably wouldn't kill me and I'd end up a quadriplegic with my mother feeding me through a straw."

So I pulled myself out of the doldrums. As a child I always thought I would die young. Nearing my twentieth birthday, I saw that I survived coming close to death and would probably continue to survive for some time. No matter how bad things were, I decided to wait to see tomorrow.

During those years, I was filled with a sense of urgency. Painting calmed me and gave me joy. My favorite days were ones when I could paint all day. At those moments, I saw depression as a vampire. There were so many books to read, so many images to paint and stories to write, and I wanted to do it all. Although I was scared stiff as a child to be alone, as the periods away from my parents grew longer, I grew to love solitude, and enjoyed my own company.

For some crazy reason, I thought it would be a good idea to spend the second summer at my parents' house and work for them as a cleaning lady. I wanted to take a break and lose myself in the monotonous, repetitive Zen of housework, and spent the long summer days ironing in the cellar, then washing and polishing Maman's house to a fine sheen. Some days, I drove to my dad's office to scrub and disinfect the chairs and instruments, then polish the floors.

It was a contemplative summer. Using the time for introspection, I read and wrote in my journal, and spent lots of time with Mimi and my relatives. I drove to Pépère's Lake to stare for hours at the water rippling on the pond. When I attempted to meditate, I still could not sit for very long. Although I pulled myself out of my depression and achieved an equilibrium that I mistook for peace of mind, underneath I was tortured.

I do not know why I chose to spend this time at my parents' house. I thought I did it to support Maman who was dreading the approach of fall when Kim would leave for college, and she would be left at home with Lori-Ann, who was still quite young. It was excruciating for her to be in the house with my father without a confidante. But during those first years away at college, I think I was also scared to be on my own. I believed in my deepest self that it was me, who was bad.

In midsummer, we took a family trip to Québec. I was overjoyed to visit the land of my ancestors where we spoke French with the locals who answered with the distinctive Québécois accent. We spent a few days in Montréal and met French Canadian artists at the outdoor markets. In Québec City, we stayed in small stone rooms in the elegant historic Manoir Richelieu hotel high above the Rive Saint-Laurent, and rode in horse drawn carriages to see first hand the historic sites of our heritage.

Then we drove several hours north along the western shore of the river to a resort overlooking the Rive Saint-Laurent near Pointe au Pic at La Malbaie, and spent several days swimming, diving, and playing tennis together. I was nineteen, Kimmy was seventeen, and Lori-Ann was thirteen but stood nearly five foot nine, and looked much older. Together, the three of us were breathtaking.

Afternoons, we vied with each other to make the perfect dive. Our competition got the attention of a slim mustached gentleman sitting with his wife and friends watching their towheaded children play in the pool. He introduced himself as Ted Turner and said he was the owner of the Atlanta Braves. Of course I had never heard of him or the "Atlantic" Braves. I stopped following sports as soon as I left home for college. Meeting Mr. Turner impressed my father much more than it did my sisters and me. Ted introduced us to his wife and their party and over the next few days we enjoyed sharing company and playing with the children in the pool. Before we left, Ted gave me their address and made me promise that I would work for them as a governess the next summer. I agreed. Over the next year, I managed to misplace the address and forgot about the promise to be Ted Turner's governess.

A few weeks after we returned to Rhode Island, on a Saturday night when I had chosen to stay home alone, I had a strong feeling that there was something wrong with me for not having a date on a weekend night. Writing in my journal, I mused that like most girls, I was only worried about a dateless Saturday night because society told me to value myself in terms of my relationships with men. Now I was discovering that I liked to be alone and my solitude was precious and freely chosen. As I packed to leave for Bard, I was just getting my balance, and ready to face the world on my own.

Sky Mother

Le Rêve d'une Jeune Fille

Mimi Parle de Son Travail

Mimi Parle des Grenouilles

Mémère's Boat

Mimi Fait la Lavage

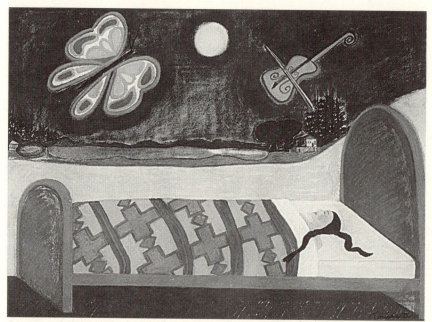

Listening to the Fiddling

Serving Cake to the Grandmothers

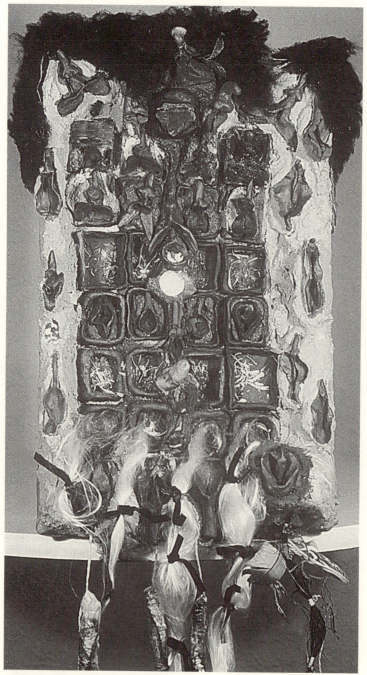

Only Women Bleed

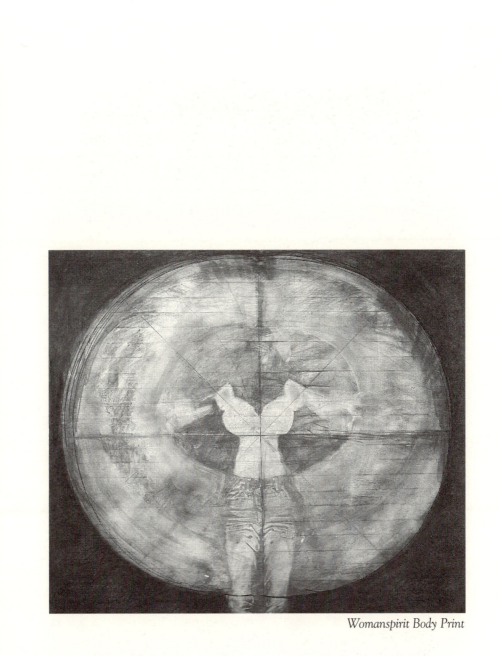

Womanspirit Body Print

Birth

Mother Earth

Medicine Egg Dream

Grandmother Leads Us to the Mountain

On the River Again

Sweat Lodge Northwest

Pink Pontiac and Painted Tipis

A Wolf is Coming

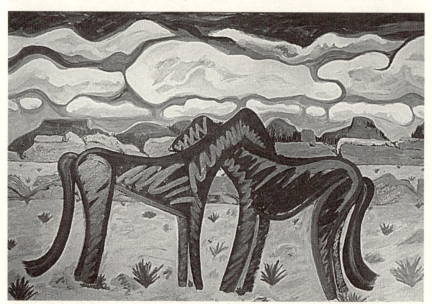

Chinle Horses

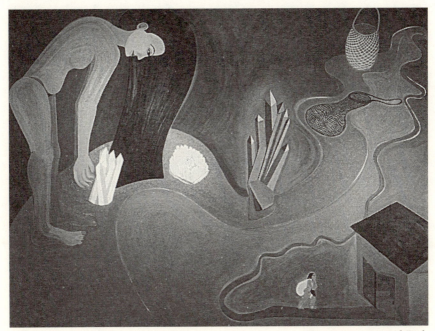

Dreaming a Crystal Path

Holding Up Half the Sky

Shima Telling Stories

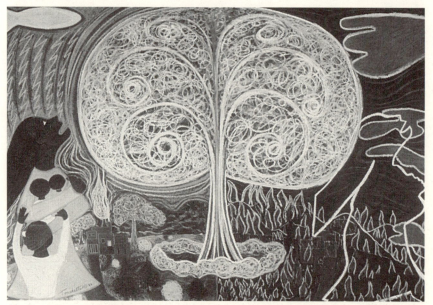

Shadow Mama in Santa Fe

We are the Same, But Different

Elk Woman at Twilight

Elk Woman with Twin Serpents

Elk Woman Gestating

Her Miraculous Birth

Deer Mother Vision

Communication about the Spiritual Path

Offering on the Snowpacked Mountain

Offering à la Mer

My Vision is My Shield

You Can Get AIDS

Confined Gestation

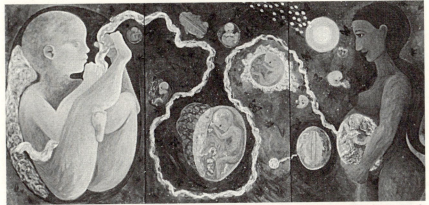

Dreaming of Her Birth

Tikkun Olam

It Took Them All to Save Her

Toxic Pain

Illumination

Fleeing with My Treasures

DEUX

My Music Man

I N THE FALL KIM AND I LOADED OUR BELONGINGS into Daddy's now embarrassing champagne colored Cadillac and my parents drove us to Bard College in upstate New York. I was transferring as a junior and Kim was an entering freshman. Archie talked without pause during the entire four hundred mile drive. Dappled autumn light vibrated around the car illuminating Kim's tense face as she sat next to me in the back seat trying to conceal her anxiety about leaving home. Lori-Ann was in her place in the front seat between our parents.

We arrived at the campus in Annandale-on-Hudson and disembarked. Archie wore pinstriped golfing pants topped by a pressed polo shirt and a pastel sweater tied around his neck. My mother dressed him. Their outfits were color coordinated. We unloaded the car, arguing back and forth. Maman criticized Archie as we cleaned our new dorm rooms in the recently-converted former infirmary. The rooms had to pass Maman's strict standards before we could unpack. At last, we finished and said goodbye. Kimmy was sad to see them go, but I was delighted when their car pulled out and I could explore the pastoral campus on my own.

The first few days at Bard were a blur, filled with the usual orientations and much standing in line. We queued up to register, meet with faculty, and to buy books and supplies. One moment stood out among the endless hours of waiting. On a crisp autumn afternoon as Kimmy and I walked down a path in front of the ancient medieval looking dormitories on Stone Row, I noticed a figure in the distance walking up the hill towards us. The slim young man strolled up the road lined with towering trees that bisected the grassy hill. The giant trees dwarfed his figure, but something about his bearing was compelling. As he neared, I gasped. Laughing, I turned to my sister and said,

"Kimmy, that is my boyfriend."

"Oh Shaall, you're so craaazy."

As soon as I saw his soulful face, I knew I had found my love. Golden ringlets cascaded down his graceful neck to toned shoulders bared under a faded army surplus tee-shirt. He wore khaki shorts, *huaraches*, and had a gas mask bag slung over his shoulder. As he neared, I saw his fine features and nicely shaped legs, but, it was his sizzling green eyes that won me over. Though he barely noticed me, locking eyes with that stranger on that hill changed my life.

In the following days, I found myself searching my "boyfriend's" piercing jade eyes out in every crowd. There were only six hundred students at Bard, so I often caught a glimpse of him at the movies, the coffee shop, waiting in the hallways to meet faculty, or on one of the paths. One sunny Sunday morning when Kimmy and I entered the dining hall, I noticed my boyfriend standing in line, and managed to slip in behind him and his friends. One of the boys turned towards me and asked if I went to Brown, and I explained I was there just for the previous semester. Martin Paisner, a junior at Brown was visiting his brother, Barry. After we introduced ourselves, the Paisner boys said they were returning to Providence that afternoon to drop Martin back at school. Maman was having a hard time adjusting to the two of us being away from home, so I asked if we could hitch a ride back to Rhode Island. They agreed and we jumped into the car. On the long ride, my elation turned to disappointment when Barry talked about how he was in love with his girlfriend at Yale. He was a little nonplussed with two new girls in the back seat and overflowed with a bravado that was far less appealing than the strong silent presence I observed up to then. His words dashed my hopes of making him my boyfriend. Still, I could not get his image out of my mind. That night, I wrote in my journal, *things are beginning to gel—understanding is dawning. Strangest coincidence—riding to Brown with a guy from Brown whose brother is a Bard freshman.* It was September 15, 1973.

In Cumberland I raided my dad's garden plot under my maple tree and brought back eggplants, zucchinis and tomatoes. We invited Barry, and one of his friends who my sister liked, to a vegetarian dinner in our infirmary turned dorm room for the next Friday night. Kim and I cooked ratatouille and *solyanka*, a savory Russian peasant dish of mushrooms, onions, and cabbage, filling the dormitory with mouthwatering aromas. After dinner, we went "down the road" to Adolph's, Bard's legendary watering hole, and danced until the wee hours of the morning. I wore the short blue gym shorts and white tee shirt that were my current uniform. When Barry drew me close and we embraced for the first time, I felt I had found my counterpart. He bent and whispered in my ear,

"Will you come home with me tonight?"

"Not tonight, but maybe tomorrow night."

I knew I could love this man. After a few beers, I was tipsy, and did not want to wake up bleary-eyed with a hang over, and risk turning a chance for a real relationship into a one-night stand. Besides I did not want him to think I was that kind of girl. In the early 1970s, making a guy wait one night was considered playing hard to get.

I returned to my narrow single bed with a huge smile. I dreamed about being in Barry's arms and his image stayed in my mind long after I awoke. No matter how many times I blinked, his earnest face and piercing eyes remained. We spent Saturday together and hiked to the waterfalls cascading into the Hudson where we shared our first kiss.

That night when we began making love, I found the other half of my heart. At seventeen, Barry was already an expert lover. To my delight and satisfaction, we made love throughout the days and nights of the following weeks, breaking apart from each other's embrace only long enough to throw on some clothes to make a run to classes or to the dining commons for refueling. It was the beginning of an astonishing romance. Although he looked more like a curly headed troubadour than a knight in shining armor, Barry rescued me.

At first I could barely believe my newfound happiness. When I looked into the cracked dorm mirror the morning after our first night of passion, I was convinced Barry would hate me if he ever saw the real me. What if he discovered that I really was a *bête* like Archie said? Although an unblemished fresh face with delicate features and big doe eyes framed by shiny cropped hair returned my steady gaze, I was convinced I was a monster and no one could love me the way I was. But Barry did, and as time passed, I found his love was unconditional.

Barry initiated me into sexual practices that would have horrified the nuns. Soon, we settled into a routine of lovemaking, classes, and study. Despite dingy walls and narrow medieval style windows that let in little light, despite the infestation of millipedes that dropped from the ceiling onto our heads eliciting shrieks as they got tangled in our hair, despite the narrow metal cot that creaked under our combined weight, the cramped dorm room was our palace.

My music man introduced me to jazz and world music, and filled my days and nights with the sound of his soulful soprano saxophone blowing long tones, scales, arpeggios, bebop riffs, and jazz torch songs. We shared a devotion to art and music, and a passion for spiritual knowledge. We read Manley P. Hall's *Secret Teachings of the Ages* locked in each others' arms, turned each other on to our favorite books on metaphysics, and shared classes on Indian religion and mysticism. We threw Chinese coins on the concrete floor of the dorm room to consult Barry's well-worn copy of the *I Ching*. He hung a simple tin silhouette of a pony-tailed girl on a leather string around his neck and said—"This is you, My Girl."

Once I met my love, I phoned my parents to share my good news. "I can't wait for you to meet him when you come for Parents' Weekend," I gushed. Shivering at the grimy pay phone in Hobson's hallway, I awaited my parents' congratulations. Their response was frigid, as palpable as a gust of wind in the drafty hall.

"What's Baaaairry's last name, Shaaleen?"

"Paisner."

"Is that Paaaisner like in Goldstein or Goldberg? Shaaleen Gail." Archie sneered.

Revulsion pushed bile into my throat and I almost retched.

By the time parents' weekend arrived, Barry and I were already an item on campus. His parents were thrilled that I gave their wild-haired son a haircut, but less excited about the relationship. Barry said, "Before I left home, my mother told me that if I married a *shiksa*, I could move into their empty house because they both would have dropped dead."

I offered my trembling hand when Barry introduced us outside the dining commons. His dad's eyes exuded warmth. Hy was dark, average height like Barry, with black tightly curled hair. Barry's mom, Sheila *née* Sigesmund was stylish, with a wide smile and direct manner, light hazel eyes, blonde hair, and fair features. Hy and Sheila were about the same age then, that Barry and I are today, but they seemed so grown up, and they were, with two children already in college. Gracious and socially adept, they greeted me politely with cautious cordiality.

Hy told me years later that as soon as he met me on those stairs he knew I had won Barry's heart. Barry's little brothers still lived at home, so I soon met Joel who was fourteen and Richard who was nine. All my life I wanted brothers and, now I had three. Barry was happy to have two ready-made sisters in Kim and Lori-Ann.

The visit with my parents was tense. Archie and Colleen tried to maintain the illusion of "Archie and his beautiful girls." Barry did not fit into their plans. Maman and even Kim seemed threatened by my new relationship. When I left our shared dorm room at the infirmary to move in with Barry, Kimmy told me she felt I had abandoned her. Maman always got upset whenever I brought friends home. She wanted me all to herself and resented my friends taking my time and attention. Barry was a potential permanent interloper. As she had always done with all our friends and beaux, Maman encouraged me to confide about Barry's real or imagined faults so I would run to her if he hurt me. But I would not let her in this time. I had found my safe harbor.

After I returned from the obligatory Christmas horrors in Cumberland, Barry and I drove cross-country in a blizzard to Minneapolis. The Paisner home was a sprawling suburban ranch house that sat on snow-covered hills sloping down to two frozen ponds separated by a lap pool. After living in New England, I was overwhelmed by the spacious beauty of the Minnesota landscape.

Inside, the house was decorated with lots of white in a minimalist contemporary style. It was a well lived-in home with newspapers strewn in the comfortable family room and fluffy towels meant to be used in the bathrooms. Their art collection included prints by Picasso, Dali, Rembrandt, a magnificent Toulouse de Lautrec poster and an original Raoul Dufy. Sheila and Hy traveled worldwide, and began collecting art in the fifties. She was a gracious host who welcomed guests with casual hospitality. Instead of busying herself with last minute cooking, Barry's mom served dinners prepared and frozen before our arrival, then sat to visit with the family and entertained us with jokes and conversation.

Books were everywhere, under easy chairs, piled high on windowsills, overflowing from bookshelves—even in the bathrooms. There were books on Judaism, but also novels, art, philosophy, social action, and history books. I stretched out on the family room's long couch with my toes touching Barry's, our noses buried in books. Sheila and Hy sat in well-worn easy chairs engrossed in their books, and the younger boys often sprawled on the rug reading or doing homework while the television droned in the background. Evenings were pleasant, with all of us reading and lifting our heads to share an interesting paragraph or a bit of family news from time to time. Often Sheila disappeared into the kitchen and return with delicious snacks and homemade caramels to *nosh* on.

I had virtually no experience with Jewish people growing up in Woonsocket. Once while selling chocolate bars for École Jesus Marie down the plat where a Jewish family had moved in, I saw candles burning in the window and three boys watching television wearing caps on their heads. Their parents sat chatting and sipping tea from a *samovar* at the dinner table. Seeing them together made me wistful. But until I met Barry, I had no idea how different Jewish family values were from what I experienced in my home. At the Paisners, I learned that peaceful Jewish homes were not the exception.

Barry's father was a gentle, intelligent, committed doctor and a marvelous storyteller who enthralled me with his tales of doctoring on the Canadian Plains. Dr. Paisner delivered over a thousand babies during his ten years as a country doctor on the plains of Saskatchewan. One time a French Canadian farmer brought the young doctor out to the prairies to deliver his lying-in wife. When they arrived, Hy could see nothing but the featureless empty plain extending to the horizon. As he followed the expectant father, Dr. Paisner noticed a ladder sticking out of a hole cut into the sod. They descended the ladder, and to the young doctor's surprise, there were two rooms dug into the earth. As Hy's eyes adjusted to the darkness, he could see the laboring mother lying on a shelf cut into the dirt surrounded by her seven children.

We left Minnesota's winter to travel south to Albuquerque. The *piñon* dotted ocher mesas were foreign to a girl who grew up among New England's green hills, and I did not imagine ever living in New Mexico. I was mesmerized by the crystalline skies, but day after day of blazing sun soon grew oppressive. I grew up with the comfort of a cloudy haze every third day and the soothing sound of rain when the clouds became sated. I felt dry and exposed in the brilliant desert. But I sensed even then, that the southwest's expansive sky could captivate me with its thunderclouds that splintered the sun's light and sent god's eyes down to the plain below.

We headed to Mexico. In Mitla, we marveled at the geometric stonework mosaics honoring the Feathered Serpent and the Jaguar in the expansive palaces. In Oaxaca the market overflowed with exotic colors, sights, and sounds, all irresistible, including a freshly opened coconut. As we rode the tour bus to Monte Alban, I did not know the sweetness I was chewing on would make me sick within hours. Soon I felt like howling in pain from acute cramps that held my intestines in a painful grip. We rushed back to our hotel. I dashed through the blossoming courtyard garden, scaled the wrought-iron stairs three at a time, and barreled into our dark room to empty my guts in the tiled bathroom.

Hallucinations flashed before my eyes. I spiked a high fever, and the visions became phantasmagoric. The patterned tiles morphed into multi-hued distortions of the *Danzantes* at Monte Alban. Huge patterned serpents, and spotted jaguars moved through the room brushing against my clammy skin as I hung over the latrine. The remainder of the month-long trip was spent in outhouses wishing Pépère Touchette had made his rounds installing toilets in Mexico.

In February we returned to campus and settled into a routine of classes and work, me painting in a new studio near the enchanted forest, and working in the slide library. Barry blew sax in the music department and in trombonist Roswell Rudd's jazz ensemble. One day as I walked down the country roads by our dorm, I was drawn to a clapboard farmhouse sur-rounded by a wild overgrown cottage garden. The magical gardener on the other side of the picket fence shared her knowledge of herbs, flowers, and vegetables, broadening my understanding of herbal medicines and indigenous plants. With her teachings, and a worn copy of Jethro Kloss's *Back to Eden*, I gathered native plants for healing in the forests and fields and practiced brewing spring tonics and herbal remedies for simple illnesses.

The graceful aging Frenchwoman who inhabited the cottage was a textile wizard. She taught weaving in a sunny back bedroom whose beds were replaced by two large harness looms and smaller tapestry looms perched on long hand hewn tables. Each loom held an unfinished intricately patterned textile. The room was a crazy quilt of color and pattern. Shelves from floor to ceiling overflowed with skeins of yarn in every color and weight. Chintz curtains dressed the shuttered windows, where vibrant delphiniums, morning glory, and trumpet vines blocked the view through the mullioned panes.

Mme. Tisserand had been a freedom fighter in the Resistance. While she wove, she mumbled in a deep gravelly voice, chain-smoked thick Gauloise cigarettes, and let the ash drop wherever it fell. Soothed by her thickly accented English, I absorbed her lessons as I counted holes, mounted the warp, and pushed the shuttle through it to form *trois couleurs, leno,* and other traditional French patterns. While I shot the shuttle back and forth, I thought of the labor of my ancestors in French villages, Acadian and Québécois farmhouses, and New England mills.

One warm afternoon I sought out Barry in his usual haunt, blowing sax undisturbed in the Bard Chapel. "Are we going to have a future together?" I began. Barry was confused. "Things are copasetic. Why fix something that's working?" I needed reassurance, and lots of it. "Do you want to stay together?" I whispered trying not to whine. We did not raise our voices, but it was our first disagreement. Making up on the dusty couch in the chapel's back room was delicious. We decided to house hunt.

On the outside, the hundred year old saltbox in Clinton Hollow was a simple homestead. It was set in a green dell in front of a studio cabin and a cavernous weathered barn that were built higher up the hill at the edge of the forest. Inside, the white farmhouse had been transformed into a psychedelic bachelor pad fit for a rock star by its long haired owner who left the remodel half done, rented it to our motley group of artists and musicians, and moved to the City. Everyone pitched in five dollars a week for groceries and we shared cooking; stir fry, or bean soup, brown rice, and *chapattis*. I killed the yeast on my first attempt at making bread, and Barry showed me how to make a fool-proof loaf. The aroma of fresh baked bread and homemade beans filled the farmhouse along with the scents of mulled cider and wood smoke.

Sharing housecleaning chores was another matter. Our housemates' idea of a clean house was far different from my Maman's but I would not be the resident maid so I got used to the dust and dirt. Maman was horrified. She stood in our rustic kitchen, coifed and dressed in a silk suit, clutching her purse and burst into tears. "I can't believe you can live in this filth. This is not how I brought you up." Art, not cleaning, was my priority. I painted in a studio that was an artist's dream with a huge picture window that often framed grazing deer.

In the summer, to pay rent and support our art and music habits, Barry and I worked at a group institution in Millbrook for abused and neglected children from the City. Each morning, I sat among the girls as they combed and braided their hair. They, like Mimi, told me stories, but theirs were about their cruel families. Each had a horrendous tale about being beaten, neglected, or sexually violated. One little feisty girl was shy about having her hair combed. After I won her over and lifted her thick hair, I saw deep keloid scars from cigarette burns dotting her neck and back like mosquito bites. Her mother had burned her repeatedly from infancy. The girls told heartbreaking stories—but each one wanted to return home to their parents.

Jaguar Woman

New York City

I TURNED TWENTY-ONE IN 1975. DURING SENIOR YEAR I struggled to find my artistic voice and grappled with periodic bouts of depression, usually instigated by conflicts with my parents.

Meanwhile, I was welcomed into a Jewish family and introduced to Judaism where I discovered a religion that supported its families and helped create peaceful homes. When Barry took me to my first Passover Seder, I repeated, "I do this because of what the Lord did for me when I was a slave in Egypt."

I delighted in sampling Eastern European recipes that *bubbies* had carried in their memories while fleeing *pogroms* in Russia clutching their little ones, with precious Shabbat candlesticks, Kiddush cups, and *Siddurs* hidden in shawls thrown over their backs. They settled in Canada because there were quotas to keep Jews out of the United States. Barry's Baba Rachel Feldman was well educated and spoke thirteen languages fluently. She fled the Ukraine after the Red Army seized her family's brick factory in Zhitomir near Kiev during the Russian Revolution. Rachel got typhus and lost all her hair. The Red Calvary was about to hang her oldest brother when a handsome lieutenant stopped the hanging saying he was not their enemy. Field Marshall Lieutenant Budenny later became a Russian general in World War II who fought Hitler's Army. At eighteen years old Rachel left Russia alone headed for Fargo, North Dakota to meet the man her parents had arranged for her to marry. En route through Poland, she fell asleep, and the Polish women slit her skirt and stole the *gelt* her mother had sewn into her hem. Somehow she got to Winnipeg, where she learned that her fiancé in America had died while she was on her way to wed him. Rachel stayed in Canada and worked in the garment factories until she met an older man from a nearby *shtetl* in Russia.

Barry's grandfather Morris Pevsner had fled Russia, the Czar's Cossacks, and his family's pressure to become a rabbi during a *pogrom* decades before. When he and his brother Louis arrived in Montreal, the customs agent renamed them Paisner. Morris journeyed to Northern Manitoba and trapped with the Cree before opening a trading post on the edge of the remote Way-Way-See-Capo Reserve. Morris' first wife had died in childbirth leaving an infant daughter, who he had been forced to put in an orphanage.

After Rachel and Morris married, they retrieved the baby girl, and at the end of winter in 1927, they had a son. Rachel's life on the Canadian frontier was grueling. The trading post was near the southern boundary of what would become Riding Mountain National Park when Barry's father Hy was two years old. Their cabin had no indoor heat, electricity, running water, or plumbing. Rachel helped Morris run the trading post, chopped wood, and burned toast on the wood stove each morning. Hy grew up speaking Cree, as well as Yiddish and English, and still loves the taste of burnt toast.

Nurtured by his intellectual mother, Hy graduated first in his class so he could be one of the few Jews admitted to medical school. There were quotas to keep Jews out of medicine too, even in Canada. In Winnipeg, Hy fell in love. Sheila was a city girl at the University of Manitoba. Her mother Lillian was a small child in the early 1900s when she hid with her family in ditches by the roadsides as they fled Russia by night. Sheila's father Henry was a first generation Canadian whose Orthodox dad forced him to quit school and go to work to support his thirteen children so he could study Torah in *shul* all day. Henry did not have much patience for organized religion, but he liked Hy as soon as he found out the earnest young man with horned rimmed glasses was a medical student. After they married, Hy and Sheila departed Estevan where he practiced as a country doctor, and she gave birth to their first two sons. They moved to Minneapolis when Barry was a boy, so his dad could study at the University of Minnesota and specialize in otolaryngology. There they connected with a group of expatriates who had moved south to Minneapolis for opportunity and the "warm weather." Surrounded by the smiling faces of Barry's extended family, I felt at home at last. Visits to Minneapolis soon became more frequent than to Woonsocket.

At Bard, Barry and I were pressured for staying together and propositioned regularly. We remained monogamous—not from moral superiority, but because we could not imagine being with anyone else. Our all-consuming passion protected us from the heartbreak many of our generation experienced. With each challenge to our relationship, we chose each other until people began to think of us as a unit, Barry and Charl. It became a compound word—Barry'n Charl—like Lucy'n Desi and Popeye'n Olive Oyl. Barry was my Romeo and I was his dark haired Juliet, although with my reedy body, I looked more like Olive Oyl, all skinny arms and legs.

On weekends, we headed down to New York City. The excitement of the Big Apple was palpable. As soon as we saw the city lights, we started talking about the geniuses in art, music, philosophy, and business who gravitated to the city from around the world. The city's neighborhoods were a vibrant encyclopedia of cultures and countries that captivated me as much as the art and music did. We explored every area, traveling on foot from Battery Park to Union Square on one weekend, investigating the area south of Fourteenth Street on another, and strolling up Fifth Avenue from the Village to Central Park the next.

New York attracted the best, and it was the place to test our mettle. When I graduated from Bard, Barry transferred to New York University, and we moved to the City. I was finally financially independent. I wore an African hat instead of a traditional mortarboard for graduation. My parents were mortified. They were even more disappointed that I was planning to live unmarried with Barry in New York City. "What will people in Woonsocket, Cumberland, and North Smithfield say, Shaaleen Gail?" Archie whined. I never cared what people in Woonsocket, Cumberland, and North Smithfield said. I was way past trying to fulfill Archie and Colleen's unrealistic dreams and on my way to pursuing my own.

I rarely returned to Rhode Island and when I did I felt less and less a part of the Touchette family. On one visit, my dad took us out to dinner in Providence. As usual, the trouble began in the bar while we waited for our table. As Archie sipped his Scotch on the rocks, Maman was chatting with the barmaid. It was clear that Colleen, who is very friendly and sociable, knew the cocktail server in the skimpy black outfit. Archie accused Maman of frequenting the bar.

"You know that barmaid, Colleen? How do you know her? You come here often, Colleen? You like to come to this bar by yourself? How else would you know the barmaid?"

"You, *trou cul*, Archie. You should know her too. She used to work for your associate. You've met her many times. You just saw her at the Christmas party at his office. How dare you accuse me of going to bars? Who do you think you are to insult me like that?"

I was no longer under Archie's control, so for me, it was just another of the many times my dad would make a fool of himself and embarrass the family in public. To my sisters, who were still very tied to my parents—it was devastating. By the time we sat down to dinner, Kim was in tears. Lori was crying too, but from laughter. Tears ran down her face and a copious amount of mucus flowed out her nose, which she kept blowing into a cocktail napkin. Oblivious, Daddy continued his *faux pas* as he baffled the waitress with his unique style of ordering.

"What's in this clam chowder? Is it the New England kind or the weird kind from Manhattan that has those squishy tomatoes? Do I like that, Colleen? Is that the kind I like, Colleen? What about this Bouillabaisse? What kind of fish is in it? Does it have celery? Or even any celery salt? Because I'm allergic to celery. My face swells up like a baboon if I eat celery salt. Are you sure there isn't celery salt in the Bouillabaisse? Sure, sure? Well, I don't think I should take a chance. Should take a chance, Colleen?"

The waitress tapped her pencil harder and louder on her order pad. Daddy paused and shrugged, "I guess I will have a steak—medium rare."

Lori tossed her sodden napkin into the air in a fit of exasperation. We all looked up, our mouths agape, as the mucus-soaked wad poised in midair, then plopped into the ample cleavage of the lady seated below us. The poor woman bolted from her seat and ran to the bathroom mopping her bosom. Kimmy was inconsolable; she sobbed while Lori-Ann and I doubled over in laughter.

After a summer in a dark loft between Little Italy and Soho, Barry and I spent four years on the Lower East Side in a bright sixth floor walk-up in one of the few habitable buildings on Second Street between Avenue B and C. It was in the most dangerous part of America's oldest ghetto, but it was what we could afford. The loft was oriented to the cardinal directions and had windows on all four sides that offered a panoramic view of Manhattan. It seemed like the perfect perch for our life in New York City. The price was right, so we wrote a check that emptied our savings accounts. We were delighted with our new loft, even after we moved in and discovered the tap water ran brown, the ancient boiler in the basement rarely worked, and harsh winds blew through the bricks that were as porous as cheesecloth. We did not care; we were young, in love, and willing to suffer for art.

Soon after moving, I had a dream about four serpents. In the dream I was sleeping in my loft bed, and I awoke and descended the ladder to the studio. I walked to the east window where I saw the East River and a large yellow snake bit me on my heels. I turned to the south, saw the twin World Trade Towers, and a white snake struck me on my knee. Then I walked to the west and looked out the window at the Hudson River, and a black snake sunk its fangs deep into the back of my neck. Completing the circle, I turned to the north, and saw the spire of the Empire State Building. A red snake reared back and attacked my eyes.

I would be injured in the same four places in real life. The first injury had already happened when I was in Providence and had surgery on my heels. A few days after the dream, I was bicycling home from my job at a dental office on Washington Square in the Village. It was fall, and it was getting darker earlier ever day. As I crossed the intersection of Avenue B and Second Street, I saw the approaching car on Avenue B run the light and race towards me. The world seemed to stop except for the rusty sedan speeding through the red light. I pedaled as fast as I could. *Pedal harder faster. Get past before it hits.* The thought barely formed in my mind when the car's front end plowed into my right leg sending me and the bike to the pavement. As I crashed to the ground, I heard a whistle shriek followed by dozens of whistles answering in unison, then the pounding sound of running feet. Losing consciousness momentarily, I awoke to a crowd of bystanders hovering over me. When I came to, the faces of my Nuyorican, Dominican, and Haitian neighbors were joined by those of the Gatos Muchachos gang. The Chinese family that owned the corner restaurant, the lesbian prostitutes from next door, the *bodega* owners, and their customers all ran out to investigate.

Everyone was chattering and shouting at each other in Spanish, English, Chinese, and patois. "I saw him hit her. He ran right through that red light. Did you see that? Look at him. Look at his eyes. His eyes are pinned. The motherfucker's stoned. Sacré Bleu. He's a fucking junkie. *Pendejo's* stoned. He just ran the light and hit that girl. What the fuck is *whitey* doing coming into our hood and hitting girls off their bikes?"

As I blinked my eyes, I saw a scruffy disheveled man with hooded eyes, looking as confused and traumatized as I felt, stumble towards me. He collapsed to his knees and began bawling while throwing twenty dollar bills around my crumpled body, and slurred, "Here take this money. Just take this money, please? You can have it all. Just don't call the police, lady. Take the money. Please," he droned like a mantra over and over again while tossing cash onto my bleeding leg. The Gatos Muchachos tightened the circle around me, the junkie, and the money—their muscles taut, jaws clenched.

All of a sudden I heard a loud cackle, "Hah. We got your balls in a vice, Hot Lips." The crowd of onlookers parted, even the Gatos moved out of the way respectfully when Fiona Williams sashayed right up to the junkie and pulled up her six foot four inches to tower over him. "Boy, do we ever. We got your balls in a vice Hot Lips, and we ain't gonna let go."

She waved her red bouffant wig wildly through the air, nearly swatting his head. Then squatted down on six-inch platforms and reached a slender arm out to me. "Don't you worry, honey. We'll take care of you. I've already called the police and an ambulance. That's their sirens now, sweetie. You can hear them, can't you? You just lie there 'til they come. They'll take you to Bellevue and fix you right up. Does it hurt much? All that blood sure does look nasty, and I mean nasty. But don't you worry, hon, I'll take care of this joker."

Fiona was so close I could smell her cheap perfume and see the five-o'clock shadow poking through her matte foundation. She glared at the cowering slob yelling, "She not gonna take your filthy money, loser. She gonna sue you." Then she turned again towards me and counseled, "Don't you take his money, honey. You gonna sue his ass." Fiona's eyes fell on the mussed mahogany wig in her fist; and her other hand went to her shining scalp. "Oops. I was so excited I ran out of the house and forgot to put my wig on. 'Magine that. And so close to work time." She adjusted her wig and turned back to the junkie who was attempting to crawl away. "Hold up, low life. You ain't going nowhere." Fiona shrieked while wagging a long manicured index finger in front of his pinned eyes. "Give me your license and registration, pronto. We got your balls in a vice, Hot Lips. You gonna pay."

She scribbled the guy's info and license number on a scrap of paper and pushed it into my bloody hand. Just then, our downstairs neighbor Harvey's bulk cut through the crowd. Relieved to see a familiar face, I asked him to give the note to Barry. As the wail of the police sirens grew louder, Fiona gave me a quick hug and said, "I'll just slip away before the pigs get here. I know you understand, honey. I live right up there on the corner, sweetie. Just come by after you get out of the hospital. You can see my Great Dane puppies. My bitch had ten and they're just adorable. We'll talk and I'll make you my special tea," she said pointing to the third floor window overlooking the intersection where a black light glowed through fluorescent beaded shades. Then Fiona pivoted gracefully and disappeared into the crowd just as the ambulance screeched to a halt and uniformed EMTs emerged with a gurney.

They quickly loaded me into the ambulance and we shrieked our way to Bellevue where I waited interminably in the emergency room surrounded by junkies, psychotics, and felons handcuffed to police guards, all the while hoping Harvey had found Barry, and that he would get to the hospital soon. Barry was frantic when he rushed into the ER. Apparently Harvey had handed him the blood soaked wad with the words, "Your old lady's been hit by a car," without bothering to mention that my injuries were not critical. I was cut up and bruised badly, but the only serious injury was to my right knee, which took the brunt of the impact.

This second bite of the serpent disabled me for two years. I could not work, had no income, and was stuck in a sixth-floor walk-up with no heat or hot water. My parents refused to help unless I returned to Clark Road, but I was determined to stay with Barry, so I borrowed and scrimped until I could work again.

While confined to the loft, except for rare times when I tackled the one hundred and twenty stairs with crutches to see the doctor, I was introduced to the eccentric residents of 223 East Second Street. Our building was the home of an amazing array of Lower East Side characters including a speed crazed couple famous in the East Village modern dance world, Alan Arbus, the photographer's ex-husband, who starred in *Greaser's Palace*, acted in Mel Brooks's *Blazing Saddles*, and played the psychiatrist on *MASH*, John Williams, a born-again Christian whose abstract paintings of monumental crosses were exhibited at the Cathedral of St. John the Divine, and Harvey Robbins, a Beat generation doper and Zen philosopher.

Harvey was a streetwise guru who shattered my suburban naïveté. When I was well enough to negotiate the two flights down to his loft, we knocked on his door to thank him for telling Barry about my car accident. Harvey opened the door with a flourish, looked me up and down, and roared, "My, aren't you a skinny bedink?" as a blast of fetid air reeking of rotten eggs, mold, body odor, stale urine, and marijuana smoke hit us head on. A television blared behind his bulk which filled the doorway partially hiding unbelievable chaos. Harvey flashed a wide nearly toothless grin and bellowed, "Great. You're just in time for the *Gong Show*."

Before the show was over, we learned that at thirteen Harvey became a heroin addict from years of dipping his pinkie into his mom's morphine prescription as he returned from picking it up for her at the pharmacy. Before being diagnosed with terminal cancer, his mother had been a beauty who easily entranced his brilliant and well-born father. But when she discovered she was pregnant, the wealthy scion refused to marry her. Mother and child were sentenced to a life of struggle and poverty in New York's underclass. Harvey's brilliance earned him a full scholarship to MIT, but he did not accept it because he could not bear to leave his dying mother. Harvey's other addiction was his old lady. When we arrived, he explained that his goddess was asleep, but would soon awake to entertain us with her beauty. He complained about all the men who could not keep their eyes and hands off his beautiful nymph.

After Harvey introduced us to the diverse and interesting people that sat in small groups conversing around his loft, we ventured out of the corner, and cautiously followed him across the floor. The entire expanse of the loft was filled ankle deep with several layers of toys, dirty clothes, junk, soiled diapers, and rotten food. Harvey explained, "Every morning I get up at dawn and rush to Salvation Army to choose toys for the kids as they take them off the trucks. Then I run home and deposit the score in the middle of the room and the kids go crazy. Look what I found today…"

As we listened, we could see that Harvey's finds of the day must have been swallowed up by the rubble of weeks and months of past scavenging as soon as they hit the floor.

We followed our new neighbor's jiggling backside to the back of the loft, and noticed there were other living beings among the chaos. A stocky toddler stood stranded in the middle of the vast garbage heap. She sucked hard on a pacifier while trying to find an empty space to place her foot. The baby's wailing and outstretched arms were ignored by her mother who lay nodding out on a filthy mattress at the far end of the room. Harvey's goddess was snoring with drool dripping onto her paisley muumuu. An upper denture floated in the glass she held upright in her hand. With a grand gesture, Harvey pointed to Sparrow, "There she is. She will be up in awhile to make us coffee. She is only half asleep. She has to stay awake to hold onto that glass to make sure I do not steal her dentures. It's the only way I can be sure she is faithful because she's vain. She will not go out without her teeth."

Then Harvey turned to the baby who had stopped her crying to play with the snot dripping from her nose, and said in the sweetest voice imaginable, "Hi Ariel, my darling. How is Daddy's little girl? Go read with your brother for awhile. Then you can come sit on Daddy's lap." The toddler beamed a smile, turned, and then determinedly made her way through the trash towards her brother. Harvey explained, "The children benefit from the mess because it requires them to develop more balance and agility than children who grow up in clean homes." The man was a veritable fount of child rearing expertise.

Cody sat happily in a corner surrounded by books. The three-year-old was totally immersed in the encyclopedia, which he read aloud to a platoon of plastic army men. Once Ariel reached him, she mimicked her older brother and both children bent bulbous heads intently over books. Nearby, their older sister Sabrina, who had a different father, lay splayed out on a king size waterbed bed sucking her thumb. The four year old fragile waif was naked except for a soaked diaper. With her free hand, she alternately twisted matted strands of her hair and scratched the lice at the nape of her neck while staring listlessly into space with sunken vacant eyes. As we passed, Harvey explained "Sparrow brought her along when we hooked up, but Daddy still loves my Sabrina—just like my own," he cooed, eliciting a weak smile.

The scene we witnessed in Harvey's loft made us dizzy. What brought these accomplished people, from Harlem schoolteachers and visionary artists to local newscasters and media figures, jazz musicians and neighborhood activists to Harvey's salon? Perhaps it was the children's charm. Maybe it was the marijuana. The smoke was good and flowed freely. No, it was Harvey who was an original.

Over the next months and years we learned Harvey's bizarre appearance was a shield to repel the unworthy. He held court in his filthy lair conducting Platonic dialogs and railing eloquently about the hypocrisy of the bourgeoisie. Harvey was an unlikely repository of brilliant thinking on a global scale. He was an expert on the history of warfare, jazz, and the natural mind's search for altered states. Something about Harvey inspired friendship and loyalty. In his Salvation Army get-ups of inflatable rubber shorts and wooly sheepskin vests or down jackets, topped by his wild savage hair and ritual markings, Harvey looked like a lunatic, but sounded like a sage. He was a *koan* incarnate.

Harvey's Achilles heel was his "old lady" Sparrow, who he idolized as a wanton sex goddess. Sparrow's drug induced haze made her think the hag reflected in the mirror was still the svelte hundred pound girl who left upstate New York for the first time at seventeen. Dressed in satin slinky numbers with plunging necklines pinned with a fake gardenia that highlighted patterns of stretch marks streaking her bosom, she'd grab a Fischer-Price Sing-a-long microphone, and entered another world where she was Billie Holiday and Janis Joplin incarnate, and said, "Ya know I'm a singer. I'd be famous if Harvey didn't keep me down with these damn kids." Most often, soon after she began crooning *Lover Man*, she nodded off between the bridge and the chorus.

Harvey could not bear to see his kids hungry. Sparrow counted on that. If she waited long enough he would find someone else to feed them. He sent Sabrina up the frozen two flights of steps to knock on my door just as the smell of *toast daughty* drifted under the door. I offered her a plate topped with butter and maple syrup. Within moments, Cody and Ariel would be at the door knocking. I loved cooking and they were fun company. Besides I could not bear to see hungry kids. While my knee healed, I was their "nanny." I took care of them for a few hours a day, got them out of diapers, and the nits out of their hair, and taught them to keep themselves clean. We began studying; letters, numbers, and reading for Ariel and Sabrina; astronomy and researching everything under the sun for Cody.

When I could walk with a cane, I took them all over Manhattan. We rode the subway after getting hot dogs at Katz's Deli, and emerged at a different magical place every time: the Museum of Natural History, Central Park, MOMA, the Guggenheim, and the Met. On weekends, we met friends for outings to the Bronx Zoo, and Coney Island. Nearly everyday, I put Ariel in a stroller from the Salvation Army and took the children for a walk, usually to Thompkins Square Park, where I watched them play on the swings and slides while keeping an eye out for junkies and derelicts among the little old Yiddish and Ukranian people who fed the pigeons. No matter how shabbily I dressed, or how dirty and uncombed I let my hair get, I could not walk half a block without the sneers, hoots, whistles, "Mamacitas" and "Ooooh Mamas" starting. No woman alone was safe in the neighborhood—no matter what time of day.

Everything was so dirty. There was the regular New York grime and soot—plus hundreds of years of neglect. Soaps and detergents were priced so high at the corner *bodega* that it was nearly impossible to get and keep anything clean. Welfare moms had to worry about the price of milk and diapers. Cleaners were not high on the grocery list. I got by in this world, but I could leave any time I wanted. Harvey pointed out, "People like you are just slumming. You're living in poverty, but it's your choice." It made me appreciate the sacrifices Maman, my grandparents and ancestors made to struggle up to the middle class.

We were sitting in Harvey's loft sipping coffee and looking at the tube, when there was a pounding knock, and the door burst open. "Just came from Adopt-a-Building bro. They're helping welfare mothers get houses over there. I did some carpentry for them." Harvey looked up from the TV and smiled,

"Barry and Charl... Bo, Kelly, and Aquay."

"Aquaybonnon." Kelly corrected.

"Right, right, Kelly, Aquaywhatever. Okay, Bo's from Puerto Rico. Did some time, but he's a good egg. This refined "lady" was born in the projects between C and D."

Bo was tall and lean, the color of bittersweet chocolate. He and Aguay had the same heart-melting smile. Under his snowsuit, the toddler was encased in a body cast. Bo balanced him in the bizarre white armor in the crook of his long forearm. Kelly had spent the day waiting at the welfare office. "They make you feel like *sheeeeet*. Made me sit there all day, *pendejos*—with this baby in a cast. Kept making me wait to fill out more forms like they don' know he has *spinal bifeda* by now, *motherfuckers*."

Kelly and Bo couldn't get married because they'd loose Medicare benefits for Aquay. Kelly stamped her foot and said, "I hate that we hafta hide that we're a family, just so Aquay can have his operations. He's had twelve already. An he ain't even eighteen months yet—doctors say he's gonna need more. Wha' the fuck we gonna do if we lose our Medicare?" She grabbed Aquaybonnon from Bo, settled him on her broad hip, and strode over to the waterbed where she plopped him down in the middle of Harvey's brood. Aquay squealed as the kids took turns amusing him and Kelly tugged his snowsuit off. After awhile, Bo pulled himself out of Harvey's recliner and announced. "Be back in awhile. Gotta help Miquel on that theater on Sixth Street just up from our place. Kelly, you come on home when you're done here. And get Aquay something to eat for God's sake." Before turning his back on her sneer, Bo bent down and whispered to us. "Nice meeting you folks. Come on by the theater on Sixth. There's a big sign out front, Nuyorican Theater—can't miss it. Come by and I'll show you around. Just got seats donated. It's looking good. And that Piñero is a damm good writer—tells it like it is."

I visited Bo and checked out the theater. Kelly and I hung out together with Aquay in her narrow railroad flat on East Sixth Street almost every day. I'd stop in with Harvey's kids on our way to Thompkins Square Park. Aquay breezed through his operations and learned to walk with a determined smiling face using little metal crutches. Barry and I built him a set of drums from discarded wooden barrels and deerskin from Soho factories to see his face light up as he banged on them. I'd bring some food to supplement Aquay's meager diet and give Kelly something to put into her stomach besides beer. We watched her soaps and the kids playing together. I hoped my company would break up the monotony of her days caring for Aquay. Drive-by shootings were becoming frequent. As I stepped off Kelly's stoop one day with Ariel in my arms and Sabrina and Cody in tow, a car whizzed by and shot up the tenement three doors down on the corner of 6th and Avenue B.

After living in our bohemian style loft, I could no longer bear being in the house on Clark Road for even one night, and visited my parents only if I could stay at the lake. Maman was heartbroken. She said I was rejecting her if I didn't love her house. "I just like staying at Pépère's Lake." Maman didn't buy it. I was lying to myself as well as to her. The deep resentment I felt about Maman's obsession with her house made me hate everything it symbolized. I couldn't admit it, but I was rejecting her—I had to.

During my years in New York my parents went through profound changes. One night, Lori-Ann called in tears. "Can you please come home this weekend? I'm worried about Mom. She cries all the time. I don't know what to do. Please come home and talk to her."

When I arrived, Maman sobbed and shook as we sat on the bed in my old room. She said she already missed me and Kim unbearably, and could not bear the thought of Lori going away to Brown in the fall, and being in the house alone with Daddy. I took her by the shoulders, and said, "Mom, I love you and will support you if you decide to leave Daddy. But you are the only one who can make that decision. If you're not going to divorce him, you have to pull yourself together. You are losing control. If that happens you won't have any say. You'll be institutionalized and strangers, doctors, will decide what's best for you." She collapsed in my arms sobbing.

Afterward Maman threw her heart and soul into the volunteer work she did since I was in high school as a catechist for the mentally and physically challenged. As the years passed she often said how disappointed she was that the time she invested in raising us had not turned out as she planned. She resented that her daughters had all moved far away and did not practice Catholicism. "I'm never going to give again where I am not appreciated," she averred, and devoted herself to building a program to train and direct volunteer catechists. The Bishop soon appointed her as lay administrator of the program for the entire diocese. She became a spiritual leader in the Church, and was anointed a Eucharistic Minister.

One weekend I met my parents while they visited friends in Massachusetts. Over the years Archie had embraced tennis with a vengeance. He played several times a week and won lots of trophies at tournaments.

His doubles partners struggled to keep the ball in the air at all costs to avoid Archie's harangue. One even dove into a corner to return a baseline shot and ended up with a compound fracture. Up to then, that had been Archie's only tennis casualty. But that weekend as he reached up to slam the ball onto his opponents' base line, Archie was his fierce self one moment, and the next—he was paralyzed. He collapsed on the court, unable to move from the neck down. The ambulance rushed him to the hospital where they diagnosed a ruptured cervical disc.

Maman and I were chatting with her friend when the call came. I drove her to the hospital, and sat at my dad's bedside. He was so frail and scared. He seemed moved by my love and concern. I think it surprised him.

For twenty-four hours Archie could not move and did not know whether he would be paralyzed for life. He was frightened. Praying fervently, he seemed to be making a deal with God. I will never know for sure, but when he regained mobility after the laminectomy, Archie seemed different.

It was as if the monster in him was deflated. He would still bicker and rant, but the brutal vicious edge had been dulled. He sneered less when we ordered at restaurants, and even fought less when he drank. Sometimes, he could even go through a visit from Mimi without insulting her.

"That was a close call, Shaaleen Gail. I had to make a deal with the man upstairs. I could not feel a thing, you know. It's good they fixed me up. That's a scary feeling you know, Shaaleen Gail. Your daddy could not feel a thing from the neck down, from the neck down. It was not funny at all. Not at all, at all, at all, Shaaleen Gail."

Once I was in New York, I sent cards and presents for holidays and birthdays, but rarely visited my parents. When I did, I could never seem to keep from being drawn into their bickering. Maman would reiterate how disappointed she was with the choices I made. The visits would end with outbursts and crying. Once I even left the cottage in a huff, yelling, "You will never see your grandchildren." I was years from even thinking about having children. For months and years Maman refused to talk to me.

One night I had a shocking flashback I tried to deny and suppress. Barry and I were making love and the creepiest image kept flashing into my mind. I saw myself as an infant on the changing table, and my daddy's face above me. It seemed to be reflected in a mirror. Daddy was shaving. I heard water running. Then I felt a big hard finger on my pipi. It hurt so much. I was crying. I heard violent knocking at the door. Maman's voice was shouting over and over again, "*Ouvre la porte, Archie. Ouvre la porte. Open the door. Ça c'est tu bons sens? Ça c'est tu bons sens?* Does that make any sense? *Ça c'est tu bons sens?*" Daddy answered, "Well excuse me. I forgot to burp up my apple seeds, Miss Please and Thank You." I heard a child's voice repeat, "I told you mommy. I told you mommy. I told you mommy."

The flashback was so creepy, I couldn't believe it. I tried to squeeze the image out of my eyes, but it kept reappearing. I did drawings of the memory. They scared the hell out of me. It couldn't be true. This could not have happened. Could it? Daddy would never have done that to me. He was too sexually repressed. I never heard of anyone doing that to a baby. I hid the drawings. And I forgot about them for many years. I just put it out of my mind.

Flashback Memory

Repatriation

I WAS DETERMINED TO LEAVE WOONSOCKET and my past behind and make a new life for myself in New York City. Though Maman whined and tried to make me feel guilty about abandoning her, I left her behind to get away from Archie. I thought I left the memories of my monster daddy behind me too. Healing from the physical wounds from the car accident, I read Dee Brown's *Bury My Heart at Wounded Knee,* relearned history from the point of view of women and indigenous people, and researched my ancestors. Dreams led me to explore the skills Mimi and Maman had been unable to teach me. Maman thought the soil was dirty. Now I reconnected with the earth, so I could teach this lost knowledge to my children. I wanted them to grow up knowing where they were on the earth in relation to the directions and the sun and moon. I wanted them to watch the paths the celestial bodies made across the sky and mark their own paths through life in relation to them.

After I rejected the Catholic Church, I needed spirituality compatible with my hopes and ideals. My ancestors' indigenous traditions resonated with my soul, and I began to reclaim them. Though I had no access to medicine men or women, powerful dreams connected me with my ancestral spirituality. The dreams inspired paintings. Native Americans who saw my art shared their knowledge of the traditions. I smudged myself with sage, cedar, and sweetgrass, practiced simple ceremonies and prayed that one day I would participate in ceremonies held in community like sweatlodge and Sundance.

My knee healed. I worked at various part time jobs, and painted full time. After a stint at the Tin Palace, Phoebe's in the East Village hired me. I was a terrible waitress. The suits, longshoremen, and theater types would pinch and slap my ass, and I slapped them back and said, "*N'touche pas.*" "Don't touch." They whined, "Can't you just give me a little? You cut your tip in half, sweetie." I got orders mixed up. People yelled. Jazz drummer Phillip Wilson who tended bar befriended me. "You go, girl. These guys are just not used to girls who bite back. This way they respect you."

People came from all over Manhattan to Phoebe's in cabs and limos dressed in all kinds of get-ups. The actors from La Mama Theater around the corner, and the cast of *Godspell* came in after every performance and broke into song spontaneously as they crowded around two small tables drinking beer. When the Lower Manhattan Ocean Club opened up, Mickey Ruskin hired me to wait tables. Like Ruskin's Max's Kansas City, LMOC immediately became the newest trendy spot to see and be seen as soon as the doors opened. Every night, NYC's glitterati rocked the place dancing to hot new bands debut. At night, Julian Schnabel pushed plates of mussels and steaks off the grill and out of the kitchen unto the stainless steel warmer before he broke other plates and clued them to huge canvases Mary Boone sold for millions. The Club was Schnabel's unlikely launching pad to a Blue Chip art career. The waitresses giggled about his antics schmoozing with the Club's famous patrons after his shift cooking was over at night. On the night shift I shook my booty to some of Talking Heads' first New York performances while balancing trays full of cocktails. Philippe Petit, who walked a tightrope between the towers of the World Trade Center, was my favorite regular. One night, I ran into the lady's room on break to see two men standing at the sink. The surly Columbians in expensive suits dripping with gold chains hovered over several huge piles of cocaine sitting on the sink. At first they stiffened. Instinctively, their hands went for their guns, but when they saw it was only a waitress, they started sweet talking me. "*Que linda, preciosa. Quiera esos?* Want some?

Quiera little toot?" "*No, gracias, Señores,*" I replied and quickly backed out the door, grabbed my tray and disappeared into the crowd.

Some part time jobs were more creative. I crocheted and beaded unique jewelry for the Tribal Arts Gallery with their African beads, and they sold them at their uptown gallery on 57th Street near MOMA. At night, I knit signature vests for Joan Vass who was just starting out as a designer. Each week, I picked up a shopping bag overflowing with wool, jumbo knitting needles, and a pattern. I was paid $12 for each finished vest that Vass sold for $90 apiece at Henri Bendels off Fifth Avenue. I was her only English-speaking pieceworker, and I am pretty sure the only one who attended Wellesley and had a BA.

I brought my portfolio of exotic handmade necklaces to one of Bendels' monthly open houses where young designers present their wares to the buyers. "This black group, this red one, that turquoise piece, and all these gray pieces are wonderful." As I saw the elegant former model smile and point to several groups of my necklaces, I was elated. But my balloon burst when she said. "We would need these pieces in quantities of at least a hundred each. Can you come back in a month with a sample trade line that you can produce in mass quantities?" It was a great opportunity, but with no capitol to buy materials and hire workers there was no way I could even imagine delivering those kind of orders in such a short time—and what would I do if they didn't sell? My heart was more interested in creating art than a product line, so, I gave my jewelry as gifts instead of turning into a mass production machine.

But I did work an assembly line. Barry and I both got jobs at a French bakery in SoHo. He left before dawn to drive the Voilá delivery truck bringing fresh croissants to the Mayor at Gracie Mansion, the ladies who created the Silver Palate, and the finest restaurants in New York City, some of whom claimed they made the croissants and delectable puff pastry in their own kitchens. I walked west on Houston Street later in the morning and stood on the assembly line making thousands of *croissants, brioches, pains aux chocolat* and *papillons* each day to the rhythm of salsa music blaring on a fuzzy radio, dressed in baker's white with flour dusting my hair and skin.

Barry studied saxophone with avant-garde jazz saxophonist Oliver Lake and performed with the Electronic Music Mobile and the People's Heritage Orchestra, a Jamaican reggae band. He rode the subway to the

South Bronx nightly to rehearse in a bizarre lounge bar that looked like it had been imported wholesale from the beach in Jamaica complete with tiki lamps, tropical decorations, syrupy rum drinks topped with colorful paper umbrellas, and big island women whose breasts and bottoms erupted out of bold floral sarongs as they danced.

Often I accompanied the band on gigs in bars and dance halls in Harlem, the Bronx, and the rest of Manhattan. When People's Heritage played for a Chinese wedding, the bass player's girlfriend and I sat in the back of the hall giggling, and washing down Southern fried chicken she smuggled in with shots of Wild Turkey. The bride's wardrobe changed as she disappeared four times to re-emerge in a new costume from an exotic traditional red Chinese wedding dress with an elaborate gilded headdress to a traditional white Western gown, a blue chiffon ball gown, and a smart silk shantung suit topped with a pillbox hat.

We were regulars in the seventy's loft jazz scene at concerts by Sam Rivers, The World Saxophone Quartet, Cecil Taylor, Sun Ra, and Ornette Coleman. At debuts of punk rock bands at CBGB's in the East village, we danced among leather clad, tattooed, and pierced head bangers. Barry played with alto saxophonist Tim Berne who introduced us to the legendary Julius Hemphill. Julius visited our loft often—he couldn't resist my tempura.

We returned to Bard for Kim's graduation in 1977. My parents, Lori-Ann, Kim's boyfriend Fred Morgan, and his parents were all there to celebrate. My sister Kim had dated J.P. Morgan's great grandson since her freshman year, and everyone expected them to marry after graduation, have their wedding picture posted in *Vanity Fair*, and take their place in Long Island society. After the ceremony, Barry and I lounged on the lawn while waiting for the grown-ups. When they arrived, we stood up and were covered with blades of dead grass. Archie and Mr. Morgan, both began picking at the grass on my bodice. "Shaaleen, your dress is covered with grass. What were you two doing on the grass? Ah-hénh- hénh - hénh?" Archie cackled. Both men pulled on my jersey dress in opposite directions at the same time, and the entire top fell to my waist exposing my breasts to the graduating class and their guests. Both men were flabbergasted. "How did that happen?"

stammered J.P. Morgan the Third. "What kind of dress is that? Shaaleen Gail. Cover yourself up." Archie shrieked. It was hilarious. Gentlemanly Mr. Morgan blushed six shades of red.

After her graduation Kim and Fred were staying at Pépère's Lake with my parents, when Kim left Fred to hang out with Archie and Colleen, and drove to Cambridge for a romantic tryst with her former chemistry professor. Hilton Weiss was on sabbatical and had a fellowship at Harvard, and Kim's first job as a chemist was at Gillette in Boston. It was one of the rare times when she would not be a "good girl." Something told her to take a risk.

After Kim's graduation, Barry and I went backpacking out West, never sleeping in a hotel for three months. After hiking in the Adirondacks, we headed north to the Laurentians, and then canoed the wild Algonquin Waterways. One evening we went for a walk at dusk and were startled by a bear cub. When we ran into the wilderness to avoid the mama bear, each lake and wooded area looked like the next, and I was lost for the first time in my life. Just when I was about to give up, I saw the fading glow of the setting sun on the tree trunks and followed them to the east to find the way back to our lakeside camp. Barry wanted to go the opposite way. He had the worst sense of direction. We'd walk up Fifth Avenue and go into a store and he would turn back down the street when we walked out of the store. I teased him, "That's why your people got lost in the desert for forty years. They went around in circles."

I felt at home on those northern woodland lakes. As we traveled through Canada and continued west, people welcomed us at Indian Reserves. We walked through the wildflower flats of Hiawatha Forest on the Upper Peninsula, camped on the Great Lakes, and then canoed the Boundary Waters that are the homeland of the Ojibwe. In South Dakota, we were invited to our first Sun Dance outside Rosebud, and in Wyoming we visited the site of the victory over Custer depicted in Mimi's painting and hiked a forty-mile loop in the Rockies. We camped in Montana's old growth forests then turned south for a sojourn among Canyonlands' red rocks. On the way we stopped at reservation towns, meeting people, sharing food, stories, and laughter. When we entered Glacier National Monument, we were awestruck by the glaciers and craggy snowcapped mountains and the thousands of waterfalls. No wonder it was sacred ground for my Blackfeet ancestors who trekked west to Going to the Sun Mountain for vision quests.

There's a snapshot of me feeding a chipmunk squatting on the edge of a cliff, my fuchsia dress contrasting with the turquoises and greens of the background's cascades and mountains.

We set out for a two week trip in Montana's Gallatin Wilderness and headed toward a pyramid shaped mountain amid the white peaks of the Rockies. Rain poured incessantly on our backs, packs, and soggy tent. We stopped for a few days of cuddling, sharing secrets, and reading aloud until we decided the skies weren't going to clear before our food ran out, shouldered the sodden packs, and slogged out of the mountains.

I snapped a photo of Barry muscular and lean standing triumphant on a ledge with the emerald pyramid mountain behind his head on the first clear day. He looks like a sun burnished mountain man with a wild red beard all long and scruffy.

When we turned east, we were transformed. This was our walkabout, our first vision quest. Returning east, I saw New York City with new eyes. It was no longer the center of the world—now it looked like a cluttered island on the edge of a vast continent.

Oil Spill

Danger
Comes Knocking

THE MYSTICAL COLORFUL WORLD I CAPTURED IN MY ART after we returned from our trip couldn't block out the dreary monochromatic reality of grimy poverty surrounding me in our loft. The Lower East Side had always been dangerous, but as time went on the danger grew. When the workers replaced the boiler, they leaned the old plates against the storefront next door where the Gatos Muchachos squatted. The gang went ballistic and accosted us at our door *en masse*. Their leader, a tall Puerto Rican in a studded denim jacket, grabbed Barry, lifted him up by the collar and slammed him against the wall. "Your workers broke our windows. You gotta pay us," he said pointing to the storefront's previously cracked plate glass. "You pay, or we're gonna beat up everybody who comes to your building. Then we'll burn the building down, little children, babies, and all."

It became clear that the bars on our loft windows were keeping us prisoners in our own home as well as keeping intruders out. When Bo, heard about the gang's threats, he told Barry, "You just have to look them in the eye and let them know you're willing to go the whole way." "The only problem is I'm not willing to kill anyone. And they know it."

We arranged for Bo and his family to move into the recently vacated loft in our building and got Adopt-a-Building to provide materials for renovation. They had barely moved in when Bo was assaulted. Kelly woke the whole building wailing from the first floor in the dead of night. Bo had been beaten into a coma by a Jamaican gang. We rushed to Bo's bedside. But he was already gone—just a shell of his former self, bruised and swollen, wrapped in gauze attached to tubes and life support systems. We were sure we were no longer safe in the Lower East Side. If Bo couldn't protect himself—how could we?

As soon as Bo's doctors told her there was no hope of recovery, Kelly took up with Omad, a very scary ex-con on parole, and moved him into Bo's loft. They were settled in for a week when her new lover held the door open for me one morning when I returned home from work with groceries. "Why don't you come in for a cup of coffee?" Not wanting to insult him, I accepted, and we chatted for an hour or so mostly about Islam and why he'd become a Muslim in prison. The next day, Kelly ambushed me in the foyer. "Omad said you're pretty and smart. If you'se so smart, wha' you gonna do with this?"

She screamed like a banshee, lunged at my head, grabbed my waist-length hair, wrapped it around her fist, and yanked it by the roots over my face like a hockey player yanking a jersey over another player's face. I screeched. The pain immobilized me. I was no street fighter and Kelly was over sixty pounds heavier than me and grew up on the streets of the Lower East Side where chick fights were a spectator sport. Taking advantage of my surprise, she delivered sharp punches repeatedly to my stunned face blackening both eyes, clawed at my face with her nails, and tore out my beaded earring ripping a permanent long hole in my ear lobe.

Barry arrived as Kelly was pummeling me. He wedged himself between us and pried us apart. We both fell backwards to the concrete floor. When Kelly fell on her fat ass—it was just the beginning of our problems.

The next day, I was awoken at dawn by Harvey's bellowing at the bottom of the stair well. "Baaaaaarrrrrrry, Omad says he's gonna kill you. Kelly's already pregnant with his baby." I froze with terror. It was my fault. I shouldn't have befriended Kelly. Why did I help her get the loft? Why did I talk to Omad at all?

As it happened, we had time off work at the bakery and were leaving the next day for a weeklong back-packing trip to the White Mountains. I spent a sleepless night tossing and turning, startling at every night sound, convinced it was Omad climbing the stairs to kill us. The next day we packed and snuck out of the loft in the middle of the night. We drove out of the City thankful to escape with our lives hoping the maniac would cool down while we were away. Throughout New Hampshire the locals stared at me with sympathy and eyed Barry as if he were a monster. They thought he was the one who beat me up and gave me the black eyes.

Up to then, neither Barry nor I had been mugged despite close calls. A break-in robbed us of our sense of security, but left our lives and valuables intact. The neighborhood had gotten more perilous after the Gatos Muchachos moved next door. Now, it was indisputable. Our time was up on the Lower East Side. The magic that had kept us safe in one of the most dangerous ghettoes in America had run out.

We put a deposit on a raw loft in SoHo on Greene Street and prepared to get out alive. With our belongings camouflaged in black garbage bags, we left in the middle of the night. The sparse space in Soho looked onto an airshaft and a brick wall. We needed a place insulated from the sensory overload New York City had become.

Soon after we settled in our loft, I became ill. After vomiting for several days, I couldn't keep any food down, and Barry rushed me to the hospital doubled over in pain. I was hospitalized for a week and fed through an IV. Even when I was discharged, I couldn't keep any food in my stomach. Indians made porridge from slippery elm bark for pregnant women who could not keep any other food down, so I whipped up the mucilaginous gunk and forced myself to swallow it five times a day. For several weeks, the porridge was the only thing I could stomach, and it kept me from starvation. But I couldn't subsist on the slime forever and the doctors' drugs were no help, so I consulted a natural health center that had just opened way out on Long Island. It was one of the first of its kind in the New York area. I didn't know what to expect, but the diminutive Korean *amma* therapist had a reassuring manner.

"There are seven energy centers up and down spine. We call them *chakras*. Each have different color—different purpose. Three lower charkas —more about body. Three upper charkas—more about spirit. Heart connects them. Very important keep heart charka open, or spirit and mind can not talk. Throat chakra is fifth—color sapphire blue—has to do with speaking truth. Can get sick here—if holding tongue. *Chi*-energy flow through all seven chakras. From there, go to *nadis*. When there is block— you get sick. I clear blocks—energy flows—you feel good."

The Korean therapist touched each chakra and massaged them in a clockwise direction. There was a deep thick knot in my solar plexus that throbbed. As she kneaded it, the pulse steadied. She explained,

"See, Chi-energy blocked here. Third charka. Hold fear here. Feel pulse. Very strong. Boom—Boom—Boom. Too strong. Everyday—you rub like this—strong circle—sunwise. Keep massaging until soft, pulse quiet— heal self."

Each visit, the healer moved energy through my chakras and *nadis*. Each visit, she taught me more about how to work on healing myself. One day, she said,

"You need leave City. Air bad for you. Never healthy until leave."

"I can't leave now," I protested.

"Then you get air conditioner. Right away. Least you can do for health."

Forks

AFTER I WAS RELEASED FROM THE HOSPITAL, writer Jamake Highwater hired me to work in his office in Little Italy amid paintings, sculpture, and a vast library on Native American culture. I didn't tell Jamake about my Indian ancestry, but my Indianess was etched on my face. One day the director of the American Indian Community House Gallery visited. The next day, Jamake confronted me. "Pete said as soon as he met you, he was sure you are Indian. Why didn't you tell me?" "I didn't want to offend you. I only have my family's oral history to document my heritage. I didn't grow up on the reservation, and did not want you to think I was one of those phonies who talk about their Indian Princess Grandmothers."

Working for Jamake I talked with fascinating people like Indian activist LaDonna Harris, author Kurt Vonnegut, his wife photographer Jill Krementz, and dancer Erick Hawkins, and met celebrities like Bianca Jagger, and Harvey Keitel. Winona LaDuke visited while she was still a student at Harvard; we connected, and became close like sisters. Besides doing research for Highwater's many books, typing manuscripts, and being an all around gal Friday, Jamake gave me the list of contemporary Indian artists to invite to be featured in *The Sweetgrass Lives On*. I wrote the artists to offer them a chance to be in the seminal book on contemporary North American Indian Art. Artists visited and brought their art, or mailed bulky packages of slides and photos. Winona's mom, painter Betty LaDuke dropped by periodically when she returned to the States via Kennedy airport after working with women artists in Africa, and we became friends and colleagues. Jeanette Looking Clear came and brought Jamake a colored pictographic abstraction. Every day was like Christmas with the mail overflowing with slides, photos, and resumés from a variety of Indian artists from well-known painters like Fritz Scholder, George Morrison, and R.C. Gorman to emerging artists like Dan Namingha, Jaune Quick-to-See Smith, and Mike Kabotie.

I persisted in the almost impossible task of locating the legendary Ojibwe artist Norval Morriseau who spent his days canoeing in the Canadian Quetico Provincial Boundary Waters rarely making contact with the outside world. Billy Soza Warsoldier was on the lam from the FBI because of his actions during the A.I.M. takeovers at Plymouth Rock, Alcatraz Island, and the BIA Building in D.C., but I searched until I got slides through George Longfish of Warsoldier's art including his infamous *Death FBI* painting. It took many phone calls to get Aberbach Galleries to agree to include T.C. Cannon's art, but I wouldn't give up. Close to publication, Mr. Aberbach agreed, and we got to use several of T. C.'s paintings including *Beef Issue at Fort Sill* for the book cover. Some of the artists, like George Morrison from Minnesota became teachers and friends. Working for Highwater, I met many artists who encouraged me to be part of the Indian art world. The expertise I developed led to a career of interesting jobs, experiences, and deep friendships. Though my highest salary during the entire time I worked for Jamake was only $3.25/hour—the experience was worth far more.

My job placed me in an interesting nexus in Soho. Everyday I walked from Jamake's office on Lafayette Street, and often passed legends like Ornette Coleman who would give me a gentlemanly nod and smile as he passed. Several times, I came upon ritual artist Betsy Damon caked with clay, clad only in layers of thousands of small cloth bags filled with earth pigment performing her *Thousand-Year-Old Woman* piece with only a circle of pigment sketched on the cobblestones separating her from scores of baffled longshoremen who crowded around.

At the copy center on Prince Street, I became friends with the handsome young Black man who worked the machines. Jean-Michel Basquiat confided he was the artist SAMO behind the block letters appearing on Soho buildings. Soon after, he became known for his confrontational graffiti. We chatted nearly every day for an hour about painting and the hypocrisy of the Soho artworld while copying Jamake's manuscripts and papers. Jean-Michel always wanted to see the art the Indian painters sent for the *Sweetgrass* book. We xeroxed the images and saw T.C. Cannon's high color cultural appropriation, James Havard's illusionist abstractions scrawled with tipis, Morrison's geometric abstractions, and pictographs and stick figures in abstract expressionist paintings by George Longfish and Jaune Quick-to-See Smith. My friend Basquiat was discovered in 1980 after I left New York City. From out west I heard about his meteoric rise to Blue Chip artist stardom, addiction to heroin, and overdose in 1988 at twenty-eight.

Maman called at the beginning of the summer in 1979.

"I think I am pregnant?"

"You're what? You are forty-five years old. You can't be pregnant. You're just going through your change."

"No, I'm pregnant. I can tell."

My sisters and I were unsympathetic. We kept telling Maman it was impossible. She kept calling. When the doctor confirmed her pregnancy, we were flabbergasted. I felt guilty for not being more understanding. We were all conflicted. Everyone but Archie, who strutted like a peacock, announcing to everyone, "Didj'ya know I got my wife pregnant? Not bad for an old goat. A hénh hénh hénh."

Daddy constantly bragged that he was always ready for sex. "You know me, Collio Jell-O, Ever Ready. Just like the battery." He followed with a lascivious laugh, "A hénh hénh hénh." Maman had tried for years to have more children with no success, then gave up and used the rhythm method, the only birth control the Church allowed. Archie marked the calendar in the kitchen with safe dates when she might agree to have sex. When I visited from college, Daddy would point to the calendar and announce, "Tonight's the night. Get ready, Colleen, because tonight's the night."

After Maman got over the shock, she looked forward to the birth of the surprise baby. She would never have an abortion. Amniocentesis was a moot point, since she could never terminate the pregnancy even if the child had a disability. Maman loved the Downe's Syndrome kids she taught about Catholicism. We tried to support her, but I was torn. If my mother had a baby at forty-six, how could I leave the East Coast like we were planning? I could not abandon my new sibling to a life without any sisters to buffer Dad's violence and Maman's obsessive control. When Colleen was two and a half months pregnant, just as she was bonding with her unborn child, and I thought I was about to have a sibling twenty-six years younger than me—Maman had a miscarriage.

That August Barry and I joined the mass exodus from the city's muggy heat and drove to Bard for a romantic weekend. We slept in Kim and Hilton's cottage in the woods and bicycled through the green paths from Annandale to Tivoli reliving memories and talking about what was next. I was twenty-five. Maman had her last child when she was twenty-four. Although she wanted more children, she had never been able to get pregnant again, until this last pregnancy that ended in miscarriage. During sleepless nights while Barry snored, I'd been asking myself, "Is it already too late for me to conceive?" Driving back to the city, we decided to start a family. Barry said, "I want to get married so the baby will have my name." He knew I didn't like the idea of marriage because it oppressed women. But we managed to live together for six years and I had maintained my independence, so I said yes.

Since our families had never met, we decided not to get married in Rhode Island or Minnesota, and settled on neutral ground in Manhattan.

"Your parents would freak, if we had a rabbi and a *huppah*." Barry pointed out.

"I would never want a priest."

We found a judge who agreed to do the ceremony in his chambers at the State Courthouse of New York. Barry thought the theme of the wedding should be *When Two Worlds Collide*.

The preparations were hurried and lonely. Maman had dreamed of a big church wedding, me wearing her voluminous lace bridal dress with its billowing petticoats that she preserved with care, and her straightening my veil as I prepared to walk down the aisle to wed whichever hometown French Canadian son-in-law she had hand picked. She was not too happy about me marrying Barry, and refused to participate in the plans because we would not get married in her church or garden.

Maman was coming to New York to meet Lori who was returning from studying in Europe. "Could you stay an extra day to help me shop for my wedding dress?" "No, the plans have already been made." If I would not wear her lace bridal dress that she kept so long for me to wear, she could not be bothered. I wandered around the city, wistfully looking through storefront windows at luminous delicate bridal gowns, too sad and shy to enter the shops and try one on by myself.

Barry's parents came to town, and we shopped. I bought a simple purple suit. At the ceremony, Sheila was surprised. "If I had known you were picking out your bridal clothes the day we shopped, I would have helped you find something more appropriate."

Our wedding day was bright and sunny until a cloudburst at sunset wet the city streets. Barry's grandmother Lillian said, "Mazel tov. It is great luck when you have a little rain on a sunny wedding day. Your joys will be many and your sorrows few."

By the end of the wedding day, I knew I was pregnant. We did not want to raise our child in New York City breathing carbon monoxide from his stroller, and thinking all trees had fences around them, so we prepared to leave the East as planned. We were moving to Canada; I even went to the Canadian Consulate and applied to emigrate. But "men plan and God laughs." Our landlord refused to let us sell our loft as promised. Barry worked with a lawyer to close the deal while I got bigger and bigger everyday. In May, we decided to walk away from our loft, and went to Minneapolis to have the baby. I flew on ahead, big with child. Barry drove our stuff cross-country. When he rolled into the driveway, he announced,

"I'm going to Law School."

"Law School?"

"Working with the attorney about the loft made me see how lawyers can help people. During the drive, I thought about what I want to do with the rest of my life. I'm too shy to make it as a musician. The late nights and drinking are not for me. I could work for what I believe in if I became a lawyer."

Indian Country and Entering the Covenant

THE EIGHTIES WERE MY TIME OF CHILDBEARING. Our first child was born in the middle of 1980 and the fourth in 1990. My days and often sleepless nights were filled with nursing babies, puréeing baby food, changing diapers, chasing toddlers, and baking birthday cakes. Throughout these years, I painted and developed my career as an artist, arts activist, curator, and writer. With enormous stores of energy, fierce determination, and the aid of bouts of insomnia, I created a life that blended art-making and mothering. When our first son was born in 1980, we marveled that he would turn twenty in the year two thousand. We couldn't imagine living through twenty years of parenting. The year 2000, the long awaited millennium, would be the year our son would enter manhood and no longer be a teenager.

Just after Jacques' birth, I dreamed I visited an ancient medicine man on the Hopi Reservation in Northern Arizona. Though I had never been anywhere in the Southwest, the landscape was identical to Second Mesa. The grandfather took me into an adobe pueblo house and introduced me to his three black-haired daughters. Then he led me outside to a ledge perched on the edge of the mesa, and pointed out the sacred San Francisco Peaks in the distance. A white egg appeared in the crystalline sky and zoomed towards us until it stopped in front of me hovering in the air. As I watched, the egg cracked open and a green snake emerged and flew at me. I gasped frozen in fear as the serpent wound itself around my leg and up my torso twisting its sinewy body until its face was just inches in front of mine. The snake locked his eyes upon me and frightened as I was, I could not break away from his gaze. But this snake was a friend and would never hurt me. He extended his tongue and touched me gently on the mouth.

The snake was a spirit helper. I painted the *Medicine Egg Dream*. When I researched its symbols I discovered it was a creation dream, and that the symbols often accompanied the birth of a child. Later that year we flew to Southern California and the terrain of the southwest was like the desert in my dream. Barry and I switched off strapping Jacques on our backs and hiked Pushawalla Canyon in the Coachella Valley. When we climbed to the ridge I could see the hike along the San Andreas Fault was shaped like a serpent's body. We were walking on the back of the snake.

Our first responsibility as Jewish parents was Jacques' *brit*. Though I wanted a son more than anything, I had no experience with newborn's penises and was surprised when I saw that boys were born uncircumcised. Moments after Jacques' birth, I found myself amid a whirlwind of preparations and plans for my son's *brit*, a word I never heard before. My mother-in-law, her cousin Auntie Arline, and the other aunties baked and cooked furiously for the ceremony on the eighth day after our son's birth.

I had a caesarean section, and was not released from the hospital until just before the *brit*. I was still on pain medication and the preparations swirled around me like a blur. When everyone arrived laden with baby gifts, *kamishbrot*, creamed herring, and honey cake, I felt so embraced by this loving family. While the Orthodox *moyel* prepared to perform the circumcision, I stood around the table with the others clutching my swaddled babe, unsure what to expect.

Shepsel, the *moyel*, was warm and comforting. I felt only a little trepidation as I handed my baby to him to be strapped onto the board where he would be bound for the ritual. Shepsel then placed my son in a chair symbolically reserved for the prophet Elijah, then passed him from his great-grandfather to grandfather to father and to his *k'fater*, Joel. I was moved to tears when Shepsel chanted the prayers that announced my son was connected to the tribe of people who began this ritual over five thousand years ago. Jacques was a member of an ancient people, and as his mother I became connected to another tradition. The *moyel* swiftly performed the circumcision. Jacques hardly let out a cry. Still the women paled, the men grimaced, and everyone heaved a sigh of relief as Shepsel handed him back to me to be nursed. A loud chorus of Mazel Tovs resounded. The walls shook as everyone clapped and stamped joyfully while singing a rousing *Mazel Tov v' Siman Tov*.

But the warm embrace of Barry's extended family could not make up for Maman's absence. Though our relationship had been strained since I was eighteen and we spent long periods estranged, it was still my mother I wanted when my baby was born. Maman said she couldn't be there because she could not get a cheap plane ticket on short notice. As my due date neared she called me several times a day to see if she should purchase the ticket. It felt like I was being nagged to deliver on demand to save airfare. Maman came to see her first grandson eleven days after his birth.

In a sweet picture Maman cradles Jacques with a wistful smile.

She never imagined her grandchildren would be raised across the country—so far from Woonsocket.

After corresponding for years, George Morrison and I met in person at an art opening for sculptor Doug Hyde in Minneapolis. Barry and I went with Jacques. When the elder Ojibwe artist entered Judith Stern Gallery beaded cane in hand, his warm smile filled the narrow storefront. George welcomed me and became a mentor and father figure. He reminded me of my Pépère Touchette, and helped fill the void that my grandfather's death had left. George was teaching at the University of Minnesota then, and attended most exhibits of Indian art in the Twin Cities. Originally from Grand Portage on Lake Superior, Morrison developed a unique body of abstract paintings, sculptures, and bas-reliefs, and gained renown as one of Minnesota's most distinguished and beloved artists. Over the years, George critiqued my work, sent his art for exhibitions I curated, recommended me for several jobs as an artist educator in Minnesota, and became a steadfast friend.

Feminist artist Harmony Hammond curated my art into a WARM (Women's Art Registry of Minnesota) exhibition in Minneapolis and I attended the opening with my newborn babe in arms. There I met Harmony and Hazel Belvo, Morrison's wife, who was a founding mother of WARM. When I showed slides of the goddess imagery I made in New York City, Hammond gave my work a positive critique. The opening was packed. But my clay piece *Only Women Bleed* elicited no comment, neither negative nor positive. Refusing to be ignored even though I was an outsider to both Minneapolis and WARM, I stood by the sculpture clutching my four-week-old, and asked each passerby, "What do you think of my homage to women's moon cycles?"

The piece had twenty-eight vermilion clay boxes, each filled with a different clay vagina to reflect the changes during the menstrual cycle. It was too strong for a gallery in the Midwest, even a feminist one. Maybe they couldn't get past the shellacked bloody tampons hanging from the bottom of the piece like scalplocks.

It was a radical action to use menstrual blood in an art piece. *Only Women Bleed* asserts that women's bodily functions can be a source of power even if they had been used as an excuse to oppress women. The shrine-like sculpture honored the sacredness of menstrual blood as the source of life women carry within our bodies. I wanted to show its beauty, and didn't think about how transgressive it would be in Midwestern society. It was my first indication that the work I harvested from my subconscious was too strong for many. The more I pushed the boundaries, delved into other realities, and explored difficult issues, the more avant-garde the art became.

We flew back to Rhode Island with nine week old Jacques to watch Kim and Hilton marry in Maman's garden. She was angelic. He was tall, handsome, and Jewish. My parents, the ma tantes, and mon oncles acted as if it were a funeral instead of a wedding. Hilton was just a year younger than Maman, divorced with two pre-teen daughters, and a vasectomy. Our bornagain, boy cousin who was Kim's favorite, berated her to tears for marrying a divorced man. It did not seem to matter to the rest of the family that Kim and Hilton were deeply in love.

We spent Jacques' first year in Minneapolis then moved to Oregon where Barry enrolled in law school. On the way we stopped at nearly every

Indian reservation, camping, visiting, and attending ceremonies. We detoured to Browning just in time for Blackfeet Nation's Indian Days and were welcomed. The people treated me like a long lost relative when they heard what Mimi told me about our grandmother being Pied Noir. They knew about the Lamberts. We got lots of invitations to share camp, food, and company between watching the dancers. We visited, ate together, and listened to stories around the fire. In the arbor wearing a borrowed shawl and moccasins, I danced to the heartbeat of the drum embraced by my relations. At my heels, Jacques crouched, stomped, and spun, imitating the traditional dancers.

We rented a farmhouse in an orchard south of Portland near the Willamette River with a view of Mount Hood to the east. Determined that my baby would have the happy home I did not, I made sure our pale green farmhouse was different from the other green house on Pearl Street. I baby-proofed it so our son could explore. I didn't want him to only hear, *no*, and *don't touch*. When he misbehaved, I gave him time outs, and made sure I kept control of my anger. If I lost my temper, I apologized.

Summers, we drove east to Blackfeet territory. In Stand Off, Alberta, Canada on a bluff overlooking the Kootenay River and Highway 2, I saw the abandoned site where David Lambert's Trading Post stood from 1830 until the mid-1970s. We camped with elder holy man Albert Wolf Child and his family. When we arrived, everyone rushed out to greet us. The men set up our tipi poles while the women directed the raising of the tipi. Camping along the river in Stand Off among my long lost relatives was idyllic. The year I was pregnant with our second son, I beaded his tiny moccasins while sitting around the fire. Several of Albert's grandchildren slept in our tipi at night, and we shared meals around the fire. When we left Stand Off, the grandmothers filled my arms with *pemmican*, and sweetgrass, the mothers with bags of Pampers, and Albert and his sons pushed gas money into our hands. "For your long trip home," We protested but they insisted. "You are our guests. You traveled so far." They were happy I had come home. I reconnected with my grandmothers' people, and brought pictures back to share with Mimi and the ma tantes in North Grosvendale.

There is a photo of me, six months pregnant, bareback astride a painted horse, with Barry on another horse, in front of the tipi we stayed in at a Blackfeet friend's place in the mountains outside Kalispell.

In Oregon on the first day at the law school, Barry and I met CeCe Whitewolf from Warm Springs, and we became fast friends. CeCe introduced us to the Portland Urban Indian community, and to her family in Warm Springs. We often drove out to Warm Springs for pow-wows and to visit with her mom who was warm and welcoming. Cece was the eldest girl in a large family, and took on mothering her siblings and their children with ease. We soon got to be friends with her many brothers and sisters, and our farmhouse was often filled with sleeping bags and bed rolls of visitors from Warm Springs. Jacques ran around the orchard with CeCe's nieces and nephews, while the grown-ups drank coffee and visited on the deck overlooking Mount Hood. Sometimes Cece's boyfriend took out his guitar and entertained everyone with cute hilarious love songs he wrote about CeCe's moist cocoa skin, full breasts, and luscious bottom, and she burst into giggles. Ron loved CeCe and wanted the world to know.

Cece taught me how to make a cradleboard for our second son. We got the plywood form, cloth, and beads at the trading post in Warm Springs and borrowed the pattern from Cece's mom. Then we cut the material for the cradleboard on the kitchen table in our farmhouse, and the rose stem for the bow from the bush in the herb garden. Cece beaded the bow; I sewed the calico and flannel pieces into a cozy bed for my baby.

For this birth, I called Maman as soon as I was in labor. She got on a plane and arrived just before the baby was delivered. She, Cece, and Barry's brother Richard, who was in college in Portland, were at the hospital with us for the birth. While they waited for me to come out of the operating room, Cece finished the moccasins I had begun beading in Stand Off.

When Sage was born, he was blue and still. It seemed to take forever for the doctors to get him to breathe. Once we heard his lusty cries and counted his perfect fingers and toes, we thought he was fine. But a few hours after birth, our baby had *focal* and *grand mal* seizures. He seemed developmentally perfect, but we had to give him Phenobarbital every night to prevent more seizures for an entire year. The doctors said they could not rule out cerebral palsy.

Maman stayed ten days and was a great help. I needed mothering. The time spent together was healing to our relationship. She had warmed somewhat when Jacques was born, but Sage's birth seemed to re-ignite her maternal instincts. She was being so sweet, I went with her to Mass one Sunday to keep her company. The priest railed about the evilness of the Jews in his sermon. Despite Vatican Council II, the anti-Semitic virulence in the Church persisted. Maman didn't understand what upset me.

An air of uncertainty hung over us about Sage's prognosis. It would take a year and a trip to the Pediatric Neurological Center in Minneapolis before the doctors would tell us that Sage was fine. The Paisners and Archie flew in for the *brit*. The Orthodox pediatrician knew the prayers, but was inexperienced with the procedure, which is usually done by obstetricians. The doctor had an attack of performance anxiety. It took him so long that Hy nearly ripped off the doc's surgical gloves and did it himself. Ultimately, it was a fine job, but there were tense moments. Barry's law school buddy who grew up on a farm slaughtering and gelding pigs passed out cold. I almost lost it when I saw his six foot four inch frame slide down the wall to the floor. My parents were so traumatized; they decided never to see another *brit*. I can only imagine how Archie described it to people in Woonsocket.

Soon after Sage was born, Cece introduced me to a group of Indians who had founded Six Directions. I curated exhibitions for the gallery and got involved in the Portland Indian community while Barry studied law and worked on the defense team for Columbia River Indian Salmon fishermen indicted in an FBI Samscam sting. We spent time at ceremonies and pow wows along the river, and in Warm Springs Longhouses.

Winona was traveling around the country speaking for Indian land claims and came to Portland with Hawaiian activist Luana Busby for the *Artistas Indigenas* conference in Portland that I was helping organize for painter and Columbia River Fishing Rights activist Susannah Santos. Winona had come even more into her own since graduating from Harvard and moving back to her dad's rez at White Earth in Northern Minnesota. Her speech at the *Artistas Indigenas* opening was concise, inspiring, and powerfully delivered. She and Luana were striking indigenous beauties with yards of thick dark hair and eyes that burned with conviction. They stayed in our upstairs guest room under the eaves overlooking Mount Hood, and we sat around in pajamas drinking coffee talking passionately about politics, the environment, and our families, while I nursed Sage.

The next day we drove past Mount Hood to Warm Springs, and walked sunwise around the longhouse at Simnasho greeting everyone with the traditional handshake. We set up the art exhibit, and visited with the gentle elder sisters who were the leaders of the Feather Religion. Winona spoke, and then we feasted, helped the ladies clean up in the kitchen, and camped under the stars outside the Longhouse at He He. Winona, Luana, Susannah, and I stood under the night sky and smudged each other with sage from the top of our heads to the tips of our toes before crawling into our tents and chatting long into the night.

In my first sweatlodge ceremony within the small willow lodge that becomes the center of the universe during the ceremony, I found the direct experience of God I hoped for when I innocently bent back my head to receive First Communion. Incense filled the pitch black lodge when the sweatlodge leader placed sage, cedar, and sweetgrass onto the hot stones. The steam stung as he poured a slow stream of water unto the rocks making visible the breath of the Creator. The ancient chants filling the lodge and the prayers of the participants seared my heart. When I exited, collapsed on the earth, and gazed up at the starry sky—everything looked alive.

Beginning with a show of traditional beaded and cornhusk pictorial bags from Cece's Nez Percé and Warm Springs' relatives, I curated a series of exhibitions for Six Directions Gallery ranging from traditional arts to contemporary abstract paintings by urban Indians of many tribes. Native poets read; traditional and fancy shawl dancers performed and local drum circles sang at the openings. We welcomed and fed the community. Never knowing what would happen next, each moment was filled with surprises. One night, I helped carve up an entire deer the men had hunted, and roasted it up for a big feed for the Portland Urban Indian Council. On other nights, I cooked fry bread and pinto beans for a ceremony or funeral with my baby Sage peeking over my shoulder from his perch on my back. And always, I laughed and joked with the women in the kitchen.

When I curated *Ancient Visions in Contemporary Indian Art* for the Hallie Ford Museum at Willamette University in Salem, we visited John Hoover on Puget Sound to pick up his carved cedar spirit sculptures. Many of the more than twenty-four artists were at the opening. Larry Beck roared in with his hubcap walruses, Lil Pitt came with her ceramic masks, and Conrad House with a bevy of University of Oregon coeds carrying his high gloss ceramics and stain-glass-like pastels. The local television station did a feature on the exhibit and interviewed the artists, guests at the packed opening, Six Direction's founding director Pete Jackson on the sweat ceremonies and prison outreach, and me on contemporary Indian art.

The medicine men asked Barry and me to host a sweatlodge for the Portland Urban Indian community in our orchard, and we got permission from the West Lynn Fire Department to light ceremonial fires to heat the stones. Brave Buffalo, aka Devere Eastman, a Lakota medicine man from South Dakota came out to supervise the building of the sweatlodge and performed the ceremonies that accompanied its erection. He conducted the first and many subsequent sweat ceremonies there. Brave Buffalo would laugh and say, "It's *hard* to be an Indian," as he poured water on the stones sending scalding steam throughout the lodge.

For over two years, I sweat two to three times a week, and had powerful dreams and visions. Sage was just an infant. When I brought him into the lodge, he would turn his head, smile a sweet smile, close his eyes, and fall asleep. When we left the lodge, he would be soft and mellow.

But the work of hosting the lodge fell hard on me at times. Getting enough blankets to cover the lodge, hauling and chopping wood, building the ceremonial fire, making prayer ties and flags, and cooking the pinto beans, *woshapi* (berry soup), and fry bread for the feast afterwards was a big responsibility. Those tasks fell to me with my friend Theresa Black Owl often helping while Jacques played in the orchard with her children. Theresa's older girls watched the littler ones as they chased the ducks through the meadow stopping to pop cherries, plums, peaches, or apples into their mouths as the fruit ripened and summer came and went. Theresa and I cooked, chopped wood, loosened our hair, and made tobacco offerings while we nursed our babies and tended the fire. Time and again I found myself in a sweat for recovering addicts and alcoholics in programs at Totem Lodge and other rehab institutions in town. Sometimes the young men would bring wood and tend the fire. In the lodge some prayed to be forgiven for the souls they sent to the other world and I hoped they repented and wouldn't hurt my family. When Brave Buffalo waved his eagle wing fan, it felt like an eagle brushing my face with its feathers. Supernatural visions and occurrences were commonplace during sweat ceremonies.

One night at three in the morning, I was awakened by furious knocking at the farmhouse door. It was Theresa with a few of her many kids in tow, and two young Lakota women I had never seen before. As soon as the glowing stones were brought into the lodge and the door flap was closed, I sensed something was unusual about this sweat. When we finished the fourth round, I crawled out clutching Sage, panting, my heart pounded audibly as the rain hit my steamy skin.

"What in the world was going on in there?"

Theresa responded nonchalantly, "Oh, they were just trying to destroy me. Those girls are descended from the original Crow Dog who killed my ancestor, Spotted Tail. The enmity between our families goes back generations. But they did not succeed." She laughed.

"I wish you had warned me."

"It was better you did not know."

Theresa often helped me prepare for the sweat ceremonies. Her dark skin glowed in the firelight as we waited for the stones to heat. The kids ran around us and we made prayer ties together. Theresa wound the red string around the tobacco offerings, and reminded me to listen carefully to the prayers and songs in the lodge.

"You have to learn all these things because someday, you'll be the one leading the sweat."

"I could never lead a sweat. I'm not enrolled."

"The spirits chose you. They don't care who's enrolled or not. That's the *white man's* way of destroying us. The spirits only care what is in your heart. The People need women like you and me to do this work."

My dreams and visions became more vibrant, and came more often. When I painted their images, people shared stories from their cultures. I had a vision of a colossal snake, four horses the colors of the four directions, and an antlered spirit woman. Theresa said, "That vision means you have to prepare to go up on the mountain." She taught me how to prepare prayer ties, flags, and a star quilt for my vision quest.

When I was invited to exhibit in shows with indigenous and Indian artists, I consulted with elders, spiritual leaders, and Indian artists who all encouraged me to participate. George Morrison told me not to worry about it. Kuiz Kalkoatl, a Huichol/Aztec medicine man said the people that mattered would see I was a person of integrity. Kuiz was a visionary artist. I gave him the first sketch I did of the antlered woman vision. Kuiz recognized the antlered woman and the snake, and said the spirit woman brought a message of peace. After seeing my art he told his translator to tell me that my family told me the truth. "Your Indian ancestress was a powerful medicine woman. You inherited her spiritual power. She's working through you."

We often drove through the Cascade Mountains, past Mount Hood to Warm Springs, and were welcomed at ceremonies and traditional funerals throughout the seasons, the Huckleberry Feast at Hee Hee, the Salmon Ceremony at Celilo Falls on the Columbia River, Indian dances in Warm Springs, and pow wows at White Swan across the river in Yakima. Barry worked part time for Jack Schwartz, one of the A.I.M. lawyers for Wounded Knee, and Pat Birmingham, a criminal attorney on the defense for David So Happy and the other Indian salmon fisherman who had been arrested in the Sam Scam entrapment case by the Feds. We often found ourselves in the conservative Columbia River courts, and at feasts and feeds along the Columbia afterwards munching on delectable alder smoked salmon, and visiting with the fishermen's families. We camped with Theresa and other dancers each summer for Sun Dance at Mount Hood. There I met Avis Archambault, a Sun Dancer, Pipe Carrier, and Native healer who worked in Phoenix doing talking circles for at-risk Indian youth.

I felt at home at these gatherings. I headed for the kitchen as soon as we arrived drawn by the familiar sounds of women laughing and gossiping as they prepared food, cooked, and washed dishes together. The first time I poked my head into the large communal kitchens of the Longhouses and offered to help, I was greeted with cautious curiosity. But I soon fit in to the rhythm of shared work. I worked hard and knew what to do, and the ladies seemed to appreciate my quiet presence. By the time I dried my last dish and took off my apron, I was one of the crew. They wished me well and sent me home laden with leftovers wrapped in foil. When I returned, I was welcomed with warm smiles and hugs.

Wherever we went in Indian Country, people asked, "Where are you from?" When I answered, "Woonsocket," they repeated, "But where are you from?" They wanted to know my tribe. It didn't matter whether I had papers, or how many miles and generations separated me from my tribal origins.

One day there was a letter in my mailbox inviting me to exhibit my art in a traveling show featuring the art of women of Native American descent from throughout the country. The exhibit was curated by a prominent

Indian woman artist and feminist artist Harmony Hammond. Though I was flattered by the invitation, I was ambivalent about agreeing to be in an ethnically segregated show, which can ghettoize artists and give mainstream institutions an excuse to continue to exclude them. And I was uncomfortable agreeing to be in an exhibit of Indian artists because I wasn't an enrolled tribal member. I wrote Harmony and Jeanette Looking Clear a six-page letter explaining everything and asked them to decide whether or not I fit their definition of an Indian artist. They decided to include me; I accepted.

One day, I went from a sweatlodge ceremony at our home for a young woman who had cancer to a ceremony performed by Lakota medicine man Martin High Bear in a large hall in Portland. During the ceremony, the medicine man was wrapped in a star quilt and bound with ropes. The entire room was blackened and hundreds of people gathered in the room were instructed to pray for the healing of the person being treated. In the darkness, unexplainable things happened.

One of Pete's colleagues offered me a ride home in his pick-up. I liked Thòmas, and his wife and children, and had no reason to refuse. We were chatting amicably about spirituality when he pulled the car to the side of the road and said, "Did you know there is power in a medicine man's sperm, and if you give oral sex to someone who has reached a powerful position in the spirit world, his power will be transferred to you?"

I laughed "You must be crazy to think I would buy that nonsense. Even if it were true, I'm sure yours, is just plain sperm."

After nearly a decade looking east from the West, I was not the same girl who left Woonsocket for Wellesley. My childhood gave me a direct experience of the French Canadian culture into which I was born. My adult life in the Indian world immersed me in the Northern Plains culture I inherited but had been deprived of by cultural genocide. It became part of me through time and experience as a young adult just as my Canuck culture had during my youth. When I left home, I would say I was part Indian or my grandmother was Indian. When I left Oregon at thirty, I said, I am French Canadian and Indian with confidence.

We moved to Arizona and lived in Navajo Nation. My self-assurance in my Indian identity solidified from living day to day on the *rez*. We lived in Diné country for four years, Barry worked for the Navajo Justice Department on the Navajo Hopi land dispute. In just over a years time, we moved our family five times; in and out of a one bedroom apartment in Tempe for a summer, a two bedroom trailer near Canyon de Chelly for a few months, a mutual help house in Chinle for a year, and one room in the Tuba City Motel for a month before we settled into a double wide prefab on the hill above Tuba, for three years.

When we reached hot dusty Chinle, we dropped our boxes at the DNA trailer, one of the few in the destitute B.I.A. trailer park not abandoned and boarded up, then continued down to Tempe where Barry prepared to take the Arizona Bar. We rented an apartment in a complex with a pool and furnished it with a rented bed, sofa, TV, table, and four chairs. The kids and I swam in the pool for half-hour intervals until the Arizona summer heat got to be too much, and then retreated to the Spartan apartment to read stories and nap. While they played and slept, I began the *Pépère's Lake* and *Mimi Combing* pastels for a solo traveling exhibition in the Northwest. At night I participated in sweatlodge ceremonies at the Salt River Indian Reservation, and talking circles Avis led in Scottsdale. After a few weeks trying to beat the one hundred twenty degree heat, I packed up the kids and visited my in-laws in Minnesota, and my parents at Pépère's Lake. Barry stayed in Tempe to study for the Bar exam.

When we returned, Barry took the Bar then we drove up to Chinle, moved into the DNA trailer and were greeted with sewage backed up into the bathtub and sinks. Once the plumbing was fixed, we settled into life on the reservation. I got into a rhythm of caring for the children and painting. The boys made friends with the Navajo kids in the trailer park as they played in the bare dirt with their Tonka trucks among the tumbleweeds. Barry's office was in a soon to be condemned building at Begay's Corner where Chinle's red sand blew in through the cinder blocks.

Within six months, a mutual help house in a line of twenty by the highway became available. We moved again. This small house was bigger than the trailer, and I converted the extra bedroom into a studio. Nearly every day I piled the boys and the neighborhood kids into the pick-up and drove to Canyon de Chelly. I sat at my drawing board creating pastels, while the children ran in the canyon and splashed in the red muddy waters of the wash.

A Lakota man passing through Chinle said all the right things about power and spirituality, and I naively invited him to a sweat ceremony. Several months later we began worrying when I kept getting mysterious illnesses. Barry's secretary Liz Benally said, "You have been witched by somebody. I'm taking you to my medicine man. He'll do a ceremony to fix you up."

Liz took me to the medicine man's hogan, and I sat on the dirt floor by the stove surrounded by velvet paintings of Jesus, JFK, and Martin Luther King, Jr. while he prayed and chanted. A smudge stick of sage burned in an abalone shell on the cook stove in the center of the house. The healer pressed a slender bone to the base of my neck. I could feel a popping release as he sucked through the bone tube extracting a pointed object. He blew through the bone into his hand, and a small jade green triangle shape lay in his open palm.

"You have been witched by someone who came into your sweatlodge. This man removed a strip of bark from the willow frame of the lodge. This man said bad medicine and cursing prayers. He burned the bark in the fire pit with the white hot sweat stones. He did this to hurt your family." I gasped. He asked, "Do you want me to send the bad magic back to this person, or up to the North Star?"

"The North Star. Why did this man witch us?"

"Evil is attracted to the light and wants to consume and destroy it. Your husband's work for the Navajo people, particularly the Relocatees from the Hopi lands, and your work with artists for Indian people—it wants to stop that good work."

I returned home, still somewhat skeptical, so I examined each willow on the sweatlodge frame. There was one willow with a strip removed that was the exact width and length the medicine man described. I looked over each of the other willows of the lodge. All were intact. There was only one with peeled bark.

In Navajo Nation I accompanied Barry on visits to interview the Relocatees. One time, we visited Helen Yazzie who wove while Barry interviewed her through a Navajo interpreter. She periodically interrupted her tale with gentle scolding or praise in her native language for her grandchildren who played with bits of yarn and spindles, imitating their *shima's* movements. Her grandbabies fell asleep in the folds of her velvet skirts while her daughters made fry bread and mutton stew nearby on the pot belly stove. I recognized the word *Nizhoni*, beauty, repeated often among the clicks and guttural sounds that were unintelligible to me. *Nizhoni*, "beauty all around," I thought. Was it like this for my ancestors weaving surrounded by family?

I learned a small part of the *Nightway Chant*, and added, "May I walk in beauty," to my daily prayers to live in a sacred manner with inspiration, compassion, introspection, and wisdom—the four teachings of the Northern Plains Medicine Wheel.

Soon after we got settled in Chinle, we traveled to Santa Fe, New Mexico where my art was exhibited in several galleries in the town over the years. On the way we stopped at artists, lawyers, tribal advocates, and activists' places around the Southwest. We visited many Indian artists from Mike Kabotie in his trailer below Second Mesa to Larry Emerson up in Shiprock. We often visited the artist who invited me to be in the Indian women's art exhibit. At her adobe spread outside Albuquerque, Jeanette gave me detailed advice about everything from which gallery to choose to how to package and wrap my pastels to send for shows, while Barry talked with her husband, and the kids played with her horse that poked its head into the studio, and with her Polish chickens until the rooster attacked Jacques and sent us all into a flurry.

After some well-reviewed group exhibitions at various Santa Fe galleries, Enthios Gallery offered to represent my art. They exhibited it in its own separate room in a gallery that exhibited John Axton, John Nieto, and R.C. Gorman. Jeanette and I talked often in those days. When I told her about the galleries that wanted to represent me, she said, "Your work will sell well at Enthios where the tour buses stop to see the R. C. Gorman's. They will get their Gorman's, and pick up one of your pastels like ice cream cones." Barry and I thought my career had finally hit. We had unending talks we called the conversation about how our lives would change when my paintings started selling.

Each summer, we went to Santa Fe for Indian Market in August, and met more of the Indian artists with whom I worked. This had its ups and downs. But I made some good friends. Ramona Sakiestewa seemed cautious when we first met, but over the years we developed a warm professional relationship based on mutual respect that turned into friendship. Char Teters, and I connected on issues, both political and artistic, and intersected on many projects. Because our names, work and politics were similar, people often confused us. Char teased. "When they like something one of us has done, I take the credit, and when they don't like it, I say, 'Oh that must have been the other Charleen.'"

Tuba City was more diverse than Chinle. After the month in the motel, we moved into a pale green house with a white picket fence on the hill overlooking Tuba City with a view of the San Francisco Peaks. There were Indians from other tribes who worked for the BIA and non-Indian doctors and teachers from all over, including Shadi Letson who taught special ed at the primary school and was married to a pediatrician at the Indian Hospital. When we met, I asked, "Where are you from?" meaning, "What tribe are you?" Shadi laughed. She looked like a hip Navajo, but Shadi was born in Okinawa—her mother was a survivor of Nagasaki and her dad was a Black Cherokee Marine from Oklahoma. We bonded right away when I saw she had the same bamboo painted china Archie had brought back from Japan. We talked about art, philosophy, religion, and education for hours. Shadi, who had attended theology school, told me about the stages of spiritual development and how only a small percentage of people can access the spiritual directly and see the connections between spiritual traditions, and the ideas common to all.

Jeanette Looking Clear called in the fall, "You have to come to this women's art conference in Minneapolis celebrating the tenth anniversary of WARM." I flew in and we both stayed at the Paisner's in Golden Valley. I felt out of place when I arrived at the conference, but then I heard someone calling my name. It was Ojibwe photographer Shelly McIntire and her mother Ellen Olson and sister Marcia McIntire both beadworkers from George Morrison's band up in Grand Portage. Hazel Belvo was not far behind with open arms, draped in hand-woven robes dyed the colors of Minnesota fields. At one meeting, Jeanette and Ellen encouraged me to speak out when the non-Indian artists complained about not having any female role models to be artists. I told them about the Navajo weavers, Hopi potters, and other Native women I lived among in Navajo Nation who had mothers, grandmothers, and even great grandmothers, and male relatives making art in the home all contributing to the survival of the family and community.

At the general session Hispanic art historian Shiffra Goldman, African American art historian Judith Wilson, and I stood and asked, "Where are the women of color?" I said, "If you are sincere about having non-white women become a part of the women's art movement, you have to be willing to give up power at all levels. You can't just want to change the way the organization looks. You have to talk about things that interest women of color. You can't just set the agenda and expect everyone to want to come to the party when you want to keep controlling everything." Shiffra tells people that the movement for multicultural inclusivity in the women's art movement was born that day in Minneapolis. In the mornings, Looking Clear and I ate breakfast in the Paisner's kitchen looking at the pond, and later hung out with Hazel in Juanita Espinosa's kitchen near Franklin Avenue. Juanita had young kids too. We connected right away.

Throughout these years, I sewed my star quilt, made prayer ties, and prayed to the Creator to send a medicine person to take me up on the mountain. We were trying to conceive another child and I wanted to fast before I got pregnant. Since I was mixed blood, I decided I needed to find a spiritual path that reflected my heritage. I trusted that the spirits who sent me the vision that told me to go up to the mountain, would show me the right path and guide me. Fourth of July weekend, we packed up and drove to the San Francisco Peaks where a huge elk cow greeted us at dusk. Barry and the boys set up a base camp, and I climbed up the mountain. For three days and nights, I fasted, chanted, prayed, smoked the pipe, sweat in a little lodge I built, and received another song and vision. We had been trying to conceive for four years. After I came down from the mountain, I became pregnant.

While I was expecting, the whole family traveled East for the holidays. It was the children's first Christmas with their Mémère and Pépère Touchette. After a slight improvement in our relationship after Sage's birth, things fell apart between me and Maman during our four years in Navajo. After one brief visit to Chinle she withdrew and rarely visited or contacted me. We lived in Tuba City three years, and they never came to see us once there. I hoped a holiday visit would mend the rift for the boys' sake. When we arrived, the air was thick with maman's resentment. The first night, she didn't get supper on the table until ten o'clock, but wouldn't let me feed the kids before she served her dinner. The boys were climbing the walls. Barry went out and got them hamburgers, and maman was furious. She refused to talk to either Barry or me for the rest of the visit.

We kept to our plans and left the boys with my parents after Christmas to spend three days at an inn on Cape Cod. It was a blessed interlude alone as we were poised between having two and three children. When we returned, Jacques rushed to the door, "Mama. Pépère hit Sage. He was in the tub and Pépère hit him."

After that I never let my parents have unsupervised visits with my children. We did not return for Christmas either. We never discussed it. My childhood was a Pandora's Box filled with demons. I spent fifteen years trying to forget it, and I did not want to reopen those wounds.

I didn't hear from them until late spring, when Archie called.

"Shaal. I was wondering if you know anything about this resort in Phoenix. They are having a dental convention and I am thinking of attending. Would you bring the boys down to see your mother and me?"

"Barry has to work, but I'll check the calendar and let you know."

"Well, okay, but you have to tell me in four hours because I have to make my plane reservations by twelve p.m. tonight or I lose the deal. Can you promise to call me in four hours, Shaaleen? Four hours. That will be twelve midnight my time, and ten p.m. your time. Don't forget it is two hours earlier there."

"Is Mom there?"

"She's real busy. She's running some kind of special liturgy on Sunday."

Whenever Maman was upset she gave me the silent treatment. I learned the thick palpable silence on the other end of the line meant she was furious. Occasionally I insisted she share what she was thinking. We said hurtful things, and both cried. It seemed cathartic, and we would say goodbye insisting we loved each other. The process became tedious. I was busy caring for my family. This dance with Maman kept getting lower on my list of priorities. The feeling of coming to an understanding through the tearful sessions was always an illusion. Thinking I made myself clear on a certain point, I would be convinced maman understood only to discover the next time we spoke that nothing I said had made the slightest impact. I could never change her mind.

Just before our third son was born, a Lakota medicine man asked me to light the sweat fire for a ceremony for our friend Shirley Waterhouse who was also pregnant. Hours later, the medicine man called and said "You are going to have to lead the sweat." The time Theresa predicted, and prepared me for, had come. Squeezed cheek to cheek in our lodge were Navajos, Woodland and Mission Indians, Maori, and Aborigine visitors. My friend, Vanessa, who was also a Sun Dancer and Shadi helped me prepare and make the mutton stew for after the sweat. We were eating afterward, and Shadi said, "I saw an eagle enter the lodge while you were chanting."

After the sweat ceremony Steve Darden a local Navajo Cheyenne spiritual leader asked me to lead subsequent sweats for at-risk youth. While I was expecting, I organized the Four Sacred Mountain contemporary Indian arts festival for Tuba City High School. Preparations were demanding, but it was great to work with the artists. We visited with Clifford Beck in his studio in Scottsdale, Mike Kabotie in his trailer below Second Mesa, and other artists when we drove across Arizona or New Mexico to pick up their work. The artists wanted to exhibit in Tuba City where the community was Indian and seeing their art could make a big impact, especially on the youth. Most Navajos and other Indians in Tuba City knew about R.C. Gorman's paintings, but this was the first time many saw an original.

Several of the forty artists sent or brought their art to our doublewide on the hill where the stack soon took up a corner of my studio. A Hopi woman printmaker came by one day when I was painting eight months pregnant with the boys running around me. I was working on *Deer Mother Vision* and engrossed in getting the expression of maternal love just right, when her arrival interrupted me. She said, "I don't know how you can do it. Do your painting and have a family. I get so drained from teaching at IAIA." "I just have to paint," I shrugged.

I took her print and stored it with the others that Barry and I later loaded into our trucks, and drove over to the high school. When we arrived there was no one to help but a custodian. Everyone else who volunteered forgot to show up. So I got out my yardstick, hammer, and nails and Barry and I hung each of the fifty or so paintings in the gymnasium. When we were almost done hanging the art, I started having contractions. It was still a month before my due date. The doctor said, "We want you to keep from delivering until at least thirty-eight weeks gestation. Have a glass of wine or beer with dinner and rest as much as possible." "Rest, with seven and five year old boys?"

Not to mention a full house of visiting artists for the arts festival. Our friends, painter David Johns and his wife, Gloria came and stayed. The boys went crazy when Billy Warsoldier arrived with a blonde in Earl Biss's red sportscar. He jumped out of the convertible without opening the door, clad head to toe in black in summer. His long black hair was darker than the clothes and ebony cowboy boots he wore. He gave me a big bear hug and said, "You searched all over to get me in that book. The FBI couldn't find me, but you got my slides. You know how important I am to Indian art." Ed Singer in his cowboy hat and Carm Little Turtle with her flowing shirts and camera came too, looking like they had stepped out of one of her tinted photographs. Clifford Beck arrived with his family including Mary Lucie, who was one of Barry's favorite co-workers at Hopi Navajo Legal Aid. Before everyone left, we sat outside with David and Gloria and some of the other artists under the carport in lawn chairs looking northwest. A perfect rainbow arched from dark rain clouds to the edge of Castle Rock's sandstone formations. Rain burst in streaks across the sky in the distance darkening the buff colored cliffs. The monsoons had arrived. We watched Gloria who looked like a figure out of an early Harrison Begay painting as she expertly sheared Jacques' pregnant goat, Daisy. The kid was born just before our third son.

That summer, I spent days on our front lawn gazing at the San Francisco Peaks over that classic picket fence. Raoul was an adorable baby with the biggest roundest eyes and head covered with down so pale he looked bald. I nursed him, then painted while he slept surrounded by the boys playing with our four white fluffy Samoyed puppies, four black kittens, and two goats. Colbert Dazzie who traveled all over the mesas with Barry translating for the Navajo Relocatees, told him. "Now your Navajo name is Barry *Tłízí Naaki*—Barry Two Goats."

Our pale green plastic house sat atop the mesa dotted with Navajo hogans and sheep camps with Castle Rock's red monoliths as our backyard. The address was "A mile and a half up the dirt road past the Tuba City Primary north of the Twin Water Towers." Nights were filled with the sounds of drums and chanting from our neighbors' peyote meetings and the silhouettes of Native American Church tipis glowed until dawn like sentinels in the four directions.

Accused

R AOUL'S BRIT WAS DAYS AWAY AND BARRY'S MOM was stranded in Madison, Wisconsin. Barry's dad was waiting in Minneapolis with her ticket to Arizona, but heavy rains in the Midwest grounded her return flight. If she missed the plane it would be impossible to arrive in Flagstaff in time for the *brit*. She called from Wisconsin. "I'm in Madison. My flight's cancelled. There's no way I am missing the *brit*, so I'm taking a cab home. Auntie Arline and my friends offered to come along to keep me company." They spent the twelve hour ride chatting and sharing stories about their grandchildren. Mom got to Minneapolis on time. She, Dad, and Great-Grandpa Henry flew in together. They arrived in time for the ceremony. My parents did not come, but Lori-Ann, Kim, and Hilton stood with me as Raoul was welcomed into the Covenant.

In the fall a phone call came from Annie Shaver-Crandall at City College in New York, "Would you be on the WCA Executive Board of Directors?" My first board meeting was in Annie's hotel suite at the 1988 conference in Houston. I brought Raoul in his cradleboard. The room was crammed with WCA board members from around the country, a mix of staunch feminist art activists, well-heeled socialites, and a few women of color also recently appointed. My plan was to observe, listen, and not talk. Until a Dallas artist spoke.

"We can not include women of color in this organization. We have to be able compete with the big boys at CAA and the quality of the work will not be up to snuff."

"You're wrong. Every woman of color in this room is connected to a network of artists of all ages whose work is of equal if not superior quality to that of the big boys. WCA should tap into these networks to discover outstanding artists in communities of color."

The perfectly coiffed and manicured bleached blonde glared. My words fell on the stuffy room like a cloudburst. The battle lines were drawn. The new African, Asian, and Hispanic board members nodded. The forces for change in WCA perked up, and the old guard clenched their fists and gritted their capped teeth. I started right then to advocate for multicultural inclusion in the artworld.

My work in the feminist and contemporary Indian art worlds and the Indian treaty rights struggles often placed me in the center of controversy. As a mixed blood Canuck I found myself in a position where I had to fight. Mimi taught me to give back to the community and because my community was marginalized and oppressed, I had to be an activist and fight the good fight.

In 1988 Barry was hired by one of the oldest law firms in the Southwest, and we moved to Santa Fe. Leaving Tuba City was hard. Some of my Navajo friends and two of the DNA attorney's had baby boys within weeks of Raoul's birth and our families bonded watching the babies play in the gardens of the Hopi village of Moenave where they stayed in stone houses at the edge of a verdant spring. We left the goats with Colbert who took them to Red Lake. As we parted Colbert said, "Now you are Barry *Hosteen Tlízí Asteen*—Barry The Man Whose Goats Have Left Him." The tribe gave him a testimonial in Flagstaff at the local steak barn. Several clients wove dazzling rugs for us. But Lena Dazzie's present meant the most. She wove "PAISNER" in block letters into the center of a small rug with black, gray, white, and red zig zag designs. Barry was moved, "It's like she wove our family name into Navajo history."

While we were packing, my parents called. They hadn't seen their third grandson yet. He was eight months old. "We have tickets to Santa Fe. Can you meet us there?" Their dates were before we could close on our new home, but they wanted to see Raoul, so I rented a house on the North side for their three night visit. We packed up, put our stuff in storage, and left early. When we reached the crest of the hill and saw Santa Fe's lights below us—we were home.

We stayed with my parents in the spacious house furnished à la Georgia O'Keeffe. Maman and I sat at opposite ends of a modern leather couch while I nursed Raoul. When I said it hurt me that she had no interest in seeing him until he was nearly a year old, Maman revealed what had been on her mind.

"It broke my heart that you moved so far from Woonsocket and Cumberland."

"There was no future for me there."

"You could have stayed. Woonsocket is reviving."

"Right."

"I decided that if I couldn't have my grandchildren nearby, it was better to keep from getting too attached to them. That way it wouldn't hurt so much," Maman admitted.

When I look back on those years when our boys were little, I remember a time that although hectic and challenging was filled with love and joy. People would say, I don't know how you do it. It was easy compared to how I grew up. Juggling my art career, teaching, running a small vacation rental business, and caring for the family forced me to become adept at organization. Despite the demands of our careers and the family, our marriage became stronger.

That summer, I was driving when a woman pulled out into the street without looking, and broadsided my car. A bolt of pain shot up my hand to my neck as my head whipped sideways from the force. I heard a male voice say, "You have been witched." The car accident injured my spine. I remembered the Four Serpents Dream. This was the third bite to the back of my neck. The doctor diagnosed a herniated cervical disc.

One day in early August, a reporter called. "How do you feel about artists posing to be Indian who really are not?"

I thought the reporter was interviewing me because of my expertise on Native art. I began explaining. "Indian identity is complex. I've known full-blood artists who weren't enrolled because their families resisted and refused to register, others because their fathers were from tribes that were matrilineal and their mothers from patrilineal nations so they couldn't be counted in either tribe. I've worked with mixed blood artists with deep ties to their reservations, and artists with census numbers who had no contact with Indian people."

He interrupted. "But how do you feel about your name being published in a list of artists that are frauds and phonies hurting Indian people?"

"What?"

"Haven't you seen this week's *Santa Fe Reporter?*"

The *Reporter* was delivered to the end of our driveway in those days. With the phone and a loaded paint brush still in hand, I walked outside and picked up the newspaper to see a front page article about a small self-appointed vigilante group called the Native American Art Association. My name was printed on the NAAA's list of twelve artists who they claimed were *fake* Indians. The hit list read like a who's who of the Santa Fe Indian art world. With the exception of me who had just arrived in Santa Fe, all the other artists were successful and well-known in the Santa Fe Indian art market. They were a diverse group with varying degrees of connection to the Indian world.

Jeanette Looking Clear had warned us at the Atlatl networking meeting in May about an artist on the warpath against non-enrolled Indian artists. I had promoted his career, like I did with other artists, and even convinced Jamake to put his art on a book cover. I didn't expect thanks. But I did not expect to be viciously attacked. The *Santa Fe Reporter* printed a retraction, but it was small and appeared weeks later on an inside page.

After I got over the shock of seeing my name in print accused of heinous crimes against Indians, I did what I knew how to do; I burned sage and prayed as I had done for years. I smudged, blessed myself, and offered my prayers to the four directions, earth, and sky. I felt calm. I knew who I was. Nothing anyone could say could change that.

Mimi was proud of her Indian ancestry and taught me to share that pride. My grandmother and other relatives never got any benefit from being Indian, even though Mimi talked about how she qualified for educational and other financial benefits from the government. Being Indian was just a fact in her life, and one for which she paid dearly at times. When she married Papi, his family ostracized her and disowned him. Mimi was convinced it was because of her Indian blood. She told me they tormented her when they saw my mother Colleen's Indian hair and eyes. Despite the cruel treatment of her in-laws, Mimi refused to deny her heritage. I thought about the discrimination my relatives and ancestors experienced, and knew I could not deny my heritage either. I called Mimi.

"Could you have been mistaken about our Indian ancestry?"

"Sweetie, I would never lie to you. I'm sure my parents told me the truth too. Why would anyone lie about such a thing? What would be the point?"

It was Indian Market again and we had a full house, Mary Lucie, and the Beck family from grandma to nieces, nephews, and grandbabies, Cheyenne Harris, a young silverworker whose family was from Moenave, painter Frank La Pena, and curator Carla Hill. There were sleeping bags and blankets all over the house and studio filled with people chatting, eating, and drinking coffee. Frank and I sat in our living room. I told him what Mimi said, and asked,

"Why can't people accept that ethnic identity is complex for people of mixed blood? We shouldn't have to choose one culture over another. Not only can we be from two cultures, we don't have any choice."

Frank said, "We have no control over who our ancestors loved and had children with. What we hope is that their relationship was one of love, and we were the result of that love that crossed between cultures."

Carla wanted to include my art in an exhibition at the Matrix Gallery in Sacramento that was specifically defined to feature women artists of "Indian descent" as opposed to tribal members. But she called a few weeks later and said, "I hate to have to tell you this, but the Hopi printmaker and a California Indian printmaker are blacklisting you. They refuse to be in the exhibit if you're in it."

"The Hopi woman who came to my studio in Tuba City? I thought she was my friend. She knows I never lied about my ancestry." I phoned her and asked her why she was blackballing me.

"If you're not enrolled, you can't show with Indian artists. You can still do all the work for Indian artists, but you can't show with us."

"Well, that's your opinion. Countless elders and medicine people told me I should believe what my grandparents told me."

I called the other printmaker in Southern California. She said. "I can't talk right now, can you call back in ten minutes?" When I tried calling back, her phone was off the hook.

I remembered the Hopi woman's comments when she dropped her art in Tuba City. She envied my creative inspiration. It was easier to falsely accuse and eliminate me from the field than to work as hard as I did in the studio. The other printmaker never spoke to me, but complained in an interview that she was excluded from the important traveling exhibit of Indian women's art that I had agonized about accepting. Now I regretted participating, especially when Jeanette virtually abandoned me and several other women in the show who were accused.

The Indian Arts and Crafts Law championed by the NAAA created a bizarre situation. I could not legally say I was an Indian artist, but everyone who saw me and my art only saw that I was Indian. I refused invitations to include my art in exhibitions and books of Native art because I wasn't enrolled, but when I contacted art venues they said they couldn't show my art because they already had their Indian art show last year and wouldn't be showing any more Indian artists for a few years.

In the end, I saw I had no control over who my ancestors chose as mates. I was as Indian as I was, no more, no less. It affected and informed the direction of my life, but I was not going to spend time and money trying to find paper proof. I believed what my grandmothers told me and if other people didn't, that was their problem.

I was determined to make the most powerful art I could, and created *My Vision is My Shield,* a triptych of an unprovoked attack with a masked evil entity stabbing the painter's back. The middle panel shows the artist sewing her heart back into her chest while looking at a shield emblazoned with a serpent. The Elk Woman points the way to the Red Road, the spiritual path, leading to the mountain.

In 1989, the doctors urged me to consider surgery for my neck injury, and I was hospitalized for a milogram to see if a laminectomy would help. When David and Gloria Johns visited from Winslow, David took me aside. His face gravely serious, he said, "I think the reason you are sick is because you have been painting serpents. In Navajo ways, we are not allowed to paint snakes. You need to scrape all of the images of snakes off your paintings and do a healing ceremony." When I reminded him that I am not Navajo, David was unmoved. "The snakes came to me in dreams and visions, David. They know I'm a painter. They clearly wanted me to paint them." I insisted. "In Navajo culture, you are not allowed to paint these visions," David repeated. He looked like one of the full blood elders in his portraits as he did a Navajo healing ceremony in our foyer, and smudged me from the earth to the top of my head.

It took years of physical therapy, Feldenkrais, acupuncture, network chiropractic, and healing ceremonies to fix my neck. During one of the drumming ceremonies, I had a vision of traveling south to Mitla, sitting in the Temple on a Jaguar skin, and praying. Two serpents intertwined my spine. I saw myself don a jaguar mask and was transformed into a jaguar who ran through the jungle, entered a cave and nursed four cubs.

The greatest sorrow of being forced to leave my birth home was lost time with Mimi and the ma tantes. But my children and I had the opportunity to interact with elders through my work recognizing elder women artists through the Women's Caucus for Art Honor Awards. The elders were diverse. Some were gracious and easy to work with, others were cantankerous prima donnas. Hopi sculptor Otellie Loloma taught Sage to make pottery; Hispanic weaver Doña Agueda Martinez welcomed our family to her tin roofed farmhouse in Medanales. We watched the ninety-four-year-old stand at her 350 year old hand-hewn loom making a colorful rag rug, and saw that she, like Barry's Navajo client, was living a life similar to that of our ancestors before the mills' wage slavery. Acoma potter Lucy Lewis moved the whole family to tears when we delivered her award to her hospital room in Acoma shortly before she died and her daughters translated her thanks in Tewa, art historian Charlotte Rubenstein later joined the Honors Committee and became a close colleague, and contemporary quilt artist Faith Ringgold cheered me on to fight to ensure that the Honor Awards went to women of all colors.

When I became pregnant with our fourth child, I was unaware of how different that pregnancy would be and continued raising the children, painting, and writing as usual. In the spring I made several working trips at the beginning of my third trimester then headed East to visit Mimi in Woonsocket on the way to a conference in New York City. I slept at Mimi's apartment during part of the visit. My parents were furious. Mimi and I enjoyed our stolen moments together. We stayed up late giggling, raided her fridge for midnight snacks, and made each other up with the wide array of Estée Lauder cosmetics left over from her days as a beautician. Mimi shared her little black book where she recorded the titles and authors of more than six hundred books she had read in the last twenty years. Like me, Mimi devoured books, and often read four or five each month. It was the last time I stayed with Mimi in her apartment overlooking the Blackstone River. Months later she was hospitalized with congestive heart failure, and then moved to a nursing home.

The stress of traveling and working took its toll. I thought I could act like Supermom and meet every challenge, but my uterus did not cooperate. The plane home from New York malfunctioned and the trip took twenty-six grueling hours. My legs and feet swelled, and contractions started two months too soon. I was in early labor. The diagnosis was an irritable uterus. The doctor was worried that my water would break, and he would have to do an emergency delivery before the baby was ready. He put me on complete bedrest for the remaining nine and a half weeks of the pregnancy. After three C-sections and a fourth pregnancy, my uterus was an irritable bitchy woman. With three active little boys, one under three, I had to stay in bed all the time except to use the bathroom. It was one of my biggest challenges. Barry's demanding law practice kept him at work at least ten hours a day. We hired a woman to care for Raoul and me during the day, and pick up the boys after school. We called our bed, the nest, and it was a nest for me, as I was the nest for my growing child.

All during my childhood, Maman asked, "What did you accomplish today?" Since I was small, I grew up measuring my value by what I had done each day and continued the habit into adulthood. It taught me I had worth only if I could produce. Doing nothing waiting for our daughter to be born, I learned I was worthwhile even if all I did was breathe, eat, sleep, and grow my baby. It was a stark lesson in being not doing. But not quite, from my bed I managed to set up exhibitions, get my writing and art published in several publications, and sketch ideas for a new series of paintings on gestation.

Liesette's Gift

AFTER LIESETTE WAS BORN, I BALANCED the contemplative work of painting with just the sound of the brush against canvas for company, and the electrifying feeling of being connected through networking with other artists. I liked being in the loop, talking with people all over the country, introducing artists to each other and to exhibition or lecture opportunities. Standing with a baby perched on my hip, a brush in my hand, and a phone wedged between my neck and shoulder, I arranged for artists to work on projects together, scheduled exhibitions, and was in touch with creative people all over the country. While I painted I wove a web of connections throughout the art world.

With four children, ten and under, I should have been overwhelmed. But as I put Liesette-Mimi into her cradleboard, I was filled with the most complete happiness I had ever felt. I had my daughter at last.

The Friday night openings were packed in those years at Indian Market, and everybody read the local rag to plan their gallery hopping. That year, a reporter asked Jeanette Looking Clear about the best Indian women painters, and she was quoted as saying something like, "Well there's me and Emmi Whitehorse. And then C.J. Wells and Charleen Touchette, but some people think that they're not really Indian." At her exhibition opening, Jeanette rushed up to me in the middle of the crowded gallery floor.

There is a picture of me sitting on my heels tending to Liesette in her cradleboard. Looking Clear bends towards us. She looks pained.

"I'm so sorry. That reporter misquoted me. I didn't really say that."

"Please do me a favor. Just don't mention my name at all next time."

Watching Mimi and Maman network when I was growing up showed me that giving back to community deepened the meaning of your life. But Maman taught me another lesson that took years to unlearn. I was often everybody's doormat, and would give too much. I was resented by some people and snubbed, which made me feel even more insecure. But instead of telling them they could not treat me that way, I asked what I did wrong or if I could do more, and worked harder to prove I was a person of integrity. Most often they just kicked me in the face again. It took me years to learn to say no. Gradually I became more selective about where I gave my time, but had to repeatedly guard against giving myself away.

Meanwhile the family grew. Liesette pranced about the house in feminine dresses and fancy hats and amused her big brothers by laughing and bouncing furiously when they played their music. We worked hard and were exhausted much of the time with feeding and cleaning up after four children, ten and under, and the phone rang at all hours for my work. But there were some nights when Barry returned home from the office to find us all dancing in the kitchen to rock'n'roll. He would take me in his arms and we danced together around the living room until the children tugged us apart.

One night the woman from The National Museum of Women in the Arts in D. C. called to say that Otellie Loloma missed the deadline for sending slides, and they weren't going to include her art in the Honorees' exhibition. "Otellie is a WCA Honoree. Her work *has* to be in the exhibition. Deadlines do not mean the same to Hopis as they do in D.C. I'll make sure you get what you need." I called Rick Hill at IAIA and made an appointment to crawl into the storage bins in the basement of the old IAIA Museum at the Santa Fe Indian School and photographed Otellie's ceramic sculptures to curate them for the exhibition. I fractured my knee skating in Los Alamos before the conference, but was not going to miss Otellie's big day, so I used a wheelchair to get me and Liesette down the runways at the airport, and switched to a cane once I got to the conference hotel.

Otellie had the time of her life in D.C. I arranged for WCA to pay for her to travel with her lifelong companion Millard Yoletstewa. She and Millard thought the mini bar in their hotel room was free for the Honorees and ran up a three hundred dollar bill tab on the WCA. They wore their traditional Hopi clothes to the exhibit opening, and Otellie basked in the kudos for her amazing hand-built pottery. She smiled and held court wearing her handwoven dress holding the ends of her Hopi *manta* beside the towering clay figures she made out of coiled clay displayed prominently in the front of the Honorees' exhibition at The National Museum of Women in the Arts.

There is a picture of Betty La Duke and me holding Liesette in her cradleboard surrounded by the Honorees. I lean on my cane flanked by the elder Honorees with their canes, Otellie Loloma, Theresa Bernstein who couldn't remember if she was a hundred two or a hundred five, Mildred Constantine, Miné Okubo, and Delilah Pierce.

I had my happy family and thought I had gotten over my childhood until the day after the Honor Awards Ceremony when I went to a panel about child abuse. The auditorium was packed as I hobbled in with the cumbersome brace on my knee. I leaned on the cane and squeezed into the only available seat in the middle of a long row carrying Liesette in her cradleboard. The panelists were introduced, then the room darkened and a black and white video image appeared on the screen. A succession of talking heads pontificating about abuse in a cold clinical tone was interspersed with the recurring image of a small boy looking up to an unseen adult pleading, "Daddy, I'm trying to be a good boy."

Something about the image and the background music smacked me in my gut. In the middle of thousands of my staid art historian colleagues, I burst into uncontrollable sobbing. I was embarrassed. I almost never cried, and never in public. I struggled out of the cramped row balancing the cradleboard and stumbled into the hall blubbering. All the denial, all the putting it behind me, all the thousands of miles and decades that took me so far away from my family and my memories of abuse, had done nothing. Burying the memories had not made them go away. I had not escaped. I carried the wound with me.

Colleagues were surprised to see me crying in the hall and asked what was wrong. No one had ever seen me cry before, and I was bawling. I shared a bit of my story between sobs. They knew exactly what I was crying about. Some started telling their own stories of abuse. For the first time, I learned there was a language for what I experienced. What happened in our family was not my fault. There were others who understood. I learned that while most families have problems, it was a matter of degree and frequency. Families like mine were dysfunctional. My sisters and I were classic adult children of alcoholics.

My parents met me and Lori at the conference hotel in D.C. Archie and Colleen decided to fly in just after my WCA events, but in time for Lori's paper at the College Art Association. The night before they arrived, Liesette and I roomed with Lori. When I told her about the revelation I had at the child abuse panel, my youngest sister said,

"Of course, you were abused. I got emotional abuse, mostly. Mom told me that she knew she couldn't protect you from Daddy, so she decided to protect me and made sure he never touched me."

When Lori was born, Maman was twenty-four years old. I try to convince myself that my mother would have protected me if she could, but she was just too young. But even as a sixteen-year-old, Maman stood up to Archie about the apartment. I was not important enough. If I had been, she would have kept me safe, whatever the cost.

Lori delivered her lecture on ancient Roman copying techniques of 5th century Greek bas-relief sculpture to a handful of classical archaeologists in a near empty hall. I walked with my dad afterwards, and started to tell him about the WCA Honor Awards ceremony, the panel of artists I moderated the day before, and the talk I gave for a packed audience.

"Well I never think that anything you do is important. Not like Lori-Ann and Kimmy. They have doctorates. You're the only one who doesn't have an advanced degree." Archie replied.

"Over three hundred people heard me talk and show my art. It would have been nice if you had been there."

"You're awful. Shaaleen Gail," he snapped.

My dad always said, "You're awful." and turned to ask others, "Isn't she awful?"

We were packing the car in the front of the hotel the next day when Lori started cussing loudly at Archie in front of my colleagues. I said, "Lori, please don't talk to our father like that." They slammed the trunk shut, and got in the car in a huff. Both my parents harangued me the entire drive to Lori's house in Baltimore. "If I don't mind if she calls me a fucking asshole, that's my business. You have no right to interfere," my dad said. I wanted to jump out at the next exit, take a cab back to the airport, and return to Santa Fe. If I had not had a broken knee with a brace and a nine-month-old in a cradleboard, I would have. Instead, I had to spend a few nights in Lori's house near her job at Johns Hopkins University until my plane left Baltimore. At some point during the stay, I blurted out, "Lori-Ann needs psychiatric help. We all do." The three of them did not talk to me for years.

Whenever we visited Kim and Hilton we spent hours trying to figure out our parents. But none of us would ever understand Archie and Colleen. We could never predict what they would do. They had created their own world. Only the two of them knew the constantly changing rules, and only they would consent to live under them. Kim said not to let them bother me.

"Why do you expect her to act any differently?" she said.

"I want the kids to have a good relationship with their grandmother, like the one I had with Mimi."

But Kim was right. I needed to detach and learn not to care or I would only get hurt. One night I saw a news feature on divorcing your parents. They said if you continue to have the same arguments that never resolve and having contact with your family is causing emotional distress, you should give up and divorce them from your life.

I did not need them. Barry and I had a good life. His parents were warm, supportive, fun to be with, and made an effort to see us. They had been like real parents to me since I was a teen. I called them mom and dad, and they knew more about my life than my birth parents did. I was a parent now—my children and husband needed me.

I went home and made raw drawings of the violence I remembered as the staple of my childhood—my daddy exploding at me, his angry face as he drank at the kitchen table then chased me around the dining room table to hit me. The art pictured me crouching in fear and showed how tiny and helpless I felt.

Drawing with charcoal and graphite, I ground the black into the paper trying to impress my anger into the image. I added red for the wine and Daddy's twisted mouth. The drawings were raw. I hid them away for years.

Before I stowed them, I showed the charcoals to a friend who knew I had chronic insomnia. As soon as she saw the images of my dad, she said, "You were probably sexually abused too. Insomnia is a classic symptom of childhood sexual abuse. You are afraid to fall asleep because sleep is associated with sexual trauma."

"That's impossible. I would remember. My dad was far too sexually repressed to have done anything so sick."

Suddenly I remembered lying awake night after night as a child staring at the ceiling frozen with fear. Still, I would not believe her. I was suspicious of the large numbers of people my age who claimed they remembered they had been sexually abused. I was not ready to remember the other drawing I hid away so many years before of the flashback of Daddy touching me.

But the next time I bathed Liesette, it struck me how vulnerable she was. I had been that helpless and trusting when I was an infant on my changing table. Perhaps he thought because I could not talk, I would never be able to tell. I can never know for sure what happened.

One story Mimi never told when she was combing her hairs was that her dad was a pedophile. I was a mother of four and Mimi was eighty-six years old when I learned that Alphonse had sexually abused my grandmother. A cousin I never met before, one of my grandmother's sisters' granddaughters was passing through Santa Fe, and stopped to meet me. Sitting in my kitchen, one of the first things she said was, "We come from a long line of sexual abuse." She said it casually, as we sat stirring our herbal tea. "Huh?" I responded more than a little embarrassed. How had she discovered the secret I had almost succeeded in keeping from myself? My long lost cousin revealed that Pépère Alphonse Lavallée was not just a philanderer—he was also a pedophile. That day, I learned Pépère Lavallée repeatedly violated all his daughters, including Mimi, several of his granddaughters and great granddaughters. I understood now why every woman in our family always spat his name with disgust.

I was not surprised. When I asked Maman and Ma Tante about their Pépère, Maman said, "I hope you aren't going to ask Mimi about that. She is an old woman now. What purpose would it serve to dredge it up?" Ma Tante said she was certain that her Pépère never touched her or her sisters because Mimi and Papi never allowed them to be alone with him. When she was a teenager, she came out in her nightgown once when Pépère Lavallée visited. Papi got so furious, he said, "Never come out without proper clothes in front of your Pépère again." Ma Tante said she knew he was not angry with her. "He just wanted to protect me from my grandfather." Mimi had been violated by her own father, but she protected her daughters.

The next day my cousin Butch called. I had not heard from him in almost twenty years. He was on a retreat in Pecos, New Mexico and visited on his way back to the airport. He had become a bodyworker, a licensed acupressure therapist, and a shamanic healer. Butch was surprised when I told him what it was really like at our house. He didn't know Archie hurt me. We fooled him too. We talked about our crazy fathers, and lovely suffering mamans. Butch impressed the boys with his karate moves; I showed him my paintings of pregnant women imagining their babies growing, and he said, "I can't wait to see what you give birth to. It's classic Jung. You're giving birth to yourself."

Otellie invited me, Barry, the kids, Jim McGrath who wrote her catalog essay, and potter Jacquie Stevens for a party to uncork the huge bottle the Grand Dame champagne company sent her in recognition of her Honor Award. The inscription read, "From one Grand Dame to another."

It was a delightful party. Otellie sat enthroned in her overstuffed chair. They set up folding TV trays, and Millard kept bringing out course after course of snack food, first Cheetos, then pigs-in-blankets, sandwich cookies, celery sticks with peanut butter, and more. Otellie entertained us with stories of teaching claywork in Second Mesa outraging the elders when she brought a pottery wheel after studying at Alfred University, then moving to Santa Fe to be one of the first teachers at the new IAIA with her then husband, Charles the renowned jeweler. She especially liked to remember when she led the students in the Indian dance troupe that performed at the White House. Otellie was everyone's mom in those days at the Institute of American Indian Arts. During her last years, she was a grandmother to my kids. We spent countless afternoons visiting in Otellie's living room or kitchen. Each week, Sage sat at the Formica kitchen table and Otellie taught him to knead the bubbles out of the clay, make a mask from a slab, and pots from snake-like coils. I sat on the couch nursing Liesette in the living room of their house, which had the same floor plan as our H.U.D.

house on the rez in Chinle, and listened. Millard said he was a priest in the Snake Kiva at Walpi on First Mesa; he made gourd rattles with the boys and showed them how to paint a gourd of *Ojojo*, the good Hopi snake entity.

When he saw my *Deer Woman* paintings Millard said, "We Hopi also have these two entities. We have that Snake and the Antlered woman in our religion too. But I can not tell you their names because you are not Hopi."

That spring, Hazel Belvo hired me as a visiting artist at the Minneapolis College of Art and Design where she was dean. I drew the *Dreaming of Her Birth* images of a giant woman facing a huge fetus in utero with different stages of a fertilized egg growing into a fetus, then a baby. George Morrison came to the public slide lecture. Afterwards he leaned forward and said, "Good work. I would like to trade a piece for one of your pastels." My mentor wanted a piece of my art. He picked my *Lightning Tree*. We hung his intricate lithograph of ice breaking on Lake Superior over our mantel.

I nominated Pueblo pottery matriarchs Margaret Tafoya and Lucy Lewis to be honored during the Chicago WCA conference to be held in 1992. The summer before I interviewed Margaret and photographed her for the catalog I was editing. She greeted me and the children in her adobe home in Santa Clara Pueblo. She was sweet and gracious. The same age as Mimi, she reminded me of her, although Margaret was more petite. One of Margaret's granddaughters promised to write the catalog entry, but didn't, so I researched and wrote the essay, and made the presentation at the Honors Ceremony. I also curated the pottery selections for the exhibition at the Chicago Cultural Center for Tafoya and Lewis' work. The conference chair, a prominent Chicago feminist artist, fought me every step of the way.

"Why are we honoring two Pueblo potters when most of the Honorees should be from Chicago? Pottery is not art. We are not a crafts organization."

"These women are the last surviving matriarchs of Southwest Pueblo pottery. We can't wait to honor them. We had to present Lucy Lewis' honor award to her in the hospital because she was too old to travel. These matriarchs should be acknowledged while they are alive. Their work is art, not craft." I had to set her straight. Lucy died a few weeks later.

At the exhibition opening people raved about the magnificent abstract sculptural forms of the Pueblo pottery. Face to face with the technical and aesthetic genius of Tafoya's huge storage jars no one could deny they were art. Lewis' dazzling intricate patterned paintings on simple forms wowed the audience. Doubly so when they heard Lucy ground the paints from earth pigments near her Acoma Sky City adobe home and formed the fine lines with a brush she shaped by chewing yucca stalks. Thousands of people saw these Indian pots embodying hundreds of years of Pueblo women's relationship to clay in that museum in the Midwest.

The next day was my birthday. I went to the College Art Association conference to hear Rick Hill's panel on Christopher Columbus and Indians. It was 1992, the Quincentennial. People were waking up to remember Indians, to just as quickly forget them in 1993. Unlike most years, there were a handful of sessions at the conference addressing Native American art. As I arrived, I ran into Jeanette Looking Clear, said a quick hi and headed around the corner for the ladies' room. Moments later from the stall, I heard Jeanette's voice as she entered the bathroom talking to someone. "Oh. I had to run in here to hide from Touchette."

This time, I was amused, not hurt. I told colleagues, "I must be a scary person for her to have to run away from me. Maybe I'll nominate her for an Honors Award?" I did. She refused to accept the award until 1997 when I was no longer active in WCA.

That summer the children and I made a rare visit to Pépère's Lake. It was the only time all four children went to my childhood retreat. My parents drove Mimi up. Liesette sat on her great grandmother's lap and listened to stories. She giggled when Mimi tickled her chanting, *La bibit…la bibit…la bibit …mange, mange, mange, mange toute la petite bébé*. The kids played in the giant sandbox Pépère made for us when we were girls, and fished in the pond. The boys caught the usual perch, catfish, and inedible sunfish, then Jacques hooked a five foot long fresh water eel that Maman cleaned, chopped, and cooked, for everyone to eat.

The visit went fairly well until my parents took us to the family cemetery in North Grosvendale. While I chased the little ones, my dad walked with the bigger boys to show them the ancient tombstones engraved with our family names. As soon as we returned I settled in the basement to be with the kids alone for awhile. Maman had refinished the dirt floored camp kitchen into a neo-colonial studio apartment. We sat on the couch.

"Mama, why do Pépère and Mémère hate Jews so much?"

I did not really know myself.

"Why do you think Pépère and Mémère hate Jews, Sage?"

"I asked Pépère who the dead guy on the cross in the cemetery was and he said, 'That's Our Lord Jesus Christ. He died for our sins. The Jews killed him.' Is that true Mama?"

"Don't Pépère and Mémère know we're Jewish? Do they hate us too?" Jacques said.

"No, of course not," I answered, feeling not so sure.

"Mama, you better tell Mémère and Pépère we're Jewish. When you're not there, they keep telling us to go to Mass and Church with them."

I climbed the stairs to talk to my parents.

"Why did you tell my kids that the Jews killed Jesus?"

"The Jews did kill Jesus Christ, Shaaleen Gail. It's in the Bible."

"The Church doesn't teach that anymore, Dad. Ma, tell him, the Church does not say the Jews killed Jesus anymore."

"The Lord Jesus Christ died for all our sins. He died for us all."

Colleen repeated. Then she shifted gears.

"You're turning the boys against my religion. They would not say those things if you did not put them in their minds."

"Our children are Jewish. All three boys had *brits*, Liesette had a baby-naming ceremony, we joined a temple and they're learning Hebrew in religious school. When you say bad things about Jews, you hurt them."

"I can not understand why they can be raised in their other grandparents' religion, but not in mine."

Had she not been listening all these years?

"Jews do not believe Jesus is God. They are being raised in their Dad's religion. Neither of their parents is Catholic."

Maman took a different tack. "I can not believe Judaism can be Barry's religion. He doesn't go to temple every Saturday."

"Going to temple is not what makes you Jewish. A Jewish person is part of a nation of people, blah, blah, blah…" I continued wearily for the thousandth time trying to explain that while I could be French Canadian without being Catholic, Barry would always be Jewish even if he did not believe in the religion. Maman refused to see the fundamental differences between the two religions. But that was immaterial. Our kids were Jewish and there was nothing she could do about it.

"No matter what you think, you have to respect our decision to raise the kids Jewish. Jacques is having his Bar Mitzvah next year."

"That's disgusting." she spat.

It was useless to discuss it further. *Foi, langue, et famille* were indivisible. Maman would never accept my choice.

I told the older boys,

"You are members of a religion that ties you to five thousand years of Jewish life. You should be proud of your Jewishness."

My astute adolescent responded, "If you think being Jewish is so great, why aren't you Jewish?"

"I'm French Canadian and Indian, and you are too." I answered, but his point hit home.

That summer, Barry's Uncle Dave died of stomach cancer and we flew to Minneapolis to be with Auntie Arline for the funeral. The service got me thinking about what would be held when I died. I certainly could not be buried in either St. Joseph's cemeteries next to Mimi and Papi in Woonsocket, or Mémère and Pépère in North Grosvendale.

I had done so many of the things a Jewish mother does to keep a *Yiddishe* home since I met Barry, but had resisted converting to Judaism. I was proud of my own ethnicity, was turned off by women who converted without religious conviction, and it was hard to reconcile the patriarchal premises of Judaism with feminism.

Barry and I celebrated Passover Seders in the Lower East Side, Oregon, Navajo Nation, and Santa Fe. Besides asking the *Four Questions* and chanting the *Four Blessings over the Wine*, we added text to compile our own Haggadah that honors many of the dispossessed tribes and oppressed peoples worldwide. Our seders are large, boisterous celebrations with Hebrew and Ladino chanting, lively torah discussion, good food and laughter. The little children dance with colorful veils, playing tambourines and drums, singing *Mi Chamocha*. We remember the goal of Manifest Destiny was the same as Hitler's goal to destroy the Jewish people. The names of the Indian nations that were extinguished are called out, and we answer, *Ho Mitakwe oyasin. All my relations.* A teenage girl reads from Ann Frank's diary and the littlest child recites Lao Tsu, *Cultivate Justice in your self and Justice will be real.*

Anticipating my first son's Bar Mitzvah, I wanted to be a full participant in the ceremony, and not just a tolerated outsider. The rabbi told me that converting to Judaism would not require me to denounce my heritage, and that the Reconstructionist movement made room for feminist ideas with the honoring of *Shechinah*, the feminine aspect of God. I decided it was time to convert and add Judaism to my already complex identity.

My in-laws, who had long ago given up hope that I would convert, were elated. They flew in for the group conversion ceremony in the fall. The rabbi called me to the *bima* as *Rachel Simcha bat Avraham v'Sara*, after Barry's dad's mother Rachel and Simcha for Sheila's mom. At temple, *bubbies* surrounded my in-laws praising their daughter-in-law, and lamenting, "My own daughter should be so observant." The ceremony was celebratory, but verged on the surreal when one of the converts, also a former Catholic, grew ashen, then began gagging and slumped to his knees holding the Torah scroll. The rabbi broke the tension, "You do know, you do not have to gen-uflect to the rabbi now, don't you?" The congregation burst into laughter.

The rabbi said, "When I was growing up I thought Judaism was just for children and old people. My parents, aunts and uncles never went to temple. We were dropped off for Sunday school, and no one went to temple after their Bar Mitzvah. If you want Judaism to be a light in your children's life, you have to make it a light in your own."

I baked challah for Shabbat and added the blessing over the children to our candle lighting ceremony. We went to temple more on Friday night, and I made *strudel, kreplach, knishes, matzo balls*, and brisket, often getting *balabusta* tips during our Friday night phone calls from mom who was the modern equivalent of a quintessential Jewish homemaker. When I lit the Sabbath candles I focused on the peace chanting the *barucha* brought and let the worries of the week drop away. It was pow-erful to know that throughout the world Jews were lighting candles and singing the same ancient blessing. The children started joining me in the chant. Barry became more involved in spiritual practice. The family studied together.

Over the years, I had developed new family traditions to give my kids good Christmas memories like making Bouillabaisse for Christmas Eve dinner, and revived old ones I remembered fondly. I bought each child new pajamas, made hot chocolate with marshmallow fluff floating on top after dinner, and we cuddled on the couch to read *The Night Before Christmas* just as my sisters and I did with Maman. The children woke up eagerly on Christmas mornings to see what Santa brought. For Christmas day dinner, I made Julia Childs' *Poisson en Croute* by wrapping a side of salmon in *brioche* dough and decorating it to look like a golden fish.

As time went on, the contradiction inherent in being Jewish and celebrating even a secular Christmas bothered me. It was a lot of work to do both Chanukah and Christmas so far from sisters, aunts, and cousins who normally share holiday preparations. Each year I phased it out bit by bit, until we just had stockings for the kids. The year I converted I tried to eliminate Christmas all together. It was fine with everyone but five year old Raoul who climbed up into the storage closet, took down the Christmas lights, and strung them on the ficus tree in the family room. Soon we reclaimed the Paisner family tradition of catching double features at empty movie theaters on Christmas Day.

My conversion brought me joy, but I knew it would hurt maman, so I avoided telling her as long as possible. Even after I married a Jewish man, I think she always hoped that as long as I didn't convert there was a chance I'd come to my senses and return to the Church. Archie made an unexpected visit alone to ski in Santa Fe after the New Year, and it was clear I couldn't keep it from them forever. At dinner during my dad's first night visiting, I sat at the table agonizing over how to tell him I had converted in just the right words when Raoul shouted,

"Pépère, Mama inverted."

"Mom did not invert, Raoul. She converted." Jacques corrected.

"That is ridiculous boys. Your mummy didn't convert." Archie said.

I faced my dad across the long table covered with white linen for Shabbat dinner, and said, "Dad, I did convert to Judaism."

My father seemed taken by surprise but he said, "Well, that makes sense for you to convert, since your family is Jewish."

When I called to tell Maman, she burst into tears. The familiar wall of silence on the other end of the line was deafening. "You know how to hurt me more than anyone. I am much too upset to talk about it." We never did.

Later Kim phoned. She was totally distraught after speaking with Maman. "Ma said, 'None of my daughters' accomplishments mean anything because none of you believe in my savior Jesus Christ.'" Kim was stunned. Nothing she had done meant anything to our mother—not the BA from Bard, the Wesleyan doctorate, the perfectly decorated clean home she kept, and the gracious way she cared for others. Kim's academic achievements, my art career, activism, and family, and Lori-Ann's BA from Brown, MA from Princeton, Ph.D. from Oxford—all meant nothing to Colleen.

In the winter of 1993 I flew to Seattle for the WCA conference. I was chair of the Honor Awards, and moderated a panel with Doña Aqueda Martinez's daughter, weaver Eppie Archuleta who was a National Endowment for the Arts Awardee, Shiffra Goldman, Dr. Helen Lucero from the Museum of International Folk Art in Santa Fe, Winona's mom Betty La Duke, and sculptor Ruth Asawa. On the panel, I revealed my newest identity as a Jew by Choice. The audience was taken aback. It didn't fit with their image of me as Indian. People always want to put everybody in neat boxes. I didn't fit in any one box. Neither did my children. I told Winona, whose mom is Jewish, that I converted. She laughed, "Didn't you have enough troubles already?"

Emily Waheneka arrived from Warm Springs, and refused to exhibit her beadwork at the Bellevue Museum in the Honorees' exhibit because she didn't want to "leave her children with strangers." After the panel, I found Emily and her family and we worked everything out.

That afternoon at the Women of Color caucus meeting, Jeanette Looking Clear denounced the Honors committee. "I went to the museum and all the other artists had their work on the wall mounted professionally except for this poor little Indian woman, Emily Wahenekah."

I said, "Jeanette, this is a complicated situation that has been taken care of. I would be happy to tell you the details in private."

She leaned forward, squinted, and insisted on airing everything right there in front of the entire circle of thirty or more women. I began. There was only so much I could do long distance from Santa Fe.

Jeanette frowned, "This is not a conversation to have in front of these people. This is an inter-tribal matter. We should only talk about it amongst ourselves."

Several people rose to my defense. The most memorable was Sandra Rowe from L.A. "These people?" The impressive Black artist from Los Angeles pulled her spine up even straighter, and looked at Jeanette, "We know who Charleen is. We've seen her keep fighting year after year. No one works harder for the Honorees, especially the Indian women. We know your name, but you haven't been around working with us."

That night at the reception, Emily's niece did a heart rending presentation about the role her auntie's beadwork played in the cultural and spiritual life of the family and community at Warm Springs that left the audience in tears. At the museum Emily Waheneka held court in her traditional wing dress bedecked with beadwork surrounded by her pictoral art in glass beads, and hundreds of impressed admirers. She felt comfortable at last and entrusted her art with the museum. Jeanette did not attend.

That night, Barry called to tell me that Otellie died. She had been hospitalized since the fall, but I thought I would see her when I returned from Seattle. The kids were upset. The memorial service was scheduled for after my return at IAIA. We went and I spoke about Otellie. Millard fell apart without her. He had started drinking when she was in the hospital. He called Barry about his legal situation. They never married and there's no common law marriage in New Mexico, so her family took everything.

"They want to kick Millard out on the street," Barry said.

"How can they do that? Millard and Otellie lived together for over thirty years."

"Otellie never wrote a will."

A few months later, Millard was found murdered in the living room of the house where we shared so many pleasant afternoons making art and listening to Otellie's stories. The police hardly investigated. The detective said, "It was just another case of a drunken Indian getting killed in a fight."

At Jacques' Bar Mitzvah when we placed the *talit* on his shoulders I knew we made the right choice to raise our children Jewish. We prayed he would follow the covenant of the *brit*, the *huppah*, and *m'asadim tovim*, doing good works. The rabbi handed the Torah first to Barry's grandpa Henry Sigesmund, then to his dad and mom, and to me. Then I passed it to Barry who gave the Torah scroll to our first son. *L'dor v'dor*, from generation to generation. We started another family tradition when Barry and I read a *parasha* from the Torah in Hebrew before Jacques took his place as a Bar Mitzvah and chanted his four *parashas*. We wanted him to know reading Hebrew and studying Torah are lifetime pursuits that did not end with his Bar Mitzvah. Everyone sang *Siman Tov and Mazel Tov*. We danced the *hora*. Friends lifted us up into the air on chairs. My parents refused to attend. Kim and Hilton represented my family.

In August Indian Market brought lots of our friends back to Santa Fe, and after doing the rounds of gallery openings, our favorite watering hole was an old cowboy bar on the top of Canyon Road. The old adobe had low ceilings so you could touch the vigas when you danced on the tables which usually became necessary as patrons filled the dance floor until dancing to the local R & B band was a group grope. Everybody went to El Farol.

Lawyers and judges drank with Indian artists, gentlemen cowboys, and plain old cowboys, and Indians. There was always a pretty señorita named Garcia or Lopez who dazzled the drinking hooting men with fancy footwork and a luscious smile on the dance floor. Friends visiting from New York went crazy over the place. Saxophonist Tim Berne said he knew he was in the West when we showed him the bullet holes in the wall behind the bar.

One night it was so crowded and smoky you couldn't see to the door from the tables in the back. We were drinking with an elder Indian painter who was a successful New York artist with a cosmopolitan air that reminded me of George Morrison.

Billy Warsoldier arrived with bear hugs for Barry and me. He had been in Aspen carousing and drinking with Hunter S. Thompson and was flamboyant as ever with his long black coat and waist length black hair. He sat down and I introduced him to our friend from New York.

"He's a painter who loves paint too. It took me months to convince his New York gallery to let him be in the *Sweetgrass* book because he does abstract art and they didn't want him in an Indian art book."

"She got me in that book when the Feds couldn't even find me. She's a warrior woman." Billy said then began talking about how he grabbed a CNN camera when they were filming an Indian Market special and photographed the wild night at El Farol's when Darren Vigil Gray's band *Mud Ponies* got the place rocking. Our painter friend stewed as the spotlight shifted to Billy. A stylist friend of ours from Hollywood approached wearing a black micro-miniskirt, turtleneck, and knee high boots—both men were captivated. Jane was petite, blonde, and unaware of the rivalry she sparked when she was drawn into one of Billy's fantastic monologues about Indians, guns, and the passion to paint. Our silver haired friend seethed. I chattered with Jane and Billy, until Barry nudged me. I looked up and heard our friend tell him, "I hate guys like that Billy Jack guy. Women just fall all over Indians like that with the long black hair. I'm gonna take my beer bottle and crack it over his head." Barry laughed and said, "I wouldn't suggest it—chances are, Billy's packing."

That fall we bought five acres in the Sangre de Cristo Mountains, not far from Santa Fe's Plaza. The land, set in a relatively lush canyon, was studded with piñons and Ponderosa pines, and faced a pyramid shaped mountain. Though it was near the top of a mountain, the plot had a perfect site for a home that was sheltered from the west winds and had views of the Ortiz and Sandia Mountains.

While we built our new home, maman sent boxes overflowing with my schoolgirl journals, papers, sketches, and letters. When I was a child, my writings, the physical words on paper, were sacred to me, and in 1973 I had written, *They should not be destroyed*. But by 1994 I forgot penning those words and thought I left my past behind, so I read them all, then destroyed the lot. I wanted to be done with my childhood. Watching the papers burn felt good. I took a break from the art world to focus on painting.

We moved into our mountain retreat, and the home I designed was suited to our family's rhythms. The older boys were teenagers and were a challenge. They could be pains in the neck and we all lost our tempers sometimes. But generally, we enjoyed each others' company and life was sweet in our aerie. Mornings looking south to the Sandias, I chanted the *Shema—God is One*. When I drove out of the canyon, I sang the *Shema* again. Some days, the big boys shouted their rap songs, and turned the radio up to drown me out, or teased their little brother or sister to get them wailing and my attention elsewhere, but other times, one of them would start singing along and the others joined in until we were all chanting as we bounced down the dirt road toward town. On the way home from school during pauses in the squabbling in the car, rattling off of reports from school, and each of the four children's complaints about pals and teachers, we practiced ABC's and multiplication tables. Descending down the last lap of the dirt road I would chant the *Shema* again in a whisper, as I saw the lights of our home silhouetted against the mountain backlit by the glow of the setting sun.

Good Daddy

Offering on the Mountain

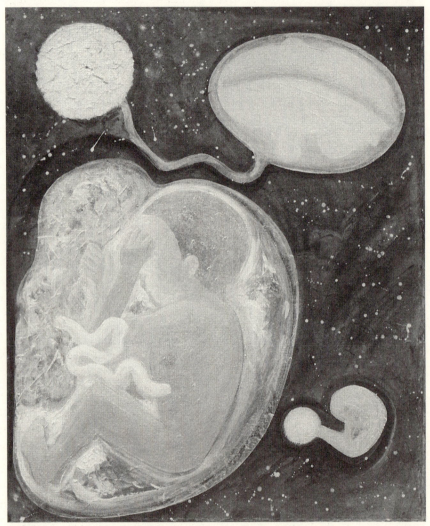

Floating in My Mother's Womb

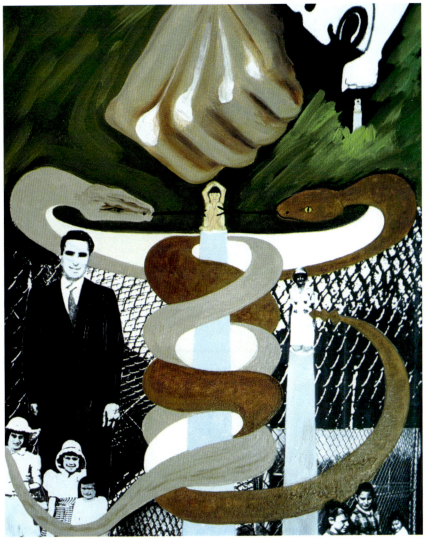

Not a Picture Perfect Family

Daddy Spanking

Daddy's Fist

Daddy's Wine Jug

Drinking Daddy

I'd Run and Run

He Always Caught Me

Daddy's Closet

The Strap

Caught in the Schoolyard

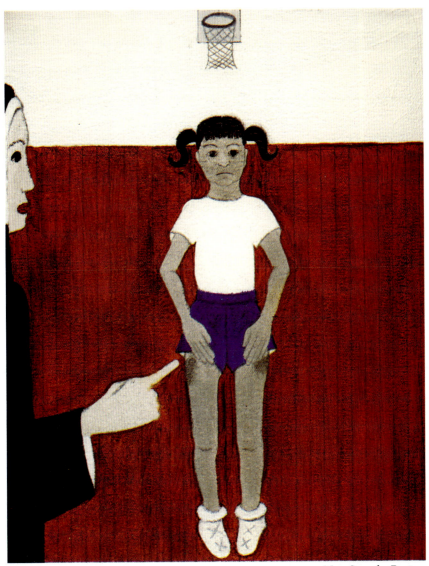

Nun Sees the Bruises

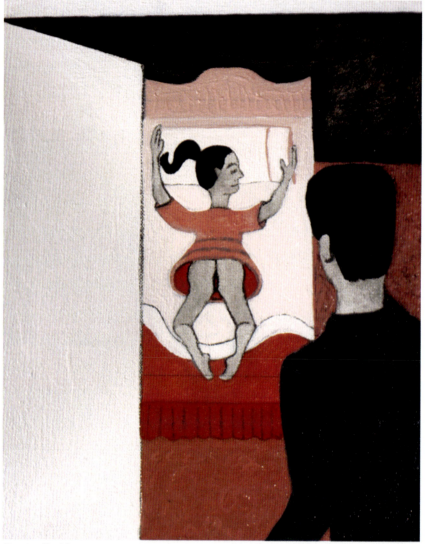

Peeping Daddy

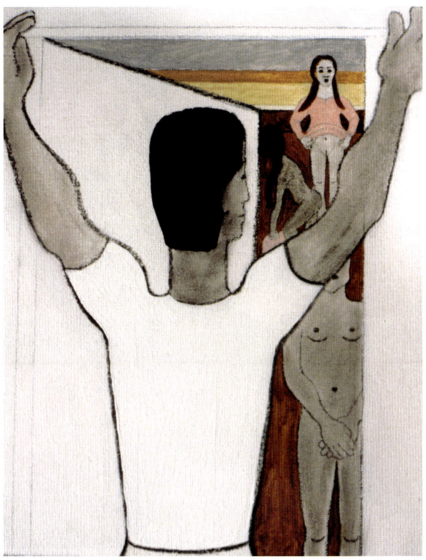

Don't Look at Us Daddy

Scary Daddy

Boom Boom Boom

Drowning Baby

Is She Alive?

Can I Save Her?

She's Alive

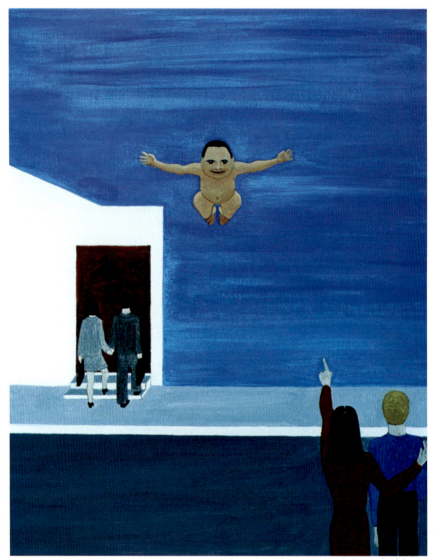

Laughing Levitating Baby

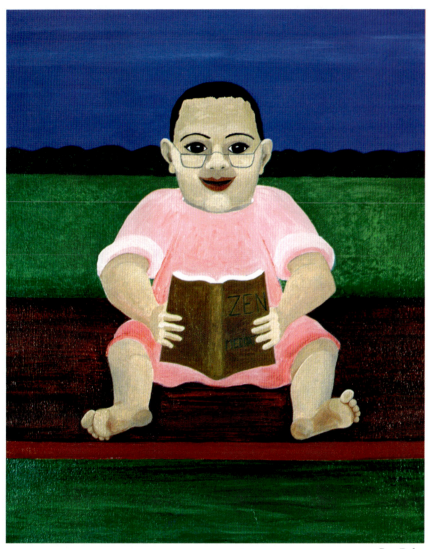

Zen Baby

Indigo Snake Tattoos

Protecting the Artist with Light

Tree of Life Ceremony

Light Shower

Depression

Rebirth

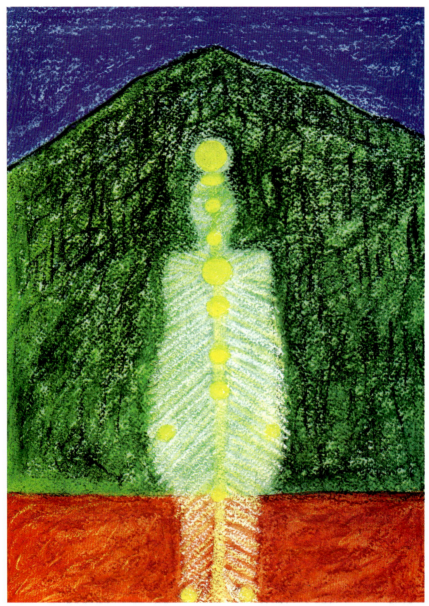

Mountain Chakras

Ocean Chakras

Water Illumination

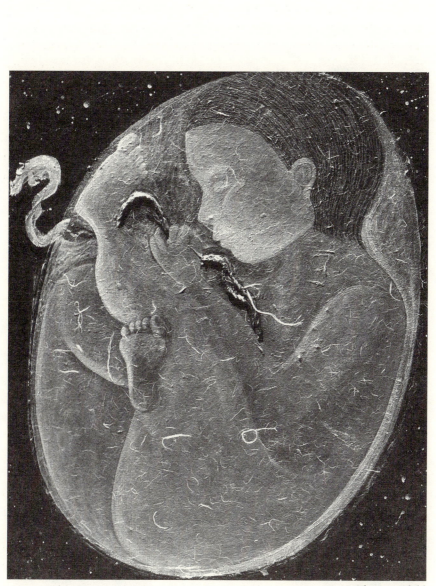

Floating Child

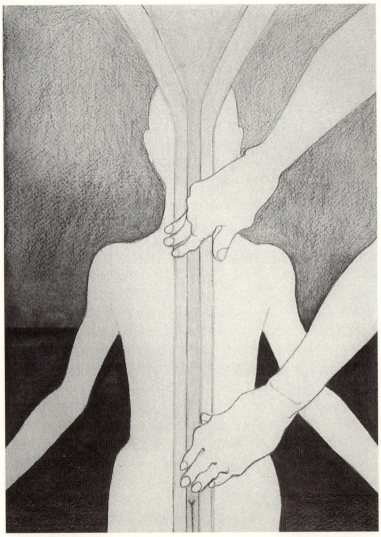

Healing Hands

Trois

Mal de Tête

THOUGH I HID AWAY THE CHARCOAL DRAWINGS and the writing about my childhood, I could not stop thinking about them. In 1994 I reworked the imagery, this time emphasizing healing and transformation. In the upper right panel of *Tikkun Olam: Healing a Shattered World*, a huge fist descends on a tiny girl crouched in a fetal position perched on a pillar. Two serpents intertwine around the column; each snake stings the girl with its tongue. Pictures of Archie's girls on Easter Sunday are dwarfed by a huge image of Daddy in a black suit. Maman kneels on a pedestal. In the upper left panel, a huge baby in utero floats intertwined with the umbilical cord and pictures of our family at Jacques' Bar Mitzvah under a *Mogen David*, and of me holding Liesette in her craddleboard. The umbilical cord and the serpents intertwine and descend to become the hair of a life size woman. A crescent moon cradles her womb. Her eyes are closed above a blissful smile. She accepts both positive and negative experiences of her past and faces the future with courage.

I painted a series of this image culminating with a ten by five foot painting. Then I drew *Good Daddy/Bad Daddy* to juxtapose the peaceful nurturing image of a father holding a newborn son and the scary one of a daddy's face and clenched fist descending on a child.

For Mimi's ninetieth birthday, I took the children to Woonsocket. It was hard to return to Clark Road in the middle of facing my childhood memories, but I wanted to celebrate with my grandmother. She was the same old Mim, aged but still full of life and still beautiful. Her hair was dark and lustrous, with some gray, but it had not gone all white. Maman dressed her for the party in an elegant white beaded dress. Mimi was so happy that night, greeting her well-wishers with grace, surrounded by the children, grandchildren and great grandchildren who adored her. Even the young waiters and the cousins' bachelor buddies gravitated to her like drones to the queen, asking questions and listening to her stories as she flirted with them. Mimi's charm transcended age, and she was most captivating at ninety.

After I returned home to Santa Fe, I continued working on the large *Tikkun Olam* painting. Making this huge piece was difficult because it was technically and emotionally complex. The four panels were covered with thick layers of paint. When I painted it, I piled huge globs of acrylics on my palette. Working with big brushes and strokes splattered stray paint up and down my arms and on my face and hair.

It was almost comical. I worked on the good memory side, and felt good, but when I did the abuse side, I felt anxious and tormented or numb. I was so frustrated, I wrote, *I can not keep doing these abuse paintings. They upset me too much. At this point, they're not helping to resolve my issues. Instead, they keep me thinking about it. It's painful and I can't take much more.* I stopped painting about my childhood.

Then the headaches began. Everyday, all day, my head ached. My forehead, the back of my eyes, and the base of my skull were dense with thick constant pain. My vision blurred. I began losing my memory. My brow grew deeply furrowed and my usual big smile was replaced by a frown. Deep dark circles ringed my eyes. The doctors could not find the cause.

When the pain began in the fall I thought, maybe I have the flu, or am drinking too much coffee, or maybe it was the glass of wine I had last night. By the next spring, I had not felt good since the Thanksgiving before, and I knew I had a serious illness. My life gradually changed completely.

When the sun came up over Overlook, everything shimmered with light and it was beautiful all around me. I was happy, but I could not enjoy life because my head hurt all the time. I became a different person. When I looked into the mirror, the face I saw was not my own. I didn't recognize myself. But no one knew what was wrong—so no one could help.

I wanted to be well. Like an amateur detective, I observed the pain, noticed what stimuli worsened or lessened it, and sought help everywhere. My sister, the chemistry professor was the first to suggest that the headaches were caused by toxins. "The headaches began in November, right?" Kim asked. "That makes sense because that's when you started keeping the windows closed. I think they are toxic headaches. The press-board emits gasses including formaldehyde and ammonia. If you were already sensitized by the paints you used, then out-gassing from the particle board could overload your system."

I called an art hazards clearing house in New York, they said headaches are common in people who worked with acrylics for two decades with no effect, then develop sensitivity to the solvent ammonia and/or the preservative formaldehyde. They told me to smell ammonia straight from the bottle, and if my symptoms got worse it meant I developed an allergy to ammonia, which is in acrylics. Sure enough, within moments of taking a whiff of ammonia, the pain in my head was like a thunderclap.

When I went back to my HMO provider with the information about the art hazards, he said, "Have your kids give you a neck rub, and take these pills. But don't take them if you have to drive. And don't take too many. They can be addictive." I drove the kids around all day, so I only took the medication at night, and only a few times. When I did, the pain got worse.

Barry's dad called. "Go back to that doctor and tell him your dad's a head and neck surgeon and your brother-in-law's a psychiatrist with psycho-pharmacology expertise, and we want you to be seen by a neurologist and have an MRI."

It was difficult to do anything when my head hurt all the time, but Barry and I got up before dawn every morning to hike up and down the mountain. I tried everything to get healthy and we were both getting in shape. But my head still hurt too much to work. This was not like me. My diet was healthy. I exercised, gave up coffee, didn't smoke, and almost never drank. No matter what I did—the pain persisted.

After years of finding comfort and inspiration in my dreams, I stopped remembering them, and woke up feeling dead inside. After a full year of constant pain, I could not function. The worst part was that I couldn't paint. Since I was seventeen I had painted through all the challenges I faced. But, not this time. I stopped painting and writing. After being active, capable, and hardworking all my life—I was a worthless lump. When I was in the grip of the pain, I was unable to sleep or think straight. The pain was so debilitating, it felt like my world was falling apart. When I wasn't tending to the children, all I could do was to stare into space and pray the misery would stop.

I went to every kind of doctor; neurologists, allergists, chiropractors and Asian medicine practitioners. They did all sorts of blood work, and three MRI's of my spine and brain. They tested my blood and urine for diabetes and hormone levels. I saw healers and massage therapists. But the pain persisted, and I kept losing weight until I weighed only one hundred four pounds—what I weighed before I had the children.

I looked so bad, people didn't recognize me. One friend was so upset by how deteriorated I had become that he insisted on paying for me to see his doctor. Native and other healers called, wrote, and visited with suggestions for ceremonies and prayers. I tried everything.

The doctors hadn't found a physical cause for the headaches, so I searched for other causes. At Women's Health Center, I asked Dr. Justina Trott if childhood memories could have triggered the pain. She said women often remember abuse when they have a baby girl and see her at different stages. "You remember what your life was like then, and how it was so different from hers. The contrast can be painful." But Dr. Trott thought it more likely that my severe symptoms had a physical cause like the toxins in the paints and advised me to take precautions. "Ventilate your studio properly, and wear a mask and rubber gloves when you paint."

Sage's Bar Mitzvah was in October, in the middle of this illness. My parents surprised me by showing up. I wore white lace. Some said I looked like an angel, but my glow was only inspired by the moment. I was emaciated and gaunt. My hair, though still long, had begun to lose its shine. My eyes were sunken deep in their sockets. I was so frail I feared I would blow off the patio with a gust of wind at the party.

It was a luminous autumn day. Jacques, Barry, and I read from the Torah then Sage chanted and gave a compassionate talk on his Torah portion.

Even my parents were impressed with the service. Maman had a few tearful outbursts when she ran out of temple and my dad scurried after to comfort her. Her theatrics elicited sympathy from a few, but everyone else seemed indifferent. Archie drank too much at the open bar. I saw Kim get exasperated and push Daddy's hands off her. I shuddered, and walked away. There were friends to greet, *crêpes* and *knishes* to check. After dusk at the sighting of the third star, we gathered under the full moon to sing with arms entwined. We circled the braided candle made from many strands that make one flame, and extinguished it into the wine for the *Havdallah* ceremony which separates the Sabbath from the rest of the week. That Shabbat was an island of holiness and light in an otherwise bleak time.

After my parents left, I remembered the Four Serpents Dream. The headaches were the injury to my eyes, the bite of the red snake. I worked on healing with the first three injuries, but never got to the core of my anguish. I avoided facing the abuse. But this fourth injury was incapacitating. I could not ignore it and continue on with business as usual. I was forced to face the memories I tried so hard to forget.

During this acute stage, I was treated by a homeopathic doctor who was dogged in the quest for a diagnosis and treatment for my headaches. The doc was a tall lanky blond with a perpetual tan as if he always just walked off the tennis court. But he was an obsessed scientist searching for clues, who refused to give up. He did all kinds of orthodox and unorthodox tests, put me on detoxifying fasts and diets, and prescribed supplements, antioxidants—even enemas. The homeopath agreed with Kim that my illness was caused by the toxins in the paints. He would not stop until he could prove it.

In the mid-1980s I had experienced problems with toxins in art supplies. After months making hundreds of pastels, sometimes two or three a day, I became sick from toxic exposure. Each time I blew pastel dust off the paper to keep the colors vibrant, I ingested poisonous heavy metals that give pigments like *cadmium* red, *titanium* white and *cobalt* blue their brilliant hues. I should have started to worry when I blew my nose and there was colored dust all over the tissue. My lungs and skin were absorbing the hazardous metals in the pigments and the solvents in the fixative. The symptoms were gastro-intestinal. The docs diagnosed a hiatus hernia, but I knew I was being poisoned. After I took protective measures, the problem subsided. As time passed, I used less oils and pastels, and did most of my art with acrylics because they were supposed to be safer.

Despite the growing evidence that my headaches were caused by toxins, the neurologist was unconvinced. "The urine and blood tests do not show high levels of metals," he asserted. But he could not offer any more plausible explanations or solutions. The process was slow because the insurance company refused to cover alternative tests. Once I started the fasts prescribed by the homeopath, I improved in minute increments week by week. But I was still in constant pain. When the headaches persisted after a year and a half of treatment, I became convinced that even if the toxins were eliminated, I would never heal if I did not face my childhood. My sister Kim disagreed.

"There had to be some good in the past. We would not have survived if they hadn't given us some nurturing. They were doing what they thought was best."

"Daddy was venting when he was drunk, not parenting."

"Well I had a happy childhood. I was a happy child."

A year after the dreams stopped, they resumed. The first were epic in scale about speaking publicly about my French Canadian ancestors at a freedom rally in New York City, and going back in time to Indian gatherings and ceremonies on the Northern Plains. But one morning I woke up gasping for breath and shaking uncontrollably with excruciating pain in every nerve fiber from the worst nightmare I ever had. When I tried to tell Barry about the frightening dream, no words could communicate the horror of this nightmare where we were separated from our children by fundamentalist Christians in flowing white robes. The nightmare seemed so tame without the dimensions of the dream world. Still every inch of my skin vibrated with burning pain where the captors had wounded me with stun guns in the dream. My heart pounded, I felt electric shocks all over my body and the pressure in my head got worse. I stood under the shower for an hour. The hot water pouring over my skull slowly dulled the ache and brought me back to the real world. After a while I remembered I had been dreaming. The pain I felt was in the same places I was injured in the dream world. For two hours I couldn't speak. I curled up in Barry's arms afraid to close my eyes, and lay there shaking for hours more before I fell asleep.

As the next weeks unfolded my dreams became multidimensional. What happened in the dreams had a physical effect on my waking body. From some dreams, I woke in pain, from others I awoke sexually aroused. Some dreams caused a painful ache and burning throughout my pussy.

My cousin Butch phoned. We hadn't talked since his visit to New Mexico in 1990. "I am glad you called," I said relieved. "I have been having bad headaches and the strangest dreams."

"I am not surprised. I thought you would be awakening."

"Awakening?"

"You are undergoing a Kundalini awakening. The serpent lying dormant at the base of your spine is rising to clear out your chakras. The dreams are around power. The secrecy is about people trying to steal power. There is a secret sexual theme. The healing you are undergoing is tied to the bigger healing of our female lineage. There has been so much violence perpetrated against the women in our family. Your healing will heal all our woman relatives back through past generations and into future generations."

"You have been repressing rage your whole life, and now you're processing it during the night. You're angry in your dreams, and your head, neck, back, and jaw muscles tighten up, so when you wake up you are in pain from clenching your jaw all night. Neuro-muscular and cranial sacral therapy would help. You are inter-dynamically separated from your family of origin, and unable to make contact with the child inside you who was hurt and is now internally raging beyond belief. You need bodywork, rage release work, and a primal, or Reichian therapist to help you scream it out. You need to let it rip. You are at a crossroads. There is great healing in these headaches."

Butch had his first shamanic dreams as a boy, but this was the first time he told me about them. "I entered a three-dimensional vortex and came out into another dimension—usually flying. There I encountered animals who embraced me, and I would go downstairs in my sleep to do rituals in the kitchen. The dreams went on for four years. They scared the heck out of your ma tante. You know my mother. She thought I was nuts. She brought me to Dr. Dashef, so I stopped journeying. But I learned then how to do lucid dreaming, and could move in my dreams. Now I go into the vortex wide awake and use it to heal. I project to people in their minds and work on them energetically."

I thought I knew my cousin. Though he still had a thick Woonsocket accent, Butch was far different from the young man who left Rhode Island decades ago for Texas to sell vacuum cleaners. "Call me anytime. So many in our family have these gifts, but most of them are afraid to open up," he added as we said goodbye.

During these last few years, I intended to call my pediatrician to ask for my childhood medical records. Perhaps he noted suspicions of child abuse somewhere in my chart. I wanted to know if he recalled anything that could help me piece together the missing pieces of the puzzle. Several times, I dialed his telephone number only to hang up before it rang. I wanted to know, but was afraid of what I might find out. Were there any marks in my file that confirmed the vague memories lurking in the back of my mind? Did he make any record of the vaginal infections, or the small slashes I made on my arms and thighs with the razor blade?

When I gathered up enough courage to call, his wife answered the phone, "Dr. Dashef died a few months back. He kept the medical records until three years ago, but they are destroyed now. You could have seen them if you had called just three years ago." I will never know what he noticed.

My illness was so acute it felt like I was going crazy. My body would start to itch all over like millions of insects were crawling under my skin. I began having swift mood swings between elation and depression, and as the days passed the shifts came closer together until I oscillated day to day, then bounced up and down, from hour to hour.

I alternated between terrors and sexual arousal. The down side was that I was attracted to other men, even strangers on the street. After being faithful to Barry since we met, I started noticing other guys. My eye would catch the muscular thigh of a long haired Indian on a motorcycle, or a dark stranger's glance across the dance floor, and I flushed with arousal and began spinning impossible fantasies in my mind. I was losing myself.

I woke one morning knowing I dreamed all night, but I could not remember any of the dreams. My pussy was sore like I was getting a bladder infection—only no infection materialized. I lost my appetite and more weight, until I weighed only ninety-four pounds. I felt nauseated with an aching pain in the pit of my stomach to match the one in my head. My arms and legs were weak and exhausted like I was getting a bad flu—but no flu appeared. It was only a matter of time before I would be hospitalized.

She Wanted to Die

Healing

I WAS DESPERATE. IT WAS NATURAL FOR ME TO TURN to alternative healing techniques, and Santa Fe was full of choices. I consulted many different healers. One thing led to another, and in addition to a psychologist, I turned to dream interpretation, vibrational medicine, bodywork, acupuncture, psychic, Ayurvedic, and Native medicine.

But first I called Avis Archambault in Scottsdale. We had known each other since we met at the Mount Hood Sun Dance, and saw each other every summer at the Big Mountain Sun Dances in the Navajo Hopi disputed area when we lived on the *rez*. Avis was a gifted healer; she would know what I should do. I asked for her counsel, as I sat on the deck off our bedroom bathed in sunshine watching the sun set over the mountain. Avis said, "Your spirit and body as well as your spirit helpers and ancestors are giving you messages to guide you through this transition. You are a powerful Native woman, a mother, artist, creative, nurturer, and teacher. You have tendencies toward Native medicine. You are already walking in that world in your paintings. Don't think of yourself as being ill or in crisis because the image we have of ourselves determines health or illness. Offer tobacco, drink sage tea, and purify your body in the sweatlodge. Follow the Medicine Wheel and learn to trust yourself."

She gave me detailed instructions to do healing ceremonies to release the images of abuse. "The talk therapy is good, but you need to do body-work because the memories of abuse are held in your body. Bodywork helps you release the pain. Call on all your spirit helpers—the snake, the eagle, the wolf, and the jaguar."

My parents hated therapists, and criticized people in Woonsocket who saw them. I had always dealt with my issues alone through my art—or by talking with Barry or Kim. I felt like a failure and so out of control that I needed to talk to a *shrink*. I didn't know what to look for or how to choose a therapist, but I knew I couldn't do it alone anymore. I took Avis' advice, trusted my gut reactions, and met several people who helped, including a Jungian psychologist who knew about shamanism. I was nervous before the first appointment.

On the drive through town to La Tierra I wondered what it would be like to tell an outsider about my family. The road led to a tin roofed adobe cottage on the mesa with a broad view of the mountains north of Santa Fe. The Jungian psychologist came out to greet me. She was petite with yards of wavy hair that sparkled with a sprinkling of silver woven throughout. Her easy manner made me feel comfortable. Once I started talking about my childhood, I couldn't stop. There was so much to tell. I began with why I came, and showed her my art.

"You have been on a shamanic journey from the beginning."

"That's ridiculous. I'm a painter. I just paint what I dream."

"There are all kinds of ways to be a shaman. You don't have to be a medicine woman to heal. Maybe you're a wounded healer, and when you emerge from this healing, you can help others who've been abused."

"It gets so painful, I want to give up."

"You don't have to break down to go through this change. Rely on healers and allies for support."

As I left, she pointed to a tree and said, "After you called me, I went outside and there were two corn snakes twined oppositely around that piñon, just like in the paintings you showed me today. I will accept you as a patient. It will take time. You'll need a minimum of bi-weekly sessions for at least a year." After a few weeks she asked,

"What would your headaches tell you if they could talk?"

"They would let out a blood curdling scream and shout, listen to me."

"Why don't you just pay attention to them?"

"Because I see myself as someone who takes care of others, not someone who needs care."

I got a knot in the pit of my stomach whenever I went to see the psychologist. I hated talking about my parents. It made me remember when and why Daddy hit me, what he said, the way I felt so bad, dirty, and evil, and how it was always my fault because I was the *bête* who wouldn't drop it. I would not stop and give in to him. I listed the litany, from embarrassment, no privacy, and constant scrutiny, to total control, anger, and violence. I told the psychologist about my constant motivation to escape and to open the doors for my sisters to break out too. When I told her how Daddy would say he had seen my *kitchewee*, and tried to see us naked in the bathroom she said,

"Your dad created a sexually charged atmosphere."

"I felt I was the one who was evil and dirty."

She leaned forward and asked, "What would it take for you to scream?"

I described Daddy hitting me and she said, "You don't seem angry when you talk about it." She was right. When I talked about it, I didn't feel anything. Even when I was doing the paintings—I was numb. I told her the memory of my daddy touching me and was on the verge of crying but couldn't. Tears welled up in the therapist's eyes. She said, "I'm amazed that someone who experienced the childhood you describe can't cry."

I was brought back to a pivotal moment as a child when I stood facing Archie looking up at his angry face. He had just slapped me. I remembered biting back my tears and vowing, "I'll never let Daddy see me cry ever again. I won't let him know he hurts me." After that moment, I almost never cried in front of my dad.

I recalled a recurring nightmare I had as a child of trying to protect my sisters from a murderer who was trying to break into our house, and told the therapist how I could never keep the intruder out. "I had a gun, the one we gave Daddy for Christmas, but no bullets. When I found the bullets, the gun was gone. I could not get the right tools together. Something was always missing."

Burning my schoolgirl journals and moving thousands of miles from my birthplace had not freed me. The memories were etched in my cells. Since I left my birth home I focused only on how lucky I was to have escaped, and buried the pain caused by those first seventeen years. But as I drove back home from the session, my eyes seared with the image of the red sun dropping behind the Pecos Mountains, I saw that I was just a way Daddy could get back at Maman.

The bodyworker said, "I work with energy. I clear out blockages to reconnect you to the deepest truth of who you are." I thought; get in touch with the truth of who I am? Yuck. Why would I want to do that?

During the sessions, we talked for awhile then I reclined fully clothed on the massage table. The bodyworker covered me with blankets and held different parts of my body. As she touched my neck, head, shoulders, or feet, she instructed me to breathe, sometimes deep, at other times more shallow. Often she moved her other hand to cover one of my chakras. Her touch was loving and maternal; I felt safe. She prayed for the Creator to keep me in the light. With her long hair and flowing handwoven robes, she looked like a new age witch, but she worked with spiritual energy in ways similar to medicine men and women. Some days she burned candles of different colors, or cleansed me with smudge sticks of sage, cedar, lavender, and juniper. I began every session convinced nothing would happen, but each time I underwent unexpected changes.

As I breathed, I went deeper and deeper until I was in a fugue state. I began most sessions not thinking about my dad, but his image often popped into my mind accompanied by more pressure in my head. One time the pain in my forehead got stronger when the bodyworker held my solar plexus, and I saw an image of my dad's face when he was young, about the same age he was when I was a baby. I felt enormous pressure throughout my body, and started breathing heavy and gasping. When I exhaled, the memory disappeared. I heard a child's voice say.

What could I have done to deserve so much pain?

I thought—you didn't deserve it. Later when the bodyworker was pressing on my legs and hips, I heard the little girl again, *I must be very bad for my daddy to do this to me.* It was such a baby way to think. When I sat up, I felt bruised all over. The bodyworker said, "You weren't bad, but horrible things were done to you. You need to hold the little girl who was hurt, and tell her she isn't bad. You are here to protect her now, and make sure nothing bad ever happens to her again."

I packed the kids up for a visit with their father's parents in Minneapolis so I could do three weeks of intensive therapy. Before they left, Liesette ran to get her favorite teddy bear that she had slept with since birth. I stuffed it into her suitcase, and she stopped me. "No mama, I want you to keep it while I'm gone. I hug this teddy when I feel sick. Maybe if you hug it, you'll feel better too."

After we dropped the children at the airport, I did healing work with the Jungian, the bodyworker, and a Swedish massage therapist trained in Reiki energy work. Every day I saw at least one practioner. I continued the cleansing fasts and supplements the homeopath prescribed, took detoxifying and herbal baths, and created my own ceremonies. Healing was almost a full time job. It was good the children were away. I needed the time alone, but I missed my babies. I woke up smiling from nights of dreaming about them. They gave form and purpose to my days and I was somewhat at sea without them. But I had to do this work alone.

I dreamed I was traveling. When I opened my suitcase it was filled with baby girl clothes and a porcelain teddy bear that opened to reveal smaller and smaller teddy bears inside it like a nesting toy. The tiniest teddy had a miniature key inside. I woke up gasping in pain, waking Barry. I told him about the deep anguish I felt, and he held me until I fell asleep in his arms.

"You need to learn how to hold yourself through the pain," the body-worker said. I did not know how to do that. I didn't even know what that meant. She explained that I had been doing all kinds of things to cleanse and heal but I needed to hold and comfort the part of me that hurt the way I held my kids when they were in pain.

"You are running on empty batteries and could nurture your children on a deeper level if you learned to nurture yourself. What would you do if Liesette was in pain and you took her to the doctors but they couldn't help, and she still said, 'But mommy it still hurts so much'?"

"I would rock her in my arms and try to comfort her."

When the bodyworker began each session, the pain and pressure in my forehead was strong, but as I breathed, the ache built up and burned even more. I tried to imagine how I could learn to hold myself. What would I need to do to get to a place where I could actually do that? I heard a voice inside me say, *I do not want to go deep into the core of my being because I hate the little girl inside me. She doesn't deserve to be comforted and held. She is bad and evil just like Daddy said.*

As a child I thought I was *la bête*—the monster who deserved to be punished—not loved and protected like good girls did. I tried to tell myself it wasn't true, and listed the ways I was good, but I discounted each. All the good things about me were ways to hide the fact that deep inside, I was *la bête*.

La Bête

Releasing

A WEEK BEFORE SUMMER SOLSTICE, I AWOKE before dawn. Waves of anguish flooded my body—shocks of fear pulsed up and down the backs of my legs. I felt these sensations on several occasions, and called them *the creepy feelings*. My head hurt so much I wanted to scream. My body itched all over, especially on my head, like hundreds of bugs were crawling on me again. I wanted to jump out of my skin. I slipped into a steaming bath hoping the hot water would soothe me, and then ate some fruit and went back to bed. Barry asked, "Are you okay?" "No," I whispered. I could not find words to describe how frightened I was. He held me tight. Feeling his strong body against my back, clutching Liesette's pink teddy like a little girl, I finally fell asleep. The next day I rose early, ate brown rice with honey and milk, and then meditated. The creepy feelings kept growing stronger. I was frightened, but knew I had to go into a meditative state if I was going to get through it. Panic hit me. This was not ordinary fear. It was blood curdling, screeching, jump out of your body with all the caps—FEAR.

I worried I would go out of my mind. When I scrunched up into the fetal position, it didn't help. Resisting made the fear worse—so I let go. My body trembled, but I slowly let myself give in to the pain. When I thought

I could not possibly bear anymore, an earth-shaking spasm coursed through my body. I shuddered. Gasps and screams burst from my larynx. It did not feel like my mouth made the sounds. They blasted right out of my gut.

After the first explosion, I was scared, but I could tell there was more to release. Once I caught my breath, I resumed meditating. The creepy feelings built up again and again until my body shuddered and whooped. The releases came in wave after wave. Some were little, and just my legs or stomach shuddered. Others were so loud and huge, my voice filled the room and my body flopped on the bed and seized for a long time. As I breathed, the spasms increased in force and frequency. They were like epileptic seizures, similar to the ones I had with bodywork, but longer and stronger. At first, the pain was strong between the releases, then it lessened after each one. I began to feel less fearful. There were over a hundred explosions before the frequency slowed, and I had the last spasm two hours later.

It took me a long time to slowly come back into the present. There was more to release deep inside, but for now the brilliant sunlight reflected off the smooth bleached linen, soft puffy clouds floated just outside the wall of windows above the shimmering mountains, and I felt drained and amazed. The pain in my head was less dense, my solar plexus felt okay, and the creepy feelings were gone from my legs.

The next day in the middle of my meditation, Maman called, and I cautiously asked her some questions about my childhood. She told me Daddy was the dreamer in the family and had weird dreams like Lori-Ann and me. When I asked if Daddy loved me when I was born, Maman tried to assure me that he did. But when I asked why he hit me so much, her tone changed.

"Well you were not easy to get along with either. It's a two-way street."

"When I was just a toddler, what could I have done that was so bad that he could justify hitting me? Didn't he hit me a lot harder than necessary?"

"I guess he did. I try not to think about that, I don't remember much of what happened back then."

Maman told me we moved to Clark Road in November when I was almost three. "You shared a room with Kimmy, and when Lori-Ann was born, you got a day bed with a matching bedspread, bolsters, and a ruffled dust ruffle." I had forgotten all about that day bed. But when I was working with the bodyworker, I often saw dark blue material with pale pink, yellow, and white nubs that were blurry, as if seen close up, and remembering that cloth filled me with fear and dread. Maman's detailed description of the bedspread on the daybed was the same as the cloth I remembered in the sessions. Maman said, "You got your own room and new furniture when you were seven. You were the only one who had your own room."

After we said goodbye, I hung up the phone and resumed my meditation. When I put my hands on my upper thighs, my body rippled with lots of small spasms and some big ones. I kept trying to close my legs to stop it. With each spasm, my neck arched and the pain grew stronger.

I saw glimpses of that bedroom and remembered I always had a creepy feeling about that room. I kept thinking about the daybed, and recalled the feeling of waiting for daddy to come into the room. A strong sense of foreboding overcame me with a feeling that something significant was connected to watching the bedroom door. I kept seeing it open, casting a sliver of light and daddy's gigantic shadow onto the bedroom walls, then close shut until the room was dark again.

I shouted *No*. My legs closed tight involuntarily, and I heard myself say, *I'm only a little girl*. I wanted to throw up. I was filled with an ominous feeling that terrible things happened in that room, and that being in the daybed had something to do with thinking daddy loved me after all.

Later, the creepy feelings started again. I kept imagining standing in the hallway facing the bedroom door seeing my little girl self on the day bed, but it was too scary and I couldn't bear it anymore. I tried to be quiet so I wouldn't wake Barry but eventually the *Nos* shaking my body woke him. He spooned me and I crawled into a fetal position and fell asleep in his arms.

I dreamed a spirit teacher stood behind me in a large room. I never saw him but sensed he was very old and small. He touched the back of my head and neck, and a sensation of power and light vibrated up my spine. I began rising into the sky, then fell very fast into a soft black void. It was a wonderful feeling of exhilaration and freedom with no fear. The old man of my dream was the essence of the good father.

Along with the talk therapy and bodywork, I burned sage, did yoga, and automatic writing, consulted Tarot cards, and threw the *I Ching*. At summer solstice I went on another vision quest on a bare rock outcropping sheltered under a majestic pine tree. Wrapped in my morning star quilt I faced each direction and prayed, fasted, and meditated watching the sun rise and set again and again. Animals visited. I had visions.

Two giant eggs appeared in the sky above me, and cracked open. One revealed a coyote. The other held a white buffalo calf. A voice said, *You must choose.*

We had been in a drought for months. It began drizzling when I went up on the mountain and rained more each day as I fasted and prayed. I offered the pipe. Hawks crisscrossed the sky. Rain filtered through the canopy of the two hundred year-old piñon dampening my hair and the star quilt I pulled over my head at night. Dawn came with ravens cawing and raindrops moistening thirsty pine needles. Wet earth smell filled my nostrils. I came down four days later. The clouds burst. It was pouring rain.

The next week at the bodyworker, I saw my face as a girl with pig tails and bangs as she held my heart charka. "I can see the history being released. It looks like energy lifting off your whole body like a white vapor. Sometimes the energy released is dark and looks like metallic filings lifting away." She burned a candle and passed it over me.

While working on healing from my childhood with the bodyworker and the psychologist, I continued appointments with the homeopath who investigated the physical cause of my illness until he proved his hunch. In 1996, nearly two years after I first got sick, the doctor confirmed that I had heavy metal poisoning. Hair analysis showed toxic levels over the charts for several poisonous metals in my system. I was being poisoned. High levels of *cadmium, titanium,* silver, aluminum, uranium, mercury, arsenic, and tin had accumulated in my system and been deposited in my bones, brain, and muscles. The toxins taxed my liver and kidneys and caused the severe pain in my back.

My doctor waved the lab report with the toxic metals blacked out on a bar graph. "I knew it was heavy metal poisoning. Long term exposure to toxins causes an overload in the body. It's like pouring water into a tea cup. Once the cup is filled to the brim, whatever you add makes it overflow. The addition of any toxins into your overloaded system triggers symptoms." The headaches got worse when I ate foods with sugar, caffeine, yeast, or wheat flour, or took painkillers because all those substances raised the toxicity level. The only way to draw out the toxic metals was by *chelating*, a procedure that had long been used successfully by doctors for children exposed to lead.

An IV was inserted into my veins to inject *chelating* chemicals that were like magnets. They attracted the metals and bonded with them as they moved through the blood stream. They could not be absorbed because there were no pathways in the body for their shape. Instead, they carried the heavy metals out of the system through the urine. The procedure itself was uneventful. I just sat and read a magazine and the chemicals entered my veins until the IV bag was empty. Once I got home, the chemical magnets started doing their work and I grew tired and my arms and legs felt leaden. My life's energy seemed to be emptying out of my entire body. My joints ached all over like with the flu. Just lifting a foot to climb the stairs was nearly impossible. This lasted for six days after the first treatment. Gradually my energy returned, and within a week and a half the headaches subsided. My head was clear for the first time in two years.

They did several *chelation* treatments. After the second treatment the recovery took longer but the symptoms were less severe. They tested my urine after each *chelation* to see how many metals were expelled. The mercury level after the third test was 11.1 ppms. Safe levels of mercury are below .2 ppms. Aluminum levels, which are tied to Alzheimer's, were even higher.

Gradually the pain in my head subsided, the ache in my back softened, the burning pain behind my eyes dulled, and my vision cleared. I became more connected to my true self day by day. There was more time without extreme pain and I was hopeful and filled with energy even when circumstances did not warrant optimism. I was remembering myself and it felt great.

Energized I wanted to make art that actually healed, and wasn't just about healing. I was excited about painting again, but anxious about the toxicity. I looked like an alien wearing a mask and plastic gloves, but I did not care. I did a diptych, one side showed me grimacing in pain with gross gunk oozing out of my open skull, the other, as I saw myself in meditation, peaceful with golden light pouring out of my head. The *chelation* cleansed the heavy metals and the pain cleared.

I dreamed I worked in a shelter for children who survived childhood sexual abuse. When I answered a knock at the door, two little girls looked up at me with expectation in their brown eyes. They were both my self at ages three and five. I could feel their feelings and hear their thoughts in my head, and knew they remembered the scary memories from my childhood that I repressed. They wanted to stay in the same bed, so I was putting fresh sheets on a double bed for them when the littlest girl said, "I can't take this anymore. It's too painful. I'm jumping."

As she dove off the railing of the sun porch, her sister grabbed her foot, but she was not strong enough to keep them from falling over the rail. I grabbed the bigger girl's ankle, but gravity pulled me over, and I began plummeting with them. A moment later I felt a jerk as an unseen woman grabbed my leg, then a jolt as several women clasped onto each woman who tried to rescue us until at last, one strong woman held us all. I could hear the firetruck's sirens blaring as it raced to save us as we dangled above the pavement. At the street level Archie was sitting in his pink Pontiac. He was the same age as when I was a child. Archie was cavalier. *She's okay. Even if she fell now, she would probably survive.*

I made a ten foot tall painting of this dream. It signaled the beginning of my healing and rebirth as an artist. When Liesette saw it, she asked if the painting was fiction or non-fiction.

"It happened, but in a dream, so it is another kind of non-fiction."

"Maman, is it a happy painting? It seems happy."

"It is happy, because the little girl was saved by all the women in her life that loved and protected her."

I was well enough to resume painting full time, and full of ideas, but I was unsure of how to frame my artistic inquiry. I never had an artistic block since I was starting out, before I found my style. The illness and healing work changed me and I needed to connect with my new voice. Once I was able to paint again there were so many images I wanted to make and I needed to get them out as quickly as possible, so I made dozens of small drawings in my sketchbook. I began with the violent memories again and drew twelve pencil sketches of the worst memories. I got out a lot of images, fast. It was just what I needed. Right after making the drawings, I felt a leap in my healing. Giving the memories physical form on paper, released their hold on me.

In a session with the bodyworker during this time, I went deeper into the fugue state than ever before. It seemed like a few moments went by, but a lot of time passed. I trusted that the therapist could get me through whatever happened and let her guide me from one layer of consciousness into deeper and deeper ones. I had several explosive releases instigated by an image, sound, or thought, and shouted *No*. It felt like I was getting so close to the core of what hurt so much inside. I kept seeing a close-up of the navy blue fabric of the daybed's spread with its little pink, yellow, and white knobby threads. My groin burned with pain, and it felt like someone was pressing on my throat and voice box. I heard my little girl voice say. "I'm going to tell. I'm going to tell. You can't stop me."

Afterwards I told the bodyworker, "I felt pressure inside my vagina like a finger was penetrating it. I felt it the last session too, but I couldn't tell you. I felt like I was going to throw up."

"I'm not surprised," she said.

"I don't want to believe what I'm remembering."

"Sometimes it makes you feel like you want to die, but you need to have courage and hold yourself through it, and the pain will pass. You need to give yourself permission to be sad without beating yourself up, or your inner self will not trust you to open up to the even more painful things you may need to remember."

For months I had a strong feeling that I was about to remember something significant that was pivotal. I kept recalling the image of me as a little girl lying in that day bed. Maman had tucked me in. I always asked her to tuck me in very tight, and tried to sleep the whole night without moving so I wouldn't mess up the covers. The room was dark except for a sliver of light by the door. I kept seeing it crack open slightly, letting light pour in. My eyes fixated on the beam of light coming into the room. My body was wracked with fear. I tried to remember what happened next. But everything went black. I was too afraid.

Telling

M Y PARENTS WERE DIFFERENT NOW. Every time I heard Maman's voice, I felt guilty about telling. I loved her, and always had despite everything. Our relationship was pretty good after all the pain and years. Telling was sure to destroy that, and I ached knowing the fragile truce we achieved would be shattered by my revealing the truth. They would deny my story and hate me.

I was sleeping better since I started making the drawings. My art had always been about healing, but now drawing the images was an actual tool for healing.

But I still got the creepy feelings almost every night. The skin on the backs of my knees, inner thighs, and groin would crawl, and the pressure built until whoops and guttural sounds burst again from deep inside me. The next morning my pussy would still smart. My third chakra throbbed with fear. The creepy feelings continued throughout the entire month of June. My pussy hurt constantly. It just did not feel right.

In the summer of 1999 my art on abuse was featured in a benefit exhibit for the Santa Fe Youth and Family Shelter. About a dozen teens from different races and backgrounds staying at the shelter came up to me at the exhibit opening and said, "I can relate to what you're saying there." "That looks like my dad." "I know where you are coming from, girl." "I sure have seen that angry face, man." "Keep doing this work, girl." Their words were gratifying. They had been there, and were glad someone was telling the story. Of all the kudos, the support, and encouragement of those wounded but tough girls and boys meant the most.

The stories people shared were so diverse, the writer who grew up tough on the streets of Philadelphia but never recovered from his alcoholic father's violence, the artist raised on New Mexico's frontier who spoke understandingly of his father's drunken outbursts, the suburban daughter who was abused by her alcoholic CEO father, the schoolteacher who cowered in a dark closet with her three little sisters while her psychotic mother brandished a meat cleaver outside the door, and the woman whose father raped her infant niece. The forgiveness they felt for their abusers was astonishing. Children have such an overwhelming need to love their parents, they can separate the person from the evil things they do.

There were many who could not bear to look at the art depicting a child's view of abuse. In Minneapolis, a close friend of my in-laws asked about my work. I told her I was writing a book about healing from child abuse and she cheerfully asked, "Is that something you are researching?" When I answered, "It's about my own experience," she blanched, and quickly moved on to talk with someone else.

A painter I had known for a decade thought I chose the topic just because I was a feminist. I could not blame her for not knowing. I had told few people. It was just not social conversation. When I did tell, I hesitated. Even people who I thought loved and supported me withdrew emotionally when I began this work.

After the exhibition closed on Canyon Road, my parents came to visit us in Santa Fe with Lori-Ann, who at the time was living in Ireland, teaching at the University of Dublin. For days before they arrived I was anxious, hoping they would be in a good mood and I could control my emotions around them. I was not ready to let them know what I was going through, and did not know if I would ever be.

I met them to take Maman and Lori to Santacafe for lunch. Liesette was seven and excited about going to the chic restaurant for a ladies' lunch. When we got settled in the car Lori-Ann asked, "Why don't you leave Liesette with Daddy?" I was not going to tell them the real reason, so I said, "She would be bored." But Lori was not going to let it drop. "She can watch television, and Daddy will take her for a walk if she gets bored." I wanted to shout, "I would never leave my precious daughter with Daddy." But I bit my tongue and said, "Daddy hit Sage when he was four years old. I don't want to take any chances with Liesette." Maman frowned and Lori-Ann bristled.

"That is ridiculous. Daddy would never hurt Liesette. You are too overprotective."

The visit was tense but short. The news in New Mexico was full of broadcasts about Catholic priests convicted of sexually abusing young boys. Archie, visibly upset, vehemently denounced the priests.

On Saturday, we got dressed up and met my parents at an elegant restaurant for a pre-opera dinner. When we arrived, Daddy said, "Va va va voom. Shaaleen Gail and Lori-Ann, you two look real sexy. Barry, you better keep an eye on your wife tonight."

I remembered telling my sisters, "Whenever Daddy hugs me too tight, I get sick to my stomach, and want to scream. When I push him away, he gives me a hurt look." They shrugged and Kimmy said, "That's just Daddy. That's the way he shows he loves us."

After we sat down to eat, I had barely smoothed my napkin on my lap when Archie began his litany of *You're so awfuls*, and *Isn't she terribles?* whenever he disagreed with what I said at dinner. But I had changed. For the first time I said: "No, I am not terrible. I'm a good person. I have hundreds of friends all over the country. If you can't see that I am good, it's your loss." Archie was speechless.

During the visit, I remarked how much Liesette looked like Lori had at the same age the day she almost drowned at Sher-Le-Mon pool in Cumberland. Archie interrupted, "You weren't even there, Shaaleen Gail."

After my parents returned to Rhode Island, my father called and mentioned it again over the phone. "You sure have a creative imagination, Shaaleen Gail. You remember all kinds of things." I snapped. "Yes I do remember all kinds of things. I remember everything—and I remember what you did to me."

I had not ever intended to let him know. I hung up the phone.

My parents did not contact me for months. Kim phoned and said, "Daddy called me. He said he doesn't understand why you're so angry. I told him to ask you himself." It was never mentioned again.

In February, I was awarded the 1998 WCA President's Award in Toronto. Harmony Hammond did the presentation. When I spoke, I began in French. *Bonjour et merci. Je veut dire merci beaucoup pour cette grande honeur dans la langue de mes ancêtres.* I told them my ancestors would be surprised that a girl named Touchette was returning to the Canada they fled to receive a big recognition, and explained why there were no other women artists in my family. I knew my mémères and ma tantes would have been proud to see me standing there getting that award. I received it for them. They taught me the importance of honoring the elders.

In Toronto, Cree installation artist Rebecca Baird took me under her wing and showed me all the First Nation hotspots and we had fun dancing to Gary Farmer's soulful harmonica at a party for Native filmmakers. Toronto's weather was the warmest of the century. I hooked up with artist Edgar Heap of Birds and we did the gallery tours and museum openings where I met lots of artists at dinners in the cosmopolitan city's cafés.

In one grotto-like Italian restaurant, a brilliant young art historian became very quiet as she flipped through my portfolio. She had been rambling articulately in a thick Austrian accent about feminist art and Carolee Schneeman moments before, then after several minutes of silence turned to me and asked if my father had seen the paintings. When I explained that I was not ready to hear his denials and be subjected to more of his virulence, she insisted, "You must show them to him. He must be held accountable for vat he did." Then, she became even quieter, and after a long pause said, "My husband is abusive. He has not beaten me, but vee get into physical fights. He hit me in front of our small children. Ven I look at these images of your child's view of your dad, I am terrified that seeing this violence might damage them." As we parted, she thanked me and said she was resolved to confront her husband about the violence and remove her children from the situation if necessary.

Grief

AS MIMI GOT OLDER, EVERY TIME WE SPOKE she asked, "How many children do you have, *ma belle?*" As time passed, she asked again and again until she posed the same question several times in one short telephone conversation. Her hearing and sight was failing, and she had not been able to hear me when I telephoned on Sundays or to answer letters for some time. Eventually, she did not even talk on the telephone, and I missed our weekly calls.

At the end of May as I was falling asleep, I heard Mimi's clear voice call my name. I knew then that I could do the work I was supposed to do. Mimi was ninety-three. A few days later, Maman telephoned to tell me that my grandmother had a bad bout with congestive heart failure that same day.

I dreamed my children and I were at a verdant farm like the Aucoin homestead in North Grosvendale. Everything was green. The children, grandchildren, and parents gathered all around. Maman and the ma tantes were there, but they were younger than now, like in their early thirties. Liesette and Raoul ran everywhere playing happily with their cousins. We were amid fields of grass edged by low rock walls, surrounded by acres of rolling forested hills. All the children passed around a baby girl. They laughed as they played with the pretty baby and she laughed too. We sat at a long picnic table like the one at Pépére's Lake only much longer. Hundreds of my relatives were there. Liesette held the baby on her hip and Raoul, Sage, and Jacques played with her, and made her laugh. Barry called on the cell phone and we chatted about the magical child.

The children passed the baby to me. She was about two months old. Her nose and eyes were wet from snot and tears. I took napkins and gently wiped her face. It took lots of napkins. She smiled when she was dry, but she was still stuffed up. I tried to teach her how to blow her nose, even though she was too young. She blew her nose right away, then beamed a smile and spoke clearly.

She put on reading classes, sat up straight, and began reading a Zen meditation book. The ma tantes were astounded. We laughed and the magical dream baby's clear musical laugh rang loudest. I woke at dawn. My laugh was clear and melodious like hers. I was energized and hopeful. When I told Barry the dream, he said.

"The baby is you with your new reading glasses."

Jacques graduated, and both Barry's parents and mine flew to Santa Fe. The evening before their arrival, I was fatigued, short tempered, and fearful. Liesette was sweet and supportive. She helped me hide the paintings about my dad. I went to bed anxious.

I awoke before dawn, smudged with sage, and prayed for cleansing, protection, and clarity. When I went to pick up the grandparents, Archie remarked how sexy I looked in my dress. Then he hugged me too tight and for too long. When I pulled away, he looked baffled. My father-in-law put his hand on my shoulder and said, "You look nice dear." I wanted to cry. Instead I put on my shades and herded everyone over to the high school stadium where we baked in the noonday sun, and watched our first son and their first grandson get his diploma. Afterwards we celebrated in the garden patio of a bistro at the end of the Old Santa Fe Trail. Barry toasted Jacques. "God said these words to Abraham, *Lechi Lach*. Go forth and prosper." I felt blessed when I looked into my son's dark eyes and sang, "And you shall be a blessing, *Lechi Lach*."

After my parents left, I avoided writing or talking about my feelings. I wanted to keep the wonderful feeling I had for weeks before their arrival. But exhaustion and a deep sadness set in four days later. At first I hoped I was just tired from working hard and the non-stop activity and high emotion of the graduation. But even after I rested, I felt more and more exhausted. The visit was pleasant on the surface, but seeing my dad and hearing his voice upset me. I noticed I never looked at him, and could not stand to hear his voice. It gave me the creeps. I avoided looking at him so I wouldn't explode at graduation, but I did not know how deeply seeing Archie affected me. After my parents returned to Rhode Island, I plummeted into another depression. It was time to process my feelings about seeing my dad and get my self back.

One afternoon I took Raoul and Liesette to see the movie *Hope Floats*. It was trite and sentimental but still got me crying buckets. When I saw Sandra Bullock dancing with her daddy who had Alzheimer's, and it flashed back to her dancing with him as a little girl, I burst out crying. I was so sad I never felt that way about my daddy.

Once I started, I couldn't stop sobbing. As we drove home, a police car whirled its lights and motioned me to pull over. I was weeping and gasping, eyeliner and mascara was running down my cheeks, my nose was leaking, and snot was bubbling out of my left nostril. I searched in vain for a tissue, settled on a page ripped out of the want ads, and was dabbing my nose and upper lip by the time the patrolman got to the window.

"What did I do wrong?" I blubbered.

"Don't cry ma'am. It's not that bad. I stopped you because you went through the red light."

I had not even seen a red light. I could not stop crying.

"Are you OK, ma'am? Is there anything else wrong? Everything okay at home?"

"I don't know," I sobbed, "I just didn't see the light. I am so sorry." I couldn't tell him I was crying because my daddy hurt me so long ago, and when I was a little girl I vowed never to let him see me cry, but now that I can cry about it—I can't stop.

At first I tried to stop crying, but then I let the tears flow. Until I looked at my mascara streaked cheeks and smudged upper lip in the rear view mirror and burst out laughing.

I had been on a plateau since the last spring where I felt great and thought I was healed, but my parents' visit revealed that I was far from done. I still had lots more crying to do. A deep sadness that seemed impossible to escape enveloped me. I was encased in a thick fog, overcome by inertia. The clarity I felt before I saw my dad was dulled by a cloud of sadness. I had to cut through it. I learned it is the task of all human beings to cut through the fog and illusion of *maya*, and reconnect with the light. The challenge is to maintain the connection, or at least, learn to rekindle it when it fades. But I could not get a hand or foothold. Even though I knew action would help, I could not take the first step. Every night I still got *the creepy feelings* up and down my legs.

I thought of the jaguar, and the rage that erupted from inside me, often righteously sometimes not. I studied the animals, their look, habits, and medicine. The jaguar, honored by the Olmec and Mayan shamans, brought me her mask to wear in a vision. The jaguar, who is ferocious, yet quiet when stalking, hunting, or pursuing.

I knew I would feel better if I painted but something stopped me from picking up the brush. It took weeks before I could paint again. One day I made a small watercolor of a healing ceremony. That little painting was not much, but it was a catalyst.

I drew sketch after sketch, and stretched dozens of small canvases. Then I hung the canvases around the studio, drew the most powerful images from my sketch book with charcoal, and painted them in batches. The first group of oil paintings was of the *violent memories*, the second of the *dreams of rescuing babies*, and the third was of the *healing ceremonies*. I had been living in a dense fog. With the images out, clarity returned.

I could feel my energy flowing more freely. My massage therapist Kristi noticed it. She grew up in Minnesota on Lake Minnetonka, and was a real Swedish masseuse. But after years practicing as a massage therapist in Santa Fe and studying Reiki and energetic techniques, she was also a powerful healer. One day she touched my crown and tailbone, and I felt a rush up my spine. Afterward she said, "I saw a broad shaft of light moving straight up through your spine. My hand could feel the energy pushing up out of your crown charka at the top of your head. Energetically, each charka is a whirling spiral of light energy. Your light is so clear—I could see them spinning."

I practiced yoga *asanas* at home upstairs in our bedroom overlooking the treetops, in the garden, and on the patio contemplating the mountain. Though we had not talked about it, Kim in upstate New York and Lori-Ann in Rome began practicing yoga at the same time. Barry and the kids did too. At home, I meditated perched atop a rock outcropping with a view of the canyon below and the pyramid shaped mountain across Arroyo Hondo.

I was asked to chant the *Haftorah* for Yom Kippur. Jews throughout the world were practicing the same ancient song that had echoed on the High Holidays for centuries. As I practiced, listening with my headphones imitating the cantor's drone, I pulled the *challah* and roasted chicken out of the oven, chopped the apples, and poured honey for the *erev* Rosh Hashannah blessing for a sweet year.

The phone rang. It was Maman, "Mimi died," she sobbed. It was her ninety-fourth birthday, September 20, 1998. Only Mimi could exit on her birthday, completing life's circle with grace. We went to New Year services at Temple, and sat in the back. Tears rolled down my cheeks as never before. The rabbi read Mimi's name at Kaddish.

She had been failing for weeks, and I had already written about the sadness of knowing I was losing her. I needed those notes when Maman and the ma tantes asked me to give Mimi's eulogy. We flew to Rhode Island for the funeral. On the flight I wrote about what an extraordinary woman Mimi was. After I finished, I took comfort in practicing the *Haftorah* chant.

I thought I was prepared for my grandmother's death. I knew she could not live forever. But I entered the funeral parlor and saw my beloved Mimi laid out in the angelic white dress she wore for her ninetieth birthday party with her once laughing face and graceful gesturing hands stilled, and burst into hysterical sobs. Since I last saw her, Mimi had lost weight making her high cheekbones and features more prominent. She looked so much like me. I broke down into heaving sobs and sunk into the ma tantes' arms as they gathered around me weeping. Mimi had held everyone together in her embrace, and now she was gone.

At the wake Lori-Ann screamed, "Don't kiss me on my neck, Daddy." When I was little, I had nowhere to go. But once I left, I missed Mimi. It made me angry that my dad made it impossible for me to visit and spend more time with my grandmother. I cursed all the years we missed when we could have been together laughing, baking pies, and making *toast daughty.*

I should have been able to watch Mimi play with my children as they grew, and see her pull them onto her lap to tell stories.

I had no choice then, I had to escape. But gathering together with my warm extended family to mourn Mimi, made me sad for what I missed. Everyone embraced and welcomed us. They were happy to see my nearly grown children, and to show me theirs. It made my heart ache that all the years and distance had made us have to introduce our children to each other as the first generation of cousins to meet as strangers.

Maman's brother's eldest son was the spitting image of my memories of Mon Oncle Gilles when he was the same age. With the same Woonsocket accent he asked if I found out any more about our Indian heritage. "I'd like to deal blackjack in the Indian casinos. Blackjack ya know Shaaleen. I'm a very good caawd playa. Been playing poka all my life, just like all the Ethiers. Pretty great huh? Wha'dya think Mim would say about all the Indians with the casinos? She never got anything but trouble from being Indian." His brothers and cousins wanted to work at the casinos too.

Ma Tante Giselle's girls' strawberry blonde kids ran around just like their mamans had at Papi's and Mémère Philomêne's wakes at Fournier's Funeral Parlor. It was odd being there after so long. The Woonsocket I grew up in was gone. French Worsted Mills now housed a Museum of Work to honor the millworkers, and the river and air were cleaner than in years. Tears blurred my view as the funeral procession wound through Woonsocket's hills past Ste. Clare's, and the diner on Hamlet Avenue, and up and down Mendon Road to St. Joseph's Church where Mimi had married, christened her children, given them away in marriage, grieved at Papi's funeral, and attended weekly Mass most of her life. The procession was miles long, much longer than most that follow hearses of nonagenarians. Mimi had made a great impression on Woonsocket, and the people came out to say farewell. In my mind, I could see Mimi's smile and twinkling eyes. It was my responsibility to be strong and carry on her legacy—but I would not return to Woonsocket.

After Mimi's funeral we faced death again when Barry was diagnosed with cancer.

La Lymphoma

I WAS AN OUTSIDER NOW. THE CANCER WAS the other woman when no real woman could ever come between us. Still she sat at his left shoulder glaring. On the left where Don Juan said Death stalks us. She was silent. As a child—Lymphomanita was probably one of those quiet mousy girls who never say anything—but seethe with envy and resentment. The kind of girl you do not notice. Why didn't I see her coming? The tumor was so small, the size of a quail's egg, but somehow we did not notice it until it was full grown. It seemed as if his back was always smooth as I stretched my arms around him when he entered me. But then one day, it was there. She—La Lymphoma—was there too—though we did not know. She had been there a long time silently growing, jealously eyeing us. She was so silent. It seemed that one day she was suddenly among us full grown, black hair blazing, swinging her full hips, and flashing her piercing black eyes. Now, we knew she was always there with us, watching, waiting for her turn. We just did not see her, didn't feel her cold breath over his shoulder as we kissed.

I researched nutrition, prepared meals of live food, and plied Barry with antioxidants and herbs. The day before Thanksgiving, the doctors cut out the tumor and sewed him up. The following weekend another doctor took out the stitches, and we flew to Vegas for a conference, and to leave La Lymphoma behind for a few days. Sunday night, I was winning at slots at Caesar's Palace, when Barry leaned back on the chair, turned pale, and said, "I think I might have burst a stitch. My shirt's all wet."

His white shirt was soaked with a rapidly growing red stain. I lifted the bloody cloth, and saw all twenty stitches split open exposing a four-inch long wound.

"It ripped apart. You'll have to get it re-stitched at the hospital."

"Can't we just get some Bandaids or Steri-strips from the security guards and go upstairs to the room so I can lie down?"

"It's wide-open, gushing blood. Steri-strips are not going to do it."

I tried to close the wound together and applied pressure with both palms as we sidled over to the security desk. The guard was on the phone, and seemed irritated to be interrupted.

"My husband is hurt and we need some help,"

When he saw the deepening blood stain the size of a loaf of bread he dropped the phone.

"Whoa. You've got a big gash there fella."

There was so much blood and the cut was so deep that I got woozy and almost passed out. All the security guards gathered around Barry who sunk to his knees, and demanded a chair before he fainted from blood loss. The EMTs came, strapped him to a gurney and rolled him out of the casino with great fanfare. I whispered in Barry's ear,

"This is perfect for you, isn't it?"

"Yeah, I hate being the center of attention."

In the ambulance, the EMTs asked, "Do you have insurance or do you want to go to County?"

"I'm fully covered," Barry shouted, and relaxed, as they steered away from County Hospital and whizzed him to the private hospital, sirens blaring. The next day we were standing under the miniature of Michelangelo's *David* back at Caesar's Palace and a female guard approached, "Are you the guy who got stabbed in the casino yesterday? They said it was a big gash."

We worried that this was just the beginning of emergency trips to hospitals, but the prognosis was good, *kina hora*. Barry had radiation treatments each morning for a month until he had a burn the size of a toaster on his back. We knew the cancer could recur, but that was out of our control. Instead of worrying we enjoy every moment. It was a rebirth for both of us.

Renaissance

A T THE RIPE AGE OF FORTY-FIVE, I was bursting with the possibilities of still becoming; becoming someone new and becoming more of my self. Though I needed reading glasses, I bought bold ones that belonged on moist twenty year old skin. Then I got great sandals with big black springs in the heels that are usually topped by young girls firm and buoyant in body. I was buoyant in my soul and spirit even if my butt sagged a bit and my skin had lost some luster. My soul was young again. I wore the shoes with bouncy springs, and shifted my weight from spring to spring, relishing the bounce in my step like a young girl.

By rights I should not have been lighthearted with what I was confronting. I had a firstborn in college, a teen in high school, a pre-teen in junior high, a pre-menarche daughter in grammar school and was approaching menopause. My career remained an uphill struggle that never gave me a moment to breathe or coast. But Mimi's death and Barry's cancer put everything in perspective.

I was ready for change. My yard of long black hair was such a part of my persona, that when I cut off two feet, three years before, Barry hated it, and Liesette cried. Now they thought my shoulder length hair was glamorous. Once Mimi was gone I was ready to give up our trademark Indian hair. "I am toying with the idea of cutting my hair and bleaching it blonde," I told everyone. Some said, "I just can't see it." "Don't ruin your black hair." "You're a beautiful Indian woman. Keep your black hair." But I was undeterred. I wanted to try it. It would be fun to begin the second half of my life as a blonde. Some got it. "With your cheekbones and eyes you could carry it off. You'd look hot." I wanted it short, platinum, and spiked like Joan Jett's to go with my black leather.

My chiropractor introduced me to a grandmotherly lady who traveled to India at age eighteen to meditate with the gurus in the caves for ten years, then meditated in Sedona for another ten years of solitude, before starting a spiritual center in Hawaii. Iswari was a psychic healer who worked with angels. She was sojourning in Santa Fe before returning to Sedona. Like bodyworkers, she moved energy, but with prayer. "I don't do anything. The angels do it," she giggled. "I used to try too hard. Once I asked the angels to do the healing, it went much faster. Now I just step out of their way."

We talked very little. I lay fully clothed on the table, closed my eyes, and breathed deeply, while Iswari called upon the Creator, the Divine Mother, all of the angels and my spirit guides. She rarely touched me, but held her hands open with palms upward. With half closed eyes she described what she saw as she tested and balanced my chakras by consulting an amethyst pendulum. Sometimes I saw similar images or colors and energy. Pain built up in different areas, and waves of energy rippled through me to erupt in little and bigger explosions like the ones I called releases. Iswari told me these spasms were releases of *shakti* energy.

She taught me how to recognize when an evil spirit attached itself to me, and how to get rid of it. The banishing ceremony was Kabbalist. A Jewish wizard friend of mine told me about it years before. It was odd hearing Iswari mispronounce the Hebrew words, but the sentiment was the same. Iswari explained cording and why it was important to sever unhealthy emotional cords that others sent out because they are needy. She said we have to cut them so your psychic energy won't be drained as matter-of-factly as she would have said, we just have to snip these threads on your hem, dear. Iswari was a diminutive sprite, but she looked formidable when she chanted and repeated. "I cut these ties by the grace of almighty God."

I prayed to find forgiveness in my heart for my dad, and saw a radiant woman with waist length hair wearing garments made of light ascend towards the west astride a white horse. "That is your higher self." Iswari said. "See how beautiful she is. You are completing an initiation from many lifetimes."

As I laid on the table Iswari continued to pray, I felt a vise grip my heart, then a ponderous weight. "Ooh I can see the angels are working on your heart. There is a double helix of light pouring out of your third chakra," Iswari said. "Now it is turning into two golden snakes. They are pulling out thousands of black squirming snakes. It looks like black gunk." The pressure started to build in my chest until I saw two lithe glowing green snakes intertwine. Iswari said, "They're intertwining around your heart chakra and light is pouring out of your heart." "That's the same image I painted after a vision on *Shavuot* years ago." I gasped as a shock of recognition hit, followed by a big *shakti* release. I felt like I was encased in a sepulcher of light. Energy cleared my heart with the force of a geyser. I was fully alive and present.

"You are taken over by the Holy Spirit. When you are releasing, other women are being healed too."

That year, I continued painting the canvases for the exhibit in New York City. Painting them was empowering, but it was hard to see the images all together on the wall, so different from when they were little drawings in my sketchbook and I could just flip it closed. I had spent my whole life trying to get away from Archie and now his image at its worst was staring at me, painted in oils on canvas, designed to last forever. There was no way I could change my mind about telling.

Barry and I flew to the East Coast together for the opening. The reception overflowed with people from every culture and color including lots of Indians, artist friends I had known since college, and my painting teacher from Bard. I felt embraced and valued. People from many different tribes and nationalities came to say how important the work was.

An aboriginal woman hugged me and said, "This art should be seen all over the world. You should take it to Australia. It would be so good for the aboriginal community to see these paintings." "And the Anglos too," her Aussie friend piped in. Coatlicue Theatre performed a riveting series of vignettes. Hortensia and Elvira Colorado pulled the enthralled audience to the depths of despair as they described scenes of childhood abuse and alcoholism. Expertly changing their voices from little children's plaintive pleas to a wide array of adult gruff, slurring, wheedling, and screaming voices, the sisters enveloped everyone in the dread and confusion of the abused child. It was so powerful I began to feel the fear build in my gut and worried I would lose it and start weeping in the middle of the crowd. Just when I thought I could not take it anymore, the Indian sisters slowly began to bring us into the light by vocalizing the power of telling the stories and joining in community to heal—they ended with a hopeful chant.

The next day at the gallery talk, people crowded close around me to see the small paintings and hear me talk. When I saw so many men, I was taken aback. Many were Indian and had the same black hair and eyes my dad did when he was young. Their sad eyes burned a hole in my chest reminding me of Daddy's. As I moved from one violent image to the next I noticed their looks of remorse, and was confused. While I spoke the knot of fear grew until by the end, my own tears were welling, like those spilling from the eyes of these oddly familiar men. Afterwards I remarked to the gallery director,

"I was surprised to see so many men."

"Oh, I sent a press release to Indian alcohol rehab centers. They sent a busload."

The experience sent me into a downward spiral. After a year of clarity, I was mired in another depression. I had worked hard to get better at crying and this sad time was a way to release through tears. In reality, things were improving. Throughout this period, I knew that I was peaceful inside. There was a fog of sadness surrounding me, but I was no longer the sadness.

In the depths of this sorrowful time, I had an irresistible impulse to create a rushing waterfall that emptied into a pond in our unfinished courtyard. Rebuilding the garden is often used as a metaphor for healing from childhood abuse. I made a huge pond that almost filled the courtyard, with a pump powerful enough to produce a sound to cleanse my soul. I paced out the courtyard that was open to the forest at the opposite end. Using a hose I drew the shape of the pond, and the boys and I dug a hole big enough to hold nearly three thousand gallons. We lugged boulders and stacked them to create a small rushing waterfall, and planted herbs and flowers around the stepping and meditation stones. It took time, but the plants grew, and soon it looked like the waterfall and pond had always been there. Wildlife gravitated to the water, and it became its own ecosystem thriving with dragonflies, songbirds, insects, and a slender garter snake that held its body upright under the waterfall like a thin man taking a shower. Hummingbirds flitted to the honeysuckle and orange monkey flowers, and dipped their fluttering wings in the falls. A red tailed hawk perched on a nearby tree by our deck railing, and eyed the koi who swam unaware.

There is a picture of Raoul and Sage, shirtless, tanned with muscles cut from stone, digging the pond with picks and shovels, and another of me and Liesette, emerging from the cold water, wet and smiling.

One day, Kristi was beaming. Her translucent skin glowed. She had just done a Watsu massage workshop with an Australian. She said it was so great, she set up an appointment for me. I arrived at Upayni Center in the barrio. The Watsu pool was in the back of some weather worn adobe buildings on land sloping to the nearly dry Santa Fe River. A fence of rough boards surrounded a hot tub, changing area, and a spacious shallow above ground pool. Beams of sunlight filtered between the branches of an overhead ramada. I entered the lukewarm water, and the massage therapist stood behind me against the plastic side of the pool. "Just relax and float. You do not have to do anything but breathe deeply, I will move your body. The water will do it all."

I closed my eyes, relaxed using my breath, and felt his arms under my shoulders shifting my body slightly this way and that as he let the movement of the water massage my body and manipulate my spine. As I breathed I went deeper and deeper to a place of utter peace. My breath relaxed. I trusted the man would keep me afloat. He embodied positive paternal love.

I felt safe like a baby should in her daddy's arms. He brought me underwater in a fetal position, and I was a babe in the womb floating in my mother's imagination. Through closed eyelids I saw brilliant light. I could feel the spaces between the molecules of my body, the water and the air—there was no separation.

After I drove off and picked up the children, I was vulnerable, and in a hurry. My four kids, and three of the boy's friends, were running all around me, each with a different request. When I asked a clerk to bend the rules, the erect young brunette assessed me with interrogating eyes under severe bangs. "No. I can not do that." She responded without a pause to emphasize that she had not listened to my request, and made up her mind to say no as soon as I started talking. Her prim manner, rigid posture, and attitude reminded me of the nuns'. Suddenly, it was Sister Dolores' pin size eyes looking down at me from under a curtain of black hair.

"What's your name?" I demanded.

"Margaret."

"Margaret, what?"

"I do not have to tell you that." She pursed her thin lips, like she was sealing them shut just for me, then puffed out her chest.

"What should I say your name is? Margaret Bitch?"

I regretted it as soon as the words shot out of my mouth. But it was too late. When she turned into Mother Dolores, anger blasted from my gut and out my throat without stopping to consult my brain. Just then a white haired old man interfered and I turned my fury on him. "This is none of your business. Stay out of it." I shouted. Blinded by rage I saw my dad in this stranger's white hair. He did not know what hit him. I was so ashamed and remorseful I wrote apology letters to everyone involved. After that, I was careful to protect myself after body work.

My nerves were raw and exposed. It was time to do an all day intensive session with Iswari. We set aside a Saturday when the kids and Barry would be out. Iswari arrived soon after dawn. We prayed throughout the day as she guided me on a journey to the depths of my childhood fears. She began, "Almighty God creator of the universe we pray for a healing for this woman and through her for the healing of her whole lineage and of all women who suffered abuse in this lifetime and all others." As the sun rose the pain and pressure increased throughout my body until it was so strong I thought I would explode. Iswari prayed, "We ask St. Germaine to shine a violet light to clear out all karmic ties between Charleen and her father."

Iswari and I sat together on the stone bench in the courtyard and I stared at the koi swimming back and forth in the pond. The rush of the waterfalls was soothing. The midday sun warmed my bones. Sobs began deep in my gut and exploded into great heaving bawling. Iswari comforted me as I wept for the little girl I used to be. My tears flowed as easily as the water over the rocks.

We walked around the garden and into the forest. Iswari said, "Let the negative energy flow out of your body through your feet into the earth." Later we sat on the patio soaking in the sun and the view. Before long the creepy feelings began building again to a dense frightening mass that permeated all my pores. The patio and landscape suddenly looked menacing.

Iswari helped me back inside and onto the couch. I crawled into a fetal position and squeezed my eyes shut tight. But I could not push out the images I saw in my memory, and could not keep out the dark palpable atmosphere that engulfed me. When I opened my eyes everything was black and white with shades of gray. The color and vitality were completely drained from my world. The home that had always been a sanctuary looked evil and sinister.

Waves of grief flooded me when Iswari took me back to my childhood and I re-experienced the terror I felt when Daddy entered my bedroom. I heard the big booming sound from my nightmare and clasped my hands on my ears. But the vile ominous sound got louder and louder in my mind. Each rhythmic beat sent me deeper into despair while Iswari held me like a baby and rocked back and forth. Suddenly I recognized the booming sound in my nightmares. It was the beating of my heart that grew louder and louder as Daddy approached.

I want to disappear. I heard my child voice say.

I was still that terrified little girl. I could hear her sob—and see her cringe.

"You are going to get it all out in this lifetime. You will never have to face it again." Iswari assured me.

"I am worthless or Daddy wouldn't do this to me. I do not deserve to succeed. That's why I give myself away," I sobbed, "I couldn't be worth anything if my daddy treated me that way."

As I cried, I comforted the hurt child inside me, and told her she was worthy. For days I was sore all over my body and slept the deep sleep of a child. Now I could see that I let people mistreat me because deep inside I believed I was totally unworthy. I tacked a post-it on my computer that said—*I am worthy*—so I would not forget.

Pardon

W E ENTERED THE MILLENNIUM WITH A SWEAT CEREMONY for our family. I chanted in the sweatlodge, and a mountain lion responded with her haunting call just yards behind the lodge as she headed down the mountain to drink at the stream below.

After we emerged from the lodge, showered, and pulled on pajamas and robes, we spent a sweet evening bringing in the twenty first century with Liesette.

There's a picture of Barry and Liesette after our midnight New Year's Eve toast. She's cozy in her robe resting her head on her dad's shoulder, smiling at me with a look of pure happiness. Her peaceful face shows she trusts her daddy and feels safe in his arms.

I was anxious about Jacques flying to Rhode Island. He was nineteen. It was his first visit to my parents without us. He called using his thickest Archie accent. His solo trip to Woonsocket gave him a whole new repertoire of Archieisms. After he finished, I asked,

"How is Mémère?"

"Mémère is like Batman. She wears a cape, and works on a computer in the basement."

"Your mémère is not a super-hero, Jacques. How's the trip going?"

"Newport was beautiful, but being with your parents is weird. Mémère tries to recruit me as her loyal henchman to pick on Pépère."

"Maybe now you understand a little bit of what I went through."

"Oh Mom, I get it now, so much, you do not know."

"They are much better than they used to be."

"Pépère asked me, 'Do you sleep naked like your mummy, Jacques'?"

Then, he lowered his usual bellowing voice to a whisper.

"Mom? Did you know I was baptized?"

"Did Pépère tell you that? Did he baptize you, or did Mémère do it?"

"He said he did it while he was giving me a bath. Pépère said he did it to all the babies. Did you know he did that Mom? And I remember now. Pépère hit Sage when we went to Rhode Island for Christmas that time because he wouldn't let him baptize him in the bathtub."

In May I was about to call Iswari, and the phone rang. It was her.

"I want you to come to a place of total forgiveness with your father. It will be a gift."

"Forgiveness? How can I forgive him?"

"Forgiveness does not mean you have to like what he did. Forgiveness is releasing the past and separating your karma from your father's so you can let him go forever and be truly free."

Daddy was usually drunk and didn't know or remember what he was doing when he hurt me. If he was abused at prep school, that made him a victim worthy of compassion. And shouldn't I cry for the little baby he was, who reached out for his maman's arms, but received only cold silence?

"By the grace of Almighty God, I forgive you, Archie Touchette, for any way that you have hurt me intentionally or unintentionally."

I remembered I was far from a perfect mother, and asked forgiveness from each of my children. I visualized extending healing and forgiveness back through all of the generations of my lineage, and from those thousands of ancestors down through me and my children, to the seven generations and more of future descendants. When I finished two hours later, I was calm.

For Raoul's Bar Mitzvah we baked dozens of pies for the party after the service. Liesette and I made and froze twenty. Then, Maman, Ma Tante Giselle, and Kim flew in early to help us make more. I wanted to relive the joy of baking with them in my own kitchen far from Woonsocket and share it with Liesette.

"Ooooh Shaleen. It is so beautiful. I am so happy for you *ma belle*," Ma Tante cooed when she arrived at our home and enveloped me in her arms. We donned aprons and began our ritual with flour. The sun streamed into the big country kitchen lighting our smiling faces as we baked pastry shells, stirred custards, beat egg whites, and whipped up meringues. Mid-July's rays lit Maman's moist, unlined skin and still nearly jet black hair. As she bent over her special recipe for "Colleen's Lemon Chiffon Pie," Maman's black reading glasses slipped down her tiny aquiline nose. She looked so lovely as she concentrated, and exactly measured, gingerly squeezed, patiently sifted, ceaselessly beat, and folded until she made the lightest lemon chiffon filling imaginable. The entire time she was relatively silent, raptly focused on her art. Occasionally she glanced up and shot an irritated glance in response to a comment from Ma Tante who still liked to tease her little sister and boss her around. Colleen lifted her head to laugh at her sister's bawdy jokes, and to beam at her only granddaughter rolling out dough. Kim stood at the stove smiling her Buddha smile. Her long silky hair fell over her eyes as she patiently stirred a custard, and then turned it into a delicious vanilla cream pie.

Ma Tante and Liesette worked on the pastry shells. My godmother was lovely as she bent to help my daughter roll out the dough. Ma Tante Giselle had aged to look like a lighter version of Mimi. At seventy-three, she had Mimi's warmth, if not her stellar beauty. She was as funny and irreverent too. We laughed and fussed over the pie shells. Kim and I giggled as Ma Tante scurried to open the oven every five minutes when the timer beeped to prick the shells to prevent the crust from bubbling. Soon Ma Tante called it *pricking time*. She pranced around when the bell rang, giggling naughtily. "Oh. Oh. It's *pricking time*. Shaaleen. *Pricking time. Prick.*

Prick. Prick. You must think your mummy's ma tante is silly? H'unh sweetheart?" she said to Liesette who was already laughing.

That midsummer afternoon as we bustled about in the kitchen, laughing, reminiscing, and telling new stories, it was as if we were moving in slow motion. The sunlight reflecting off the flour dust in the air enveloped us all in a glow. We made memories to cherish. They would fortify Liesette in her life, as mine of rolling dough in Woonsocket did for me. Together, Maman, Ma Tante, Kim, and I taught her skills so she would know she was from a culture where the women made pies, and that she could nurture and delight with the work of her hands.

But she also learned something else. Maman and Ma Tante worried about the pies every step of the way and fretted that they wouldn't be perfect. Seeing how excessive the sisters were in their constant striving for perfection made me remember how their fussing affected me and my sisters as girls. Ma Tante hovered over Liesette, scrutinizing every move as she rolled out the dough. Kim and I rolled our eyes as Ma Tante corrected Liesette's efforts. I could see my daughter tense up at the criticism as she tried her best. When she turned to me and asked, "Is this pie crust okay, Mama?" I remembered Mimi and answered, "It's absolutely beautiful, *ma belle*," and she hugged me in relief.

On Friday night at Shabbat dinner at temple, Maman lost her composure and burst into tears. My dad and Ma Tante rushed to comfort her. I checked on her briefly. "If you're crying because you hate us being Jewish I can't change that. But I love you, and do not want to make you sad." Colleen just kept crying non-stop. Barry' parents were sympathetic. "I don't know if I would be so gracious if it were the other way around," my mother-in-law admitted. She felt lucky to be *schepping nachas*, feeling the pride only your children can give you.

The road into the canyon was lined with cars and the party was already going on when we arrived after saying our goodbyes at the temple. It was a moveable feast at our home with family and friends celebrating on the sun-drenched mountain by the ponds. After the ceremony releasing my father, I retained my poise, and it did not bother me as much to be around him. I maintained my boundaries, and protected Liesette when he tried to hug her too tight and long. When he protested, I flashed jaguar eyes and pulled her to me with grace, and then we slipped into the crowd.

The pies displayed in tiers in the dining room drew the children who gathered around with mouths watering. Pairs of crispy apple pies, succulent peach, and juicy berries of every variety made the first layer. Buttery apple tarts, pecan, and walnut pies were on the second. Meringue topped Key limes, velvety coconut, and vanilla custards with Maman's famous Pumpkin Chiffon pies were raised on a third tier. Colleen's Lemon Chiffon pies towered above the rest. The chiffon was almost five inches high atop a perfect crust. Each bite was a precious jewel that melted in your mouth. The guests fought over the last pieces. "Did you taste that Lemon Chiffon?" was heard in awed tones as friends and family wandered among the gardens and ponds. If there had ever been any doubt about Maman's preeminence as a pie maker, it was dispelled with this magnificent confection. Colleen was still the indisputable Pie Queen.

There is a picture of me, Kim and my parents that Barry snapped as they left. My dad's hair is totally white. His nervous grimace is the only eerie reminder of the monster he was when I was a little girl. Colleen is perfectly attired and coiffed as always. My parents are faded versions of their younger selves, with vacant smiles. Kim and I are strong and vibrant.

As she kissed me goodbye, Ma Tante took both my hands and said, "I'm so glad you found Barry and made a happy marriage and family."

Iswari told me we hold our memories in our hair. It was time to cut mine off. No one recognized me. Barry loved it. "It reminds me of when we first met," he flattered. I enjoyed slipping through Santa Fe unrecognized without my long dark locks. My eyes were clear. I practiced *asanas* daily, and became a yoga teacher. I got my smile back. In November I cut my hair even shorter, spiked it, and bleached it blonde. Platinum. I figured it would make it less shocking when it grew in almost all silver by spring. People I had known for decades walked right past me. One friend kept blinking, stared deeply into my eyes for a solid minute, and said, "I'm sorry, I know I know you, but I can't place you."

In 2001, the Paisners gathered in Chicago to celebrate my in-laws fiftieth. Maman called. "You know our fiftieth anniversary is coming up next March too." The next winter, two of Maman's friends started contacting me. "We don't know if you know, but it's your parents' fiftieth anniversary coming up. We want to know if you're planning a party for them," they said on phone messages, emails, and notes in the mailbox. Kim and Lori-Ann got the same missives. Kim scheduled elective surgery, Lori-Ann had the ready made excuse, she lived in Rome. The three of us decided to give them dinner and a night at the Sheraton Hilton in Providence where they had their wedding party. I called to see if they liked our present, and Maman said,

"It was okay….. But we could not enjoy it because none of our children were here."

I had had it.

"Maybe you should ask yourself why none of us wanted to be there."

CLICK.

Their friends sent out engraved invitations for a big anniversary party for them. Ours had a handwritten note inserted that said, "We are saving a seat for you, in case you change your mind."

In early June in the year two thousand two, or 5762 on the Jewish calendar, I awoke just before dawn in our aerie atop a mountain, beside the man I have loved for nearly thirty years, a man I will love for whatever is left of my life. We made love to the sounds of Marvin Gaye crooning, "How sweet it is to be loved by you."

Later, Barry and I sat outside on our patio. We had just finished lunch.

"You are always there for me. I couldn't have gotten through this without you."

"We did it together babe. You've been there for me too."

Wildfires ravaged Northern New Mexico. Slurry bombers with buckets flew overhead, and I remembered the Viveash Fire that burned Los Alamos two years before.

The winds changed. Abundant dark rain clouds floated like boats overhead, and a soft drenching rain cooled the summer air. The smell of wet earth entered the house and our thirsty lungs through open doors. At dusk Liesette and I picked pansies in the garden and watched the koi swim in and out of the lily pads. The scent of honeysuckle was heavy in the dampness and the rain formed rings of movement on the pond's surface.

Liesette said, "Mama is love. She loves everything. She loves us. She loves daddy. And she loves all the plants, the animals, the dogs, the cats, even the fish."

"I'm so happy you see me that way." I laughed.

"At the beginning when you were little it was bad, but now it keeps getting sweeter and sweeter everyday."

That night I dreamed Liesette and I swam with orcas. We were deep in the ocean surrounded by dozens of the glistening black and white beasts. The whales frolicked and rubbed up against us. We could breathe underwater as we cavorted in the water with the magnificent whales. One of the orcas enveloped me with her fins. Her gaze was pure mother love. I awoke content and filled with joy.

Swimming with Orcas

L'Dor v'Dor

THE MÉMÈRES WOULD SMILE TO SEE LIESETTE cuddling with her daddy. So many generations of pain, secrets, and rage paid the way so my daughter could sit safe and protected in her daddy's arms. I was not the first girl to be abused in my family. Many lived through much worse. Some did not survive. When I remember what my French mémères and pépères, and Indian grandmothers and grandfathers endured, I can understand why some unleashed their hurt on their families.

How did love and cruelty become so entwined, so inextricably connected that they were like right and left hands, or even right and left sides of the same face? How did cruelty become such a natural part of the family that love was used as the excuse to hide it? How did loyalty become defined as refusing to tell? It would be easy to say it started with my father's drinking, but that is too simple. The damage started long before Archie took his first drink.

It could go back to my father being sent away to boarding school when he was barely twelve years old—or when Maman opted to exchange the cruelty of poverty for that of my father's temper—or when her maman encouraged her to marry the tall handsome up and coming dentist. It could have begun even earlier when Mimi, desperate for a better life for Colleen than her own as a millworker's wife, painted her daughter's thirteen year old face and entertained her suitors. Or maybe it was when Mémère Louisia never quite recovered from childbirth. She was always on some kind of medication for her nerves. Maybe Mémère had a bad reaction to some of the pills she popped, or the bottle of red wine she drank alone in the dark. Maybe she lost her temper and turned her rage upon her only son without warning.

It is not just about my family. It is tied to all my relatives and ancestors who suffered oppression. The women of my lineage connect me to five hundred years and twenty generations of French Canadian culture in North America, countless centuries and lifetimes of Indian wanderings on this continent, and innumerable ages of peasant life in France. Along with a legacy of dysfunction, I can draw on rich cultural traditions from all my ancestors—French, Blood, Québécois, Eastern Woodland Indian, and Acadian. Though rife with struggle, each strand of my peoples' history was also a tradition of fortitude.

Although merely an unrecorded footnote in the bigger history of the meeting of French and indigenous people, my story can not be complete without considering the intimate personal moment when Pépère Lambert met his Pied Noir beauty and convinced her to be the mother of his children. Through her, I am linked to her mother and grandmothers who foraged and cared for children and valiant horse stealing husbands while they set up and broke camp season after season, year after year, in their strenuous nomadic life following the buffalo across the Northern Plains. And back through time from daughter to mother to grandmother in an unbroken line of Indian mothers who faced the same struggles birthing, nurturing, and protecting their children through centuries of wanderings.

The sorrowful part of my grandmothers' legacy goes back to those women of the Blackfeet Confederacy who were kidnapped and raped, stolen far from their territory as spoils of war in the continual battles against the Cree, Flathead, and Crow, and to those taken as prisoners of war who were traded into slavery to warriors from other tribes or French Voyageurs. And to the wives whose dignified faces were mutilated when their husbands cut off their noses to punish infidelity. The heartbreak can be traced to the pitiful mourning of the clan mothers and grandmothers who wept and keened cutting their hair and slashing their flesh and clothes repeatedly throughout 1819, when the Coughing Epidemic killed a third of the Blackfeet. And to their daughters who mourned inconsolably in 1837 when smallpox infected trade goods brought in by whites on the hated railroad wiped out two-thirds of those who had survived, and any hope of retaining their land and resisting Western Expansion.

My grandmother also came from generations of proud Blood women who helped create a society where a woman could divorce an abusive husband simply by removing his belongings and placing them outside her tipi. And through her I draw inspiration from those virtuous women who fulfilled their vows to put up the Medicine Lodge for the Sun Dance Ceremony. And from those who gathered sweetgrass and sage on the endless plains for the ceremonies and trudged deep into the steep mountain forests to find flat cedar and herbal medicines. And from the humble ones who took on the grave responsibility of caring for the Medicine Pipe Bundles and their painted tipis. And spinning back through the generations ultimately to the brave girl who married Thunder and patiently learned the songs and ceremonies of the Pipe he gave to her as a gift to the People. And even to those animals who offered their skins and medicine songs to be remembered in the ceremonies. Ultimately connecting everyone back to *Oki*, the Creator Old Man who together with Old Woman made the people from lumps of clay, determined how they would live, and taught them what they needed to know to survive. To *Oki*, who decided that they would not live forever so they would learn compassion for one another.

My story is also connected to my Aucoin, Hébert, Lavallée, and Lambert ancestors who were among the three hundred *picked men* and *engaged bachelors* from Brittany recruited by order of Cardinal Richelieu in the 1600s to settle Acadia because of their reputation as strong, hard-working, religious people. I am descended from the settler Martin Aucouin and five generations of peace-loving Acadians—and tied to the untold stories of the Indian women and the French Filles de Roi who married the *picked men* who left France and braved the Atlantic voyage to settle in Port Royal in Acadia, the home of the legendary Evangeline immortalized by Longfellow.

In Acadia, the pépères and mémères worked and lived together, fishing, trapping, and cultivating fields communally and sharing equally the fruits of their work. They reclaimed the marshlands for farming and became experts at building and repairing dykes. Only a few knew how to read or write, but they knew how to live cooperatively. The women welcomed orphans into their modest clean homes and cared for the needy and elderly. Their communities were relatively free from crime for generations. They lived in a simple state of innocence and equality and were opposed to war and violence.

Five generations of Aucoin women strove to create a peaceful life in Nova Scotia in little Acadian towns like Grand Pré and Cobequid until the Expulsion of 1755 when all Acadians who refused to deny their heritage and swear allegiance to England were expelled. They left behind mementoes of our Acadian family history that are lost to their descendants forever. When they sought justice and compassion on both sides of the Atlantic— they found it nowhere and left us with a new history of bitter exile.

So naturally, to understand how Mémère Louisia, who was so proud of her Acadian heritage, could raise her hand against Little Archie, I must also remember what happened to my gentle Acadian ancestors on that fateful day, September 5, 1755 when they were ordered to congregate at the Catholic Church at Grand Pré at exactly three o'clock in the afternoon. Huge ships were moored in the harbor. British soldiers surrounded the church to prevent escape. Those who refused to take an oath of allegiance to England were herded onto the waiting transport ships with bayonets at their backs, deported immediately, and permanently banished from their beloved L'Acadie.

I am tied to the pépères and mémères who stood helplessly as the British separated families, and took them away forever from each other and their tranquil homeland. And to those who saw the glow of the flames and great billows of smoke rise from their church, mills, homes, and barns burning to the ground on the receding shore as they sailed out of the sheltered harbor.

Pépère Pierre Aucoin was among the two thousand Acadians who escaped into the woods. I imagine he survived by hiding in the brush by day starving on what little he could forage in the Canadian forest in late September. Pursued doggedly by soldiers who hunted the fugitive Acadians like animals, he fled, bushwhacking through the dark forest at night until, clothes in tatters barely concealing his nakedness, feet frostbit, and bleeding, he finally found refuge at the village of St. Pierre Les Becquets in Quebéc.

I am also tied to those who stayed behind hidden deep in the forests protected by their Indian friends, who watched while everything that was left behind was burned or stolen by the British soldiers and settlers. They saw their enemies plow the land they cleared of boulders, harvest the fields they reclaimed from marshland, let the dykes they maintained crumble into ruin, pull the nets they made in from the sea, and sleep in the beds where they conceived and pushed out their babies.

My heritage is also connected to the ones who were shipped back to exile in France, unwelcome and shunned in their motherland as well as betrayed repeatedly by the French government. And to the countless cousins like Ann Aucoin who drowned when the overloaded ships sunk to the ocean floor. I am also tied to the even unluckier cousins who were sold into slavery in the West Indies. And to the ones who died in the unbearable heat of Santo Domingo where they emigrated after the colony of New York refused to welcome them. And to the one hundred and thirty-eight who left exile in France only to die in the tropical inferno of French Guiana on the coast of South America. And to the ones who fled slavery in the Deep South with the Blacks on sugar and cotton plantations in Georgia. And to the two hundred and thirty seven Acadians who died of smallpox when they sat captive aboard transport vessels for three months in Philadelphia's harbor. And to the brave ones who were taken as prisoners of war to England and held in concentration camps in port cities like Liverpool. And to the more than two thousand Acadians who were deported to Massachusetts and labored like slaves under the harsh treatment of the Bostonians. And to the sixty brave families who left Boston and marched eighteen hundred miles back to Acadia on foot, pregnant women, children, and all. And to those few broken souls who survived the trek home, only to be forced to continue wandering like ghosts of a quickly fading past from village to village—finding refuge in none.

I can trace my lineage directly to cousins who sailed on some of the seven ships carrying Acadians back to the States, like *Le Bon Papa* with Francoise Aucoin tightening sails and swabbing decks as a seaman. And to the Aucoin, Touchette, Lavallée, Lambert, and Hébert cousins who were carried from exile in France to Louisiana to rebuild lives shattered by their exodus from Acadia in communities like Lafourche, St. Landry, and St. Martinville where they came to be known as Cajuns. Their descendants' names now clutter the phonebooks of Lafayette and other Louisiana towns.

But understanding my heritage would not be complete without considering my Woodland Indian ancestors' contribution to my gene pool. My Voyageur pépères' Indian wives passed down genes that had no defense against smallpox, influenza, diabetes, and alcoholism. But we also benefited from their genetic legacy. Their distinctive facial structure is echoed in our faces and classic hawk-like noses. Their legendary fierceness in battle is evident in my son Sage's fearlessness as a wrestler. The deep connection to the earth and clan survived among the ma tantes and mon oncles at the camps around Pépères' Lake. The trail linking us to our woodland ancestors was blurred and nearly erased by cultural genocide—but they etched their legacy onto our genes and determined who we are.

So, my roots, as with so many other Canucks, may be connected to the Abenaki and Six Nations of the Iroquois Confederacy whose matrilineal structure and Council of Clan Mothers selected the chiefs and kept them accountable to the tribe. And to the clan mothers who raised strong capable girls and taught them to make every decision guided by the wisdom of the previous seven generations always considering the impact it would have on the next seven generations into the future. And to the families who were entrusted with caring for and feeding the False Face and Corn Husk entities. And to the shamans who danced and sung their ceremonies bringing the world into harmony for healing, ensuring the return of spring, the success of the harvest, and the proper sequence of the seasons. And to the mothers and grandmothers who cultivated the fields, carefully planting the Three Sisters together as their ancestors taught them so the beans' vines would wind around the sturdy corn stalks and the broad squash leafs would shade the roots. And to the women who tanned deerskin and fashioned moccasins so their men could move noiselessly through the forests and return home safely to the Longhouses. And perhaps even to the Ojibwe who paddled silent canoes on woodland lakes and rivers braving mythical creatures to bring huge lake trout and sturgeon home to their *wickiups*.

It is linked to the fierce warriors who allied with the French and fought the French Indian Wars from the late 1600's until 1763 to expel the British invaders from their ancestral lands, and lost. But it is also tied to the healers who gathered medicinal herbs in the forests, and the beadworkers who beaded the secrets of the plants into decorative patterns to teach their daughters and granddaughters herbal medicine.

Just like it took generations to make a man like Archie, it took generations of mothers and grandmothers to make women like Philomêne and Mimi. Generations of strong women came before us, like Philomêne's maman, Mémère Philomêne Lambert, and her full blood mother who married and became Suzanne Lambert leaving her Kainah name behind. From Mimi's stories, I imagined her stuffing her Indian name deep into her memory until she could barely remember its syllables as she traveled thousands of miles from home and each year passed without hearing the sounds of her Native language. Having no one to speak with, she probably forgot, word by word, until the only time she heard it was when she dreamed of her grandmother telling her Blood stories about *Oki*. When she awoke from these dreams she would smell a trace of burnt sage and sweetgrass. When Suzanne's babies were born, she probably sang Blackfeet lullabies to soothe them to sleep and tried to teach them simple words as they grew. But there were no adults to talk with, and when her children grew older they were embarrassed by her strange words. Eventually, she spoke only French.

I wonder how she felt when she packed her belongings on a *travois* and left her tribe to follow her Frenchman East. Was she in love with the dapper stranger with the dark mustache and eyes who spoke a curious melodious language and was clad in buckskins with curling floral beadwork made by Indian women of the People of the Dawn she heard about in warrior's tales? Was he as exotic to her as she seemed to him? Was it love at first sight? Did his difference attract or repel her? Maybe she was a practical girl who noticed his rifle and saw a good hunter and provider for her yet-to-be-born children. She may have chosen to marry outside her tribe because she thought the future was with the newcomers with their powerful weapons and strange ways. Or maybe she was an adventurous girl who wanted to see what lie in the land where the sun rose. She could have gone unwillingly too, wrenched from her family as a bartering chip in the new economy the Voyageurs imposed on the Plains. Or worse, she could have been raped, if not by Pépère, then by other drunken Voyageurs, or by warriors from rival tribes who raided villages for slaves and horses. If she were one of those battered ones, she hid her sorrow well, and kept her secrets as she prayed her rosary and walked down the hill to Mass each morning until her one hundred fourth year.

It did not start with my family or with Mimi's either. It must be linked to the generations upon generations of oppression back to the explorers and adventurers who trudged and portaged the uncharted forests, rivers, and woodland lakes trapping, and trading with the Abenaki, Mohawk, Iroquois, Ojibwe, Lakota, Cree, and Blackfeet—back to the Voyageurs who met and married, seduced, or raped the Indian women who bore their children. Sojourning in towns throughout French Canada along the Rivière Saint-Laurent, they married and birthed their babies in places with mysterious names like Yamaska, Sorel, St. Hyacinthe, St. Damase, and St. Robert. I wonder how many of those women made love matches, and how many cowered in the face of their *espousés*, and how many *half breed* children got the brunt of their parents' despair.

Or it may be rooted farther back in the struggles of the starving ancestors from nearly every province and all four directions of France who tired of trying to pull nourishment from that land and left the Haute-Pyrénées, the provinces of Anjou, Poitou, Champagne, Normandy, Provence, Bretagne, and the Rhone Valley to take their chances sailing to New France, seeking cultural and religious freedom, adventure, and economic opportunity. And back to the *p'tite* courtesan Marie Touchet spreading her legs for King Charles IX on brocade sheets so her family could eat cake while an ocean away, Abenaki women greeting Voyageurs with gifts from the sea and forest received love or betrayal in return, on back through the generations to the first molested girl and raped woman.

Always it goes back to the women, struggling to put food in the stomachs of their many children, to keep warm clothes on their backs, and shoes on their feet. And to the men, who labored with no relief to feed their large families in the unexplored Canadian wilderness. To the pépères who broke their backs tilling infertile lands, trapping, and hunting in the piercing solitude of frozen forests, or fishing, trawling, and laying lobster traps from fishing boats on the frigid maritime seas. And to the fathers who were so downtrodden by political oppression and poverty that every vestige of their self-esteem was destroyed. Feeling powerless, beleaguered by the wailing of too many hungry mouths to feed, they tried to dull their anguish with alcohol and gambling, but often ended up venting their frustrations on their wives and children.

Ultimately, it goes back to the Catholic Church that gave them all solace even as it created, supported, and benefited from the conditions oppressing them. Patterns—patterns of oppression and reacting to oppression and internalizing oppression until men are drinking and beating women and children to forget the humiliation of their lives, and women are manipulating and sacrificing those children to have some semblance of control over theirs.

All those centuries produced Archie. The miracle was that he wasn't worse. Suddenly the image of my father's angry monster face was transformed into his maman's raging lipstick red mouth, and it was little Archie cowering defenseless instead of me, and I understood we were both just links in an unending chain of cruelty handed down generation to generation on back through the decades with the Lavallée girls vainly clenching their thighs closed against their daddy, the workers sublimating themselves to the mill bosses, the Acadians herded and separated with bayonets, the Québécois fleeing persecution in Canada, the Blackfeet dying of smallpox wrapped in US Army blankets, the Mohawk women and warriors dispersed from Six Nations in another diaspora, and the French peasant women struggling to feed and protect their daughters from rapists, marauders, and marquis.

Like my French and Native ancestors, my path led me far from my birth home and culture. Like my Indian grandmothers, I met and married a handsome stranger and adopted his ways and religion. But unlike them, I found a sweeter way of life to bequeath to my daughter.

How did it get to the point where men and women are at war, and their children are the swords they wield against each other? It is not just about my family and my ancestry. I don't know when it started, but I do know where it is ending. It is stopping right here with me. I choose a different legacy for my children to pass generation to generation. I was not the first girl to be abused in my family. But I will be the first to say, *c'est fini.* No more. It stops here with me.

Elk Woman's Shield

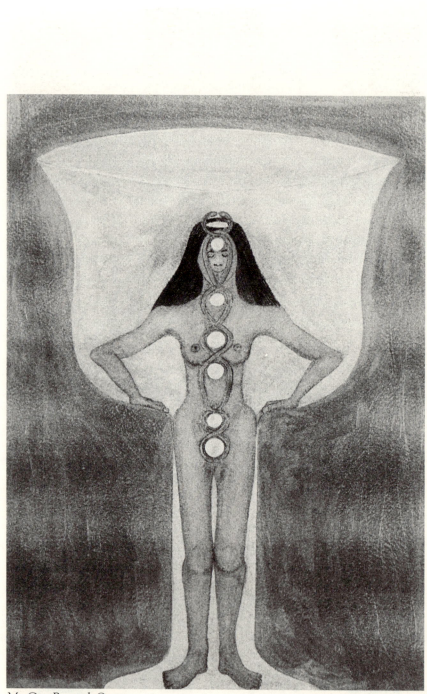

My Cup Runneth Over